THE CHASTENING OF THE LORD

OF THE LORD

THE FORGOTTEN DOCTRINE

BOB SORGE

OASIS HOUSE • KANSAS CITY, MO

THE CHASTENING OF THE LORD: The Forgotten Doctrine
Copyright © 2016 by Bob Sorge
Published by Oasis House
PO Box 522
Grandview, MO 64030-0522
816-767-8880

Editors: Katie Hebbert and Edie Mourey
Cover designer: Joel Sorge
Typesetter: Dale Jimmo
Special thanks to Jeff Ell and David Ray for their help with the manuscript.

ISBN: 978-1-937725-40-2
Library of Congress Control Number: 2016901505

For information on all Bob's books, see page 287.

www.oasishouse.com
twitter.com/BOBSORGE
facebook.com/BobSorgeMinistry
Blog: bobsorge.com
To see Bob's films, go to youtube.com, and enter a search for "Bob Sorge Channel"

Dedication

I dedicate this book to my wife, children, and grandchildren because every redemption story in the Bible was all about the family.

To Marci – because you have endured steadfastly with me in the crucible. We share the same inheritance.

To Joel and Anna – because you have looked to God in your chastening.

To Ben and Katie – because you have an inheritance in our story.

To Michael – because you will follow my faith when you see the outcome of my conduct (Heb 13:7).

To Audrey, Noah, Alexander, and Maxwell – because you will change your world.

To Emma and James – because you are marked by God for holy purpose.

Contents

- Does God ever chasten His children with sickness?
- Does sickness draw people closer to God?
- During His earthly ministry, Jesus never made anyone sick but only healed the sick. If Jesus chastens by wounding us, why didn't He wound anyone during His earthly ministry?
- During His earthly ministry, Jesus never made anyone sick in order to teach them something, but healed everyone. Are you saying He now makes people sick in order to accomplish a deeper work in their lives?
- Are there times, then, when it's God's will for us to be sick?
- If sickness or infirmity is sometimes God's will for our lives, wouldn't that mean we should ask for even more of it?
- If God is partly responsible for someone's infirmity, would it be wrong to ask for healing? Would that be asking God to do something contrary to His will?
- If someone who is sick, infirm, or afflicted asks me to pray for their healing, how can I know whether they are being chastened by God or attacked by the devil?
- If an afflicted person asks me to pray for their healing, and I sense they are under the Lord's chastening, how should I pray?
- Are there times when it's not God's will to heal someone right now?
- If there are occasional times when it's not God's will to heal a certain person right now, why did Jesus heal everyone immediately?
- The Lord said, "My people are destroyed for lack of knowledge" (Hos 4:6). Does that verse mean, at least in part, that some believers die in their infirmities because they lack knowledge about God's will to heal?
- Okay, so some believers are afflicted because they are in a chastening process with God. If they ask me to pray for

- If we say that infirmity is sometimes God's will for our lives, aren't we rendering void the work of the cross and, specifically, the healing that His stripes purchased for us (1 Pet 2:24)?
- I have an infirmity. The possibility that it has been given to me by God is really killing my faith. How can I even believe for healing now?
- If Jesus always wants to heal those He lames, why was Jacob not healed of his limp?
- If we fail to heed the Lord's chastening, will He continue to chasten in our lives until we finally get it?
- Does God hit?
- What was Paul talking about in 1 Corinthians 5:5 when he said to deliver a man over to Satan for the destruction of the flesh so that his spirit may be saved?
- Someone once asked, "Are the consequences of an addiction a result of God's chastisement?"

Introduction

This treatise on the Lord's chastening is written, not as an academic study, but as the gleanings of a man who is under the chastening hand of God. This is personal for me.

I realize this book isn't for most people. I wrote it, not to be a popular book, but to be a stake in the ground for personal reasons with the Lord.

Why am I calling it *the forgotten doctrine*? Because the Holy Spirit did in Hebrews 12:5. I explain that in the first chapter.

Today, the word *chastening* is falling into disuse. Even so, I prefer it over *discipline* in this work for two reasons:

▶ It's a more precise word than discipline. Discipline includes a variety of verbal and non-verbal elements, whereas chastening focuses specifically on non-verbal correction through physical means.

▶ It's the word that has been chosen by the New King James Version in Hebrews 12, which is the translation I'm using in this book.

The main purposes of this book are:

▶ To promote the reputation of our amazing heavenly Father as good, tender, loving, and wise. He loves us enough to discipline us.

▶ To provide understanding, comfort, and hope for those who are being chastened and perhaps straining to process the intensity of their trial.

When in Bible college, I wasn't prepared by my mentors for the Lord's chastening. When it hit my life, I was catapulted into deep crisis and became desperate to understand what was happening to me. Now that I've had years to ponder and process, I write this book in the hope it will be a resource for you in the day of the Lord's kind corrections.

I labor zealously in this book to properly represent our gracious heavenly Father, and that's because it would break my heart to depict Him in a way that skews or caricaturizes His goodness. When it comes to correcting your children, it's really important to you that your heart be portrayed accurately by others. For example, I would be deeply offended if someone looked at how I raised my kids and told others I was aloof, distant, and uninvolved—or even worse, abusive, capricious, and over-demanding. No one who paints me in those terms knows me. My desire is to write this book in a way that the Father says, "Yes, that's who I am."

Our Father is determined to give us, literally, the entire *universe*! But He knows blessings given to untrained vessels actually hurt rather than enrich. He loves us too much to give us the promotion without the pruning. In His love, He chastens so that we might gain the mountain of our inheritance without self-destructing.

Since I'm writing for those in a fiery trial, I realize this book won't seem relevant to everyone. Proverbs 27:7 says, "A satisfied soul loathes the honeycomb, but to a hungry soul every bitter thing is sweet." Sometimes, God starves us out of our satisfied state so that we become desperate for Him. For some, the truths of this book will seem bitter. But if you're desperately hungry for God, you will likely find the truths of these pages to be amazingly sweet.

Chastening is a biblical metaphor to help us understand the nature of the fiery trial we're experiencing, but it's not the only helpful metaphor. Scripture also speaks of sifting, pruning, the refining of gold, the wilderness, exile, the potter's wheel, etc. It's likely that no single metaphor fully interprets our trial, so chastening is probably not the only thing going on in our lives. However, a clear understanding of God's purposes in chastening can be extremely helpful in the journey.

May I offer one word of caution? Please don't read only part of the book and suppose you understand its full message. To grasp this book's message, you must read its entirety. The message builds up to the last chapter. If you choke on something midstream and set the book aside, you could miss the very thing that will bring it into focus for you. This is one of those books that gets better the deeper you get into it.

This book is divided into two parts. Part One is an expository journey through Hebrews 12:1-13, which is our primary compass on this subject. Part Two explores a variety of related questions, such as Paul's thorn in the flesh.

If you've been asking, "God, what are You doing in my life?" then this book may be exactly what you need in this moment.

PART ONE

An Exposition of Hebrews 12
(the chastening chapter)

1

The Forgotten Doctrine

The chastening of the Lord is the forgotten doctrine of the church. I'm not meaning to sound sensational, as though it's the *only* doctrine we've forgotten; I'm meaning simply to reflect the Holy Spirit's witness in Scripture:

> And you have forgotten the exhortation which speaks to you as to sons: "My son, do not despise the chastening of the LORD, nor be discouraged when you are rebuked by Him. For whom the LORD loves He chastens, and scourges every son whom He receives" (Heb 12:5-6).

What do we mean by *the chastening of the Lord*? We mean the way God redemptively uses adverse circumstances to correct and discipline His children for their progress and maturity. His rebukes are His verbal (spoken or written) corrections and His chastenings are His nonverbal (circumstantial) corrections.

What did the Lord mean by, *You have forgotten*? He meant we have forgotten.

My first impulse was to argue with this word. "Lord, I don't think You mean that we've literally *forgotten* Your chastening; I think You're saying that we haven't given it as much emphasis as we should."

But the Holy Spirit was clear. "No, you've actually forgotten it." The Holy Spirit testified that we haven't simply neglected it, we've actually forgotten it.

Think about it. When was the last time you read a book on the subject, or heard a sermon on it in church? You're not likely to find it on a podcast or online link, and it's not likely to be the topic of a TV preacher's message. It's not the kind of message people throng to. As an author, let me be blunt—it's not what you write about if you're trying to sell a lot of books. It's simply not a feel-good, meet-your-felt-needs, popular message.

I would like to suggest eight reasons why the church, in teaching and discipling believers, has forgotten about the chastening of the Lord.

1. We Don't Know His Judgments

The Lord spoke through His servant, Jeremiah, "'My people do not know the judgment of the LORD'" (Jer 8:7). That might be a hard pill to swallow, but the Lord did not mince words with Jeremiah. *Judgment* is a legal term. It refers to God's judicial decisions and the actions He takes in accordance with His decisions.

According to 1 Corinthians 11:32, chastening is one way the Lord's judgment is expressed. When He chastens, God takes specific action to procure a desired result in one of His children. In broad strokes, however, the body of Christ doesn't understand how the Lord judges His people through chastening. If you speak to believers about this, you may quite possibly get a response similar to Peter's, who said of Christ's cross, "Far be it from You, Lord; this shall not happen to You!" (Matt 16:22). Perhaps Peter thought he was being positive and full of faith when he declared that no calamity would befall Jesus, but Jesus recognized the sound of Satan's voice and said to Peter, "Get behind Me, Satan!" (Matt 16:23). Peter didn't yet know the Lord's judgments.

When we don't know the Lord's judgments, we tend

to ignore such a prospect and then end up forgetting about it.

2. We Don't Want a Chastening God

We have forgotten about the Lord's chastening because the natural man, in his carnality, doesn't want a God who chastens. He wants a soothing, non-invasive God. He wants a God of his own creation—made in his own image. He thinks that if God parented more like him, He'd be a better Father for it. The carnal man supposes himself more merciful than God and would rather that God dispense with the whole chastening thing.

Think back to when you were a youngster. Suppose someone had asked you, "Would you like parents who spank or parents who don't spank?" If you had the choice, what would you have taken? Given the choice, I would have definitely opted for non-spanking parents.

But I didn't get to pick. My dad spanked. And now, in the hand of my heavenly Father, I realize once again that I have no choice. God spanks.

Something inside us, however, doesn't enjoy this aspect of God's parenthood. We wish He didn't chasten. Maybe that's one reason we've forgotten it.

3. Our Theology Doesn't Make Room for Chastening

Thirdly, some of us have forgotten about His chastening because we have constructed a theological framework that doesn't have room for it.

There are some theological positions that can't bend far enough to include a well-rounded doctrine of chastening. If you were to bend them to include it, the entire theological system would break. For example, I'm reminded of an advertisement I saw some years back for a Bible school that was being launched by a ministry famous for being *happy*. One line in the ad read, "We invite all those who want to become pastors without tears." When I read that line, my heart sank. That Bible school had a vision for raising up pastors who would be so happy they would never shed tears. Obviously they had little space in their theology for the chastening of the Lord, because when God chastens there are likely to be many tears. A pastor without tears? A pastor who doesn't weep over our nation and world, who doesn't weep over the harvest, who doesn't weep over the hardness of his or her heart, and who doesn't weep in intimate communion with Jesus? Tragic! The ministry that started this Bible school is just one example of those who have theological positions so important to them (in this case, being filled with faith and joy) that they are unable to bend enough to embrace chastening.

When our theology can't accommodate chastening, our tendency is to find ways to discount or discredit it. By the time we've finished disparaging this aspect of God's ways, we've basically dispensed with it. And once dismissed, it's easily forgotten.

4. We Have Neutered Chastening

It's hard to find a believer who doesn't believe in God chastening at some technical level. But some have so narrowed the definition of chastening that they have removed its teeth.

In the understanding of some believers, chastening becomes an inconvenient slap on the hand that doesn't really mark or disrupt a believer's life. "If God chastens you," they might say, "then just repent and move on." The way they cast this doctrine makes the consequences so bland as to render it irrelevant to most believers. Chastening becomes such an insipid concept that it's brushed aside and forgotten.

5. We Don't Think We Need It

Further, we've forgotten the Lord's chastening because we haven't thought of ourselves as needing it.

"Why would the Lord need to chasten *me*? We're talking about *me* here. Pure, sincere, devout, zealous, committed, prayerful, likeable, faithful *me*. God might need to chasten those other guys, but I'm not like those guys. I'm watchful. I'm listening. All He needs to do is speak to me. I don't need chastening to get the message."

Are you saying that you are better than Job, or Joseph, or Jacob, or Joshua, or Jeremiah, or Jonah, or John, or Jesus? If you esteem others better than yourself (Phil 2:3), would you not consider that if they needed chastening you might need it too?

But if you view yourself as not needing it, you're likely to forget about it.

6. We Have Discarded Our Children's Rod

I see a sixth reason why some have forgotten about the Lord's discipline. Caving to cultural influences regarding child rearing, some believers have forsaken the proper use of what the Bible calls *the rod*. The next step, after that, is to forget that God uses a rod.

The Bible strongly advises us to chasten and discipline our children, as seen in these examples from the book of Proverbs:

> He who spares his rod hates his son, but he who loves him disciplines him promptly (13:24).

> Chasten your son while there is hope, and do not set your heart on his destruction (19:18).

> Blows that hurt cleanse away evil, as do stripes the inner depths of the heart (20:30).

> Train up a child in the way he should go, and when he is old he will not depart from it (22:6).

20

Foolishness is bound up in the heart of a child; the rod of correction will drive it far from him (22:15).

Do not withhold correction from a child, for if you beat him with a rod, he will not die (23:13).

The rod and rebuke give wisdom, but a child left to himself brings shame to his mother (29:15).

Incredible pressure has arisen in recent years to compel believers worldwide to stop administering corporal (bodily) punishment—*the rod*—to their children. Some nations have laws against any form of corporal punishment, with serious consequences for parents who disregard those laws. In some nations, parents have been arrested and their children taken from them because they spanked. Under that kind of pressure, some parents have stopped using a rod.

For the sake of clarification, I want to emphasize I strongly oppose parental abuse that uses excessive force to vent frustrations upon children. I am grateful when I hear of how abused children have been saved from horrific home lives. Parents who use spanking to strike back at their children must repent before God and to their children. One couple was imprisoned for beating their adopted daughter so severely with a "rod" that she died from her wounds. Such a story is repugnant and horribly abusive, and is not what the Bible has in view when it speaks of the rod. Biblical child discipline is tender, loving, proportionate to the offense, purposeful, formational, and administered in wisdom rather than anger. In other words, it reflects the heart of God in the way He disciplines His children.

The global resistance to biblical corporal punishment is actually fueled by a demonic design to caricaturize it as oppressive, barbaric, and abusive. Why? Because if we will believe that it is cruel and harsh to discipline our own children, then we will consider it cruel and harsh when God disciplines us. And Satan wants the goodness of God's Fatherhood to be blasphemed. Then, when God chastens us, rather than cooperating with His good purposes and coming through as a polished arrow in His hand, we are liable to become spiritual casualties with a root of bitterness in our hearts that defiles others (Heb 12:15).

Additionally, when a generation lacks appreciation for the proper exercise of child discipline, it will become deeply offended when God exercises His judgments in the earth in the final hours of human history. The Bible portrays God's end-time judgments as righteous and motivated by extravagant love, but Satan wants people to view them cynically—as inordinate, heavy-handed, and tyrannical. He wants the earth to share his rage against God.

The Bible teaches us to discipline our children because, as we do, we begin to see the good intentions of our Father toward us. Furthermore, when parents discipline their children properly, they experience the full range of emotions that naturally attend proper chastening, such as noble desire, zeal for godly conduct, tender care for personal development, compassion for immature weakness, pain of heart that we must inflict pain for a noble purpose, etc. When we feel the depths of all those emotions, we understand some of the noble motives that move Abba Father's heart as He chastens us.

Some don't experience this aspect of God's character because they have refused to use the rod on their children. When we spare our rod, it's not long before we have forgotten about how God disciplines us with His rod.

7. We Won't Acknowledge Instances of Chastening

Another reason we have forgotten about God's chastening is because we have looked at contemporary instances of it and concluded, "That's not God." Some have even been offended at the suggestion God's hand was involved.

It's so easy to look at what God is doing in someone's life, misdiagnose it, and wrongly conclude that God is not involved. Most of us have probably had a turn at making this mistake.

Jeremiah tackled this one head-on when he wrote,

> They have lied about the LORD, and said, "It is not He. Neither will evil come upon us, nor shall we see sword or famine" (Jer 5:12).

In context, Jeremiah predicted that God was going to use Babylon to discipline His people by invading Jerusalem and taking the people back to Babylon as captives. Jeremiah's contemporaries, however, couldn't believe that God would use a nation as evil as Babylon to chasten His people. According to their theology, God simply didn't do such things. So they said, "It is not He. God's not doing this."

We said the same thing about the cross of Christ. We looked at Christ's cross and surmised, "This much we know: This is not God. God doesn't do this kind of thing. If Jesus were the Son of God, this wouldn't be happening to Him. This cross is explicit evidence that this Man is not the Messiah. If He were the Son of God, God would never allow the crucifixion of His own Son."

Then, when Jesus resurrected from the dead, we went, "Oops. Maybe God does do this kind of thing after all."

Like Job's friends, believers have been misreading God's chastening for centuries. David said of his antagonists, "They persecute the ones You have struck, and talk of the grief of those You have wounded" (Ps 69:26). In other words, they spoke negatively of people's calamity because they didn't realize the trial was actually perpetrated by God and was a token of His favor. That's why David prayed that they would "know that this is Your hand—that You, LORD, have done it!" (Ps 109:27).

It's tempting to look at instances of God's chastening (such as with David and Job) and conclude, "God doesn't do this kind of thing to those in whom He delights." The next step is to forget altogether about chastening.

8. We Struggle to Reconcile Chastening with Goodness

I've saved for last the biggest reason why we've forgotten the chastening of the Lord: We haven't known how to reconcile His chastening with His goodness.

When we look at chastening, we see things such as pain, suffering, trouble, loss, restriction, and diminishment. And when we think of God's goodness, we envision things like increase, enlargement, provision, abundance, open doors, favor, increasing faith, and abounding love. The two lists appear to be polar opposites. It seems contradictory to us that God could be good while also orchestrating circumstances we experience as evil.

But God is good! He is good in His intentions and also in His activities. We will trumpet the goodness of God, even in a day when the kingdom of darkness is trying to smear God's reputation. Nothing will ever pry this confidence from our grip. God is good, all the time.

Would a good God take my child's life? Would a good God permit cancer? Would a good God take away my career? Would a good God allow a bankruptcy? Would a good God not stop my spouse from divorcing me? Would a good God remove me from ministry? That a good God might allow or orchestrate catastrophic tragedies in our lives seems contradictory and paradoxical. In our perplexity over this paradox, some have discarded and forgotten His chastening.

To reconcile God's goodness with His chastening, we must acknowledge this fundamental quality of His nature: *God never suspends any attribute of His character in order to express another of His attributes.* For example, He doesn't set aside His mercy in order to exercise judgment; He doesn't compromise His truth in order to exercise His grace; He doesn't suspend His love in order to demonstrate His wrath. In every circumstance, He always embodies the fullness of His every attribute. Said another way, *He is holy.*

When we look at an actual instance of His chastening, however, we struggle to see how *that* could be good. When God made Joseph a slave and a prisoner after he had done everything right, how was that good? When God took Job's ten children from him, how was that good? When God struck Uzziah with leprosy, how was that good? How was it good when God took Samson's eyes, or when He raised up an enemy against David, or when He gave Paul a demonic thorn in his flesh, or when He designed an excruciating death for His Son?

None of those trials appear to us, on the surface, to be good. But we must agree with God's word that they were good. God is good every time He chastens—even when we can't see it at the time. His chastening and His goodness are not mutually exclusive, but are exercised simultaneously.

When God chastens, therefore, it's not just that He doesn't *violate* His goodness; it's that He specifically *expresses* His goodness. He is so good that He refuses to avoid chastening.

As I studied this topic, there was one verse that I struggled to reconcile with the biblical doctrine of chastening. The challenging verse was Proverbs 10:22, "The blessing of the LORD makes one rich, and He adds no sorrow with it." This verse declares that when God enriches us with a blessing, that blessing doesn't have any sorrow attached to it. I didn't know how to reconcile that with biblical chastening because almost every instance of chastening in the Bible was attended with sorrow. If chastening is a blessing from God, producing eternal fruit in our lives, then why does it come with sorrow attached to it?

After years of pondering this question, here's my best answer. The chastening of the Lord is not a blessing. When God blesses you, He truly blesses. And when He chastens, well, He truly chastens. They're not the same thing. Now, the chastening of the Lord produces a blessing *in the end*, for those who have been trained by it (Heb 12:11). But in the moment it's not a blessing, it's a trial. The cross was not a blessing given Jesus by the Father; it was a grievous trial marked by great anguish and sorrow. However, because He endured the trial, He attained to the joy that was set before Him, and now His joy knows no bounds (Heb 12:2).

To see the distinction between the Lord's blessing and His chastening, let me use myself as an example. If my son asks for a blessing, I'm not going to give him a spanking. For a blessing, I might give him some money or a gift, but I wouldn't give him a spanking. Does that mean there is no benefit in a spanking? No. There are many benefits that come out of chastening. But in itself it's not a blessing, it's a trial.

But even the trials God sends into our lives spring from His goodness toward us. There is no contradiction between His goodness and His chastening.

God's Goodness in the Babylonian Captivity

Virtually all of us struggle, at some point in our journey, to see the goodness of God in chastening. This was also true of the Israelites at the time of the captivity. God chose to chasten His people by sending them to Babylon for seventy years, after which time a remnant returned to Jerusalem.

At first glance, the destruction of Jerusalem was one of the most horrific, devastating events of Israel's history. The temple was razed to the ground, the city of Jerusalem was leveled and burned, many were killed, and the people of Judah were taken captive to Babylon. The entire nation struggled to see God's goodness in such a dreadful experience.

And yet, I want to emphasize God's goodness in orchestrating their seventy-year captivity. See His goodness as reflected by Jeremiah:

> Thus says the LORD, the God of Israel: "Like these good figs, so will I acknowledge those who are carried away captive from Judah, whom I have sent out of this place for their own good, into the land of the Chaldeans. For I will set My eyes on them for good, and I will bring them back to this land; I will build them and not pull them down, and I will plant them and not pluck them up. Then I will give them a heart to know Me, that I am the LORD; and they shall be My people, and I will be their God, for they shall return to Me with their whole heart" (Jer 24:5-7).

The captivity came with much sorrow, and yet God used the word *good* three times in the above passage to describe His work in the lives of the captives. The day came when God's people saw that it was God's goodness to lead them into captivity. They were changed because of it, preserved through it, and then restored to Jerusalem after it. The chastening was a trial, but in the end His goodness came into focus.

Who was under God's rejection? Actually, those who had *not* been taken into captivity but had remained back in Jerusalem. Of them the Lord said, "I will deliver them to trouble into all the kingdoms of the earth, for their harm, to be a reproach and a byword, a taunt and a curse, in all places where I shall drive them. And I will send the sword, the famine, and the pestilence among them, till they are consumed from the land that I gave to them and their fathers" (Jer 24:9).

God's view of chastening is counterintuitive to ours. In our eyes, the Babylonian exiles were suffering God's wrath, and those living in freedom back in the land of Israel were the favored ones. But to God, it was exactly the opposite—The exiles were the favored ones.

How could the destruction of Jerusalem and the seventy-year captivity be considered good? Here are a couple good things that came out of them. The hearts of Israel were turned back to the Lord. The idolatry that had plagued Israel for centuries was almost entirely seared away. Their return to Jerusalem began a sequence of developments that ultimately prepared the nation for her Messiah to come. That last point, in itself, made the captivity something consummately good.

His plan was never to do them evil, as He said through Jeremiah, "For I know the thoughts that I think toward you, says the LORD, thoughts of peace and not of evil, to give you a future and a hope" (Jer 29:11).

The Lord expressed similar intentions regarding the Babylonian captivity through the prophet Zechariah:

> For thus says the LORD of hosts: "Just as I determined to
> punish you when your fathers provoked Me to wrath,"
> says the LORD of hosts, "And I would not relent, so again
> in these days I am determined to do good to Jerusalem
> and to the house of Judah. Do not fear" (Zech 8:14-15).

The focus in Zechariah 8 was on the sovereign *determination* of God. God was determined to chasten and purify them through the judgment of captivity. But God was equally determined, after the chastening was complete, to do good to Jerusalem and bring His people back there.

When you realize how determined the Lord is to do whatever it takes to bring His people into His holy purposes, you begin to tremble all the way through. He is a determined God who chastens so He can bring us forward into His good blessings.

Therefore, "Do not fear" (Zech 8:15). You're in good hands!

Fearing the Lord's Goodness

The prophet Hosea, in speaking of the Babylonian captivity, brought together two strange bedfellows in his prophecy: the goodness of the Lord and the fear of the Lord. Here's the verse:

> Afterward the children of Israel shall return and seek the
> LORD their God and David their king. They shall fear the
> LORD and His goodness in the latter days (Hos 3:5).

It seems rather odd, at first glance, that we would fear the Lord's goodness. What does such an idea mean?

In context, God spoke through Hosea of bringing Israel unto Himself in the wilderness of Babylon for a specific purpose—to turn her from idolatry. Babylon would be Israel's "house arrest," during which God would win back their hearts. After the seventy years, the children of

Israel would return to Jerusalem and seek the Lord and David their king.

Sometimes, we don't see God's goodness until *the latter days*, that is, until after the story is written. While we're in it, we might struggle to understand everything that's happening. But there will come a time in latter days when we will connect the dots and realize what God has been preparing.

But why would they fear the Lord's goodness after their return from captivity? Because they would realize the great lengths to which God was willing to go in order to reclaim their hearts. He invoked dreadful measures to regain their loyalty—even unto the destruction of the temple and seventy years of exile in a foreign land. Looking back on the terrifying ordeal, and realizing the whole thing was God's goodness, the people of God would fear Him. What fierce zeal fills God's heart! He is fully determined and utterly relentless until He has a people who love Him with their whole heart. The measures He is willing to employ to produce wholeheartedness are, to be blunt, terrifying. Such goodness sets you to trembling.

When Jeremiah spoke of the return from Babylon and how God would restore the city of Jerusalem, he also used the ideas of *fear* and *goodness* in the same verse to describe how the nations would view God and His ways: "Then it shall be to Me a name of joy, a praise, and an honor before all nations of the earth, who shall hear all the good that I do to them; they shall fear and tremble for all the goodness and all the prosperity that I provide for it" (Jer 33:9). The nations will tremble, after God restores Jerusalem, because they will realize it was God who orchestrated Jerusalem's captivity. The restoration confirmed God was the one who instigated the captivity. People don't fear the restoration; they fear the discipline that must be endured in order to gain restoration.

Resurrection confirms that the crucifixion was designed by God. Restoration validates captivity. Healing confirms that the chastening was from God. This is the principle behind Psalm 40:2-3, "He also brought me up out of a horrible pit, out of the miry clay...He has put a new song in my mouth—praise to our God; many will see it and fear, and will trust in the LORD." Why would men look at the new song and fear? Wouldn't the new song about God's deliverance make them joyful? No, says David. They will fear, because the deliverance proves God was involved from the start in orchestrating the horrible pit. And if God did it to David, He might do it again. To them. That's why they'll fear.

There is something awe-inspiring and fearful about the goodness of God. The holy God we serve is so good that He is willing to do whatever is necessary to win our wholehearted love and fashion us into useful vessels for His service.

I have sought to show, in this opening chapter, how God's chastening is an expression of His goodness. Not all have been able to see this, however. In their zeal for defending God's goodness, some have set aside the doctrine of the Lord's chastening. And in doing so, have forgotten this valuable doctrine.

Let's agree with the Holy Spirit's witness in Hebrews 12:5. *"Yes, Lord, we have forgotten Your chastening. Please bring it back to our remembrance, and help us understand the goodness of Your heart to chasten us."*

2

It's Time to Remember

When the Holy Spirit tells us we have forgotten something, it's because He wants us to remember. Look again at Hebrews 12:5:

> And you have forgotten the exhortation which speaks to you as to sons: "My son, do not despise the chastening of the LORD."

It's time to be jarred awake. If ever there was an hour in which the church needed to understand God's ways in chastening, it's now.

We must put away our forgetfulness!

I want to suggest three reasons why, now more than ever, we must recover the doctrine of chastening. The first reason is this: *God is going to intensify His chastening in the church in the last days.*

God's Chastening Will Increase

Hosea was one of the biblical voices who pointed to this end-time reality when he said, "They shall fear the LORD and His goodness in the latter days" (Hos 3:5). Immediately before him was the Babylonian captivity, but he saw beyond that event to end-time events that would be similar in dynamics to the Babylonian captivity. He foresaw how God would increase His chastening in the last days, and even though it would be an expression of His goodness, it would also be very intense. The grievous nature of the trials would cause believers to fear such goodness—goodness that is willing to do whatever it takes to gain the wholehearted devotion of His people.

The Babylonian exile is very instructional in helping us understand the Lord's chastening—a truth I will revisit repeatedly in this book. When you're chastened of the Lord, the exile becomes amazingly relevant.

In the last days, more and more believers will become desperate to understand the Lord's chastening. As they experience it, they will grow in understanding and become able to impart understanding to others. Who better to make sense of chastening than someone who has been chastened by Jesus?

This is what made Jeremiah such an effective mouthpiece for the Lord. He experienced chastening firsthand, and it gave him authority to speak of the judgments that were about to come. It was because of the intensity of the cup Jeremiah drank that the nation was ultimately able to receive his message.

An unbroken prophet announcing judgment is intolerable. A broken, weeping prophet announcing judgment can be heard. Forerunners who announce the coming judgments at the end of the age will themselves have to drink a bitter cup first so that the body of Christ can receive their message.

Like Hosea, Jeremiah wrote about the Babylonian captivity. But he foresaw it pointing ultimately to something much later: An escalation of the Lord chastening His people in the last days. He pointed to it twice:

> In the latter days you will understand it perfectly (Jer 23:20).

> In the latter days you will consider it (Jer 30:24).

Daniel was another biblical voice who was shown an escalation of trouble in the lives of God's people in the last days.

> "And those of the people who understand shall instruct many; yet for many days they shall fall by sword and flame, by captivity and plundering…And some of those of understanding shall fall, to refine them, purify them, and make them white, until the time of the end; because it is still for the appointed time" (Dan 11:33,35).

Daniel was affirming that God will use fiery trials to refine and purify His saints at the end of the age.

In addition to Hosea, Jeremiah, and Daniel, Jesus also spoke of increased chastening in the last days. That was His implicit message in Revelation 3 when He addressed the church at Laodicea. Many interpreters agree that as the last of the seven letters to the seven churches, the letter to the Laodiceans (Rev 3:14-22) is especially relevant to the church that will greet Christ's second coming. If they're right, then Christ's message to the end-time church was, "As many as I love, I rebuke and chasten. Therefore be zealous and repent" (Rev 3:19). In essence, Jesus was saying, "I have a specific message for My beloved saints at the end of the age. I will love you enough to rebuke and chasten you. The forces at work in the final hour will necessitate that you experience My chastening hand."

We have it on the authority of the Master Himself, therefore, that chastening will be an integral part of how He will bring His church to maturity at the end of the age.

Let me add this comforting word, though: *Revival is also going to increase in the last days!* Trouble is not the only way He renews His church, He also uses revival. Get ready—God is going to pour out His Spirit like never before. Even though trouble will increase, God will pour out His Spirit on all flesh in unprecedented glory.

> "And it shall come to pass afterward that I will pour out My Spirit on all flesh; your sons and your daughters shall prophesy, your old men shall dream dreams, your young men shall see visions. And also on My menservants and on My maidservants I will pour out My Spirit in those days" (Joel 2:28-29).

Increasing revival and chastening—what an incredibly intense and exciting time to be alive! The landscape before us demands we remember that the Lord chastens.

He Starts with the Church

A second reason we must remember His chastening is because God brings judgment to the church first. He starts with us, then visits the world. If you're a disciple of Christ, this is relevant to you personally. You really do want to remember this!

> For the time has come for judgment to begin at the house of God; and if it begins with us first, what will be the end of those who do not obey the gospel of God? Now "If the righteous one is scarcely saved, where will the ungodly and the sinner appear?" Therefore let those who suffer according to the will of God commit their souls to Him in doing good, as to a faithful Creator (1 Pet 4:17-19).

When Peter speaks of God's judgment beginning at His house, He is referring to chastening. First Corinthians 11:29-32 identifies chastening as a form of judgment. Now, not all judgment is chastening, but all chastening is judgment. It is the loving judgment of God designed to accomplish a good purpose in the lives of His children.

God's judgments can be incredibly intense—because He is so thorough—and thus can appear excessive to some. Peter indicated (above) that the righteous, experiencing this kind of intensity, are "scarcely saved"—that is, they seem to barely survive. If the righteous barely survive in the day of judgment, what will the ungodly do? I can't imagine facing His judgments without the help of the indwelling Holy Spirit! And yet, Revelation 16 reveals that such a day is coming to those who don't obey the gospel.

Jeremiah 25:29 clearly states that, when God brings calamity to His people, it means the entire world is next. God is intense with His children, but even more severe with the wicked. Even then, however, His judgments are altogether merciful, for they carry an inherent call to repent.

If Jesus doesn't chasten His bride, she will be too immature and shallow in her experience to partner with His end-time purposes. Her chastening, therefore, will be her training ground. She will come to understand and appreciate the kindness, reasonableness, and necessity of God's end-time judgments.

Let me illustrate my meaning with David and Moses. Only a chastened David[1] could write the imprecatory Psalms[2] against the wicked. Only a chastened Moses[3] could release God's judgments upon Pharaoh in meekness. Chastening made them useful partners in judgment. In the same way, a chastened bride will actually participate with Christ in His end-time judgments of the world.

Not only does Jesus chasten, it's the first thing on His agenda for His church. He starts with us. Therefore, it behooves us to put away our forgetfulness and take this doctrine to heart.

---

1   I am thinking primarily of the ten years David ran for his life from Saul, although David's chastenings were not confined to those ten years
2   The imprecatory Psalms are those in which David calls forth God's judgment upon the wicked. For examples, look at Psalms 7, 35, 55, 58, 59, 69, 79, 109, 137 and 139.
3   I have in view the forty years Moses lived in the Midianite wilderness and tended his father-in-law's sheep.

Many Are Unprepared

Thirdly, we must recover the doctrine of chastening in this hour because the Bible predicts a great falling away at the end of the age. While believers have fallen from the faith throughout history, there is yet to come a turning away from the faith so widespread that Paul called it *"the* falling away."[4]

> Let no one deceive you by any means; for that Day will not come unless the falling away comes first, and the man of sin is revealed, the son of perdition (2 Thess 2:3).

When Jesus spoke of this falling away, He gave us insight into why it will happen:

> And then many will be offended, will betray one another, and will hate one another. Then many false prophets will rise up and deceive many. And because lawlessness will abound, the love of many will grow cold (Matt 24:10-12).

Of the reasons Jesus gave for the great falling away, the first one was that *many will be offended*. What will offend believers at the end of the age? The chastenings of Jesus. *Believers who have no theological grid for understanding His chastening hazard falling away from their faith.* We must be intimately acquainted with Jesus the Judge if our love is to remain fiery and pure in the last days.

We must remember the doctrine of the Lord's chastening, therefore, because:

▸ His judgments will increase dramatically in the last days.

▸ Judgment will begin at the house of God.

▸ Many will be offended and fall away.

By the grace of God, we will remember. We *must* remember!

4   See also 1 Tim 4:1-2; 2 Tim 4:3-5; 2 Pet 2:1-3.

3

The Cross and Chastening

Yes, we've forgotten the chastening of the Lord (Heb 12:5). But now, let's back up and examine that verse's context—which is the foremost passage in the Bible on the topic of the Lord's chastening. Here's how Hebrews 12 launches:

> Therefore we also, since we are surrounded by so great a cloud of witnesses, let us lay aside every weight, and the sin which so easily ensnares us, and let us run with endurance the race that is set before us, looking unto Jesus, the author and finisher of our faith, who for the joy that was set before Him endured the cross, despising the shame, and has sat down at the right hand of the throne of God (Heb 12:1-2).

Referring to the heroes of our faith that were mentioned in Hebrews 11, the writer called them "so great a cloud of witnesses." They suffered trials, troubles, and enemies, but at the end of their race they came through witnessing to the faithfulness of God. He brought them through and completed their stories. The Christian life is depicted in this passage, therefore, as a *race*.

We are all in a race to find our place in that cloud of witnesses. This is why, according to verse 1, we lay aside every weight that might slow us down and put away every sin that might trip us up. We are racing to gain a testimony that witnesses to the delivering and sustaining power of God.

The most inspiring Hero of all is Jesus Himself (v. 2). He has finished His earthly race and is now frontrunner in the cloud of witnesses. Having endured the cross, He sat down at the right hand of God where He witnesses to the goodness and faithfulness of God to raise Him from the dead (Heb 10:12-13). He says to us, "Run! The Father will help you. He will enable you to press through every trial, overcome every obstacle, and obtain the complete testimony He has for you."

I want to begin our study of Hebrews 12 by showing how the writer drew a distinct connection between the cross of Christ and the Lord's chastening. The cross is specifically mentioned in verse two, and it continues to be the unifying motif in the verses that follow.

The writer mentioned three things that can hinder our race if we're not guarded: hostility from sinners (v. 3), sin (v. 4), and the chastening of the Lord (v. 5). For the first of those, look at verse three:

> For consider Him who endured such hostility from sinners against Himself, lest you become weary and discouraged in your souls (Heb 12:3).

As we run our race, Jesus wants us to endure any hostility that might come to us from sinners, just as He did during His earthly pilgrimage. If we're not careful, hostile people can weary and dishearten us in our race and we can become tempted to quit. The greatest hostility Jesus experienced was at His crucifixion. It seems obvious, therefore, that the writer still has the cross in view in verse three. Now to verse four.

> You have not yet resisted to bloodshed, striving against sin (Heb 12:4).

In our race toward the cloud of witnesses, we are exhorted to strive against sin because it can trip us up mid-stride. When the writer mentioned bloodshed, He had the bloodshed of the cross in mind. Jesus resisted to the point of bloodshed, but we haven't done that yet. In verse four, therefore, we see that the writer didn't change topics. He was still writing about the cross. Now, as we go to the next two verses, notice that the cross continued to be the theme of the writer's focus.

> And you have forgotten the exhortation which speaks to you as to sons: "My son, do not despise the chastening of the LORD, nor be discouraged when you are rebuked by Him. For whom the LORD loves He chastens, and scourges every son whom He receives" (Heb. 12:5-6).

In our race toward the cloud of witnesses, the writer reminded us of the chastening of the Lord. If we lose perspective on His goodness in chastening, we can lose our way. This third potential hindrance to our race (after the hostility of sinners, and sin) loomed so large in the writer's eyes that he took nine verses to develop it. That which gripped him is now going to grip us in this study.

By starting in verse five with the conjunction, *And*, the writer helped us perceive that he was staying on topic. He was continuing to speak of the cross. The topic of the cross naturally took him to the Lord's chastening. He wanted us to understand that when we are chastened of the Lord, we are identifying with the cross of Christ. The connection between the cross and chastening was secured even further by use of the word *scourges* (v. 6), which is the same word used to describe the scourging of Jesus at His sentencing.

Furthermore, many translations place no paragraph break in the first six verses of Hebrews 12, viewing that section as one contiguous paragraph. The theme of the cross flows consistently throughout.

Here's my point. The writer of Hebrews 12 put the cross and the chastening of the Lord together in one pot. Dealing with the cross naturally brought him to the matter of chastening.

Two Sides of the Cross

As already stated, when chastened we are identifying with Christ's cross. For that statement to make sense, though, I need to explain the two sides of the cross. Some theological camps tend to emphasize just one side of the cross and can even become adversarial toward those who favor the other side. The wise won't polarize toward just one side, however, but will recognize both sides of the cross in a holistic way.

What are its two sides? The substitutionary nature of the cross and the identificational nature of the cross. Let me explain.

The Substitutionary Nature of the Cross

The cross was first of all a substitutionary work of Christ. He suffered certain things, in our place, so we would never have to. As our sacrificial Lamb, He became our substitute and died in our place. As Paul wrote, "For indeed Christ, our Passover, was sacrificed for us" (1 Cor 5:7). Peter added, "For Christ also suffered once for sins, the just for the unjust, that He might bring us to God" (1 Pet 3:18). In saying Christ suffered *for* us, both writers were pointing to the substitutionary work of the cross.

In what ways did Christ suffer *for* us? Consider these aspects of His substitutionary sacrifice:

▸ Jesus was punished that we might be forgiven. "The chastisement for our peace was upon Him" (Isa 53:5).

- Jesus was wounded that we might be healed. "When evening had come, they brought to Him many who were demon-possessed. And He cast out the spirits with a word, and healed all who were sick, that it might be fulfilled which was spoken by Isaiah the prophet, saying: 'He Himself took our infirmities and bore our sicknesses'" (Matt 8:16-17).

- Jesus became sin that we might become the very righteousness of God by faith. "For He made Him who knew no sin to be sin for us, that we might become the righteousness of God in Him" (2 Cor 5:21).

- Jesus died our death that we might receive His life. "But we see Jesus, who was made a little lower than the angels, for the suffering of death crowned with glory and honor, that He, by the grace of God, might taste death for everyone" (Heb 2:9).

- Jesus became poor so that we might inherit His riches. "For you know the grace of our Lord Jesus Christ, that though He was rich, yet for your sakes He became poor, that you through His poverty might become rich" (2 Cor 8:9).

- Jesus suffered that we might share His glory. "For it was fitting for Him, for whom are all things and by whom are all things, in bringing many sons to glory, to make the captain of their salvation perfect through sufferings" (Heb 2:10).

- Jesus endured being forsaken by God that we might have the Father's acceptance. "My God, My God, why have You forsaken Me?" (Matt 27:46). "To the praise of the glory of His grace, by which He made us accepted in the Beloved" (Eph 1:6).

▸ Jesus was made a curse that we might be freed from the curse of the law of Moses. "Christ has redeemed us from the curse of the law, having become a curse for us (for it is written, 'Cursed is everyone who hangs on a tree'), that the blessing of Abraham might come upon the Gentiles in Christ Jesus, that we might receive the promise of the Spirit through faith" (Gal 3:13-14).

▸ Jesus bore the wrath of God against sin so that we might be saved from wrath. "But God demonstrates His own love toward us, in that while we were still sinners, Christ died for us. Much more then, having now been justified by His blood, we shall be saved from wrath through Him. For if when we were enemies we were reconciled to God through the death of His Son, much more, having been reconciled, we shall be saved by His life" (Rom 5:8-10).

The work of purchasing our salvation was done entirely and exclusively by Jesus at the cross. We don't do even one percent of the work. Christ, and Christ alone, has procured our salvation. This is the glorious truth of the substitutionary nature of the cross.[1]

The substitutionary work of the cross is a glorious message that thrills and rejoices our hearts. Its glory and wonder can't possibly be overemphasized.

And yet, it's not the complete message of the cross. To proclaim the cross in its fullness, we must also herald the second side of the cross—its identificational nature.

---

[1] To study more about this, I suggest the series, "The Divine Exchange," which can be found at http://www.derekprince.org. I also recommend Rod Parsley's book, *The Cross*. One of the best Bible passages to study is Isaiah 53.

The Identificational Nature of the Cross

Jesus suffered on the cross, in this second sense, to show us how. We share in His sufferings by drinking a similar cup from the Father's hand. The substitutionary side of the cross makes us exuberant with relief; the identificational side of the cross, however, sobers us with Jesus' call: "If anyone desires to come after Me, let him deny himself, and take up his cross daily, and follow Me" (Luke 9:23).

In his first epistle, Peter brought together both sides of the cross in exquisite symmetry. To see how substitution and identification come together, his is the linchpin verse. He wrote, "For to this you were called, because Christ also suffered for us, leaving us an example, that you should follow His steps" (1 Pet 2:21). Peter said Christ suffered *for us* in a substitutionary manner. It followed logically, therefore, that we should follow His steps of suffering. *Christ's substitution assumed our identification.*

But Peter wasn't done. He hammered this nail a second time: "Therefore, since Christ suffered for us in the flesh, arm yourselves also with the same mind, for he who has suffered in the flesh has ceased from sin" (1 Pet 4:1). Again, since Christ suffered *for us*, it followed naturally that we should have *the same mind* and be prepared to suffer *in the flesh*.

Peter continued, "Rejoice to the extent that you partake of Christ's sufferings, that when His glory is revealed, you may also be glad with exceeding joy" (1 Pet 4:13). The privilege of suffering with Christ should cause us to rejoice.

When we recognize that the sufferings of the cross were both substitutional and identificational, we are faced with a very important question. How can we know whether a certain kind of suffering is something Jesus suffered so we never have to, or whether it's something He suffered so that we would also know how to endure that same suffering? In other words, if I'm suffering, how do I know whether it's something I should seek to be delivered from because Christ bore it for me, or whether it's something I should endure because I am partaking with Him in His sufferings?

That is a huge question with implications explored throughout this book. For now, let me supply a short and cursory answer by further quoting Peter. "Therefore let those who suffer according to the will of God commit their souls to Him in doing good, as to a faithful Creator" (1 Pet 4:19). The principle could be stated like this: If you are suffering according to the will of God, you are partaking to some extent in the sufferings of Christ, for He also suffered on the cross according to the will of God. If, however, it is not God's will for you to suffer as you presently do, then you should claim His promises of deliverance and contend for the benefits of His substitutionary work on Calvary. For a fuller answer, please stay with me in this book.

My focus in this book is to help us understand the identificational nature of the cross. Do not suppose that, since we won't dwell on the substitutionary side of the cross, I consider it of lesser significance. Far from it! There is nothing more precious to my soul than the glorious ways in which Christ suffered *for us*. To stay on task, however, this work will center on how we suffer *with Him*.

Again, when chastened we are suffering *with Him* because the Father deals thus with all His children. Now that we're clear on this, let's pick up with Hebrews 12:5.

4

Do Not Despise Chastening

Our passage says Jesus corrects us in two ways:

And you have forgotten the exhortation which speaks to you as to sons: "My son, do not despise the chastening of the LORD, nor be discouraged when you are rebuked by Him. For whom the LORD loves He chastens, and scourges every son whom He receives" (Heb 12:5-6).

Jesus corrects through chastening and through rebuke. This mirrors the words of Jesus in Revelation 3:19, "As many as I love, I rebuke and chasten."

His rebukes are expressions of His lovingkindness and care. The psalmist described it like this, "Let the righteous strike me; it shall be a kindness. And let him rebuke me; it shall be as excellent oil; let my head not refuse it" (Ps 141:5). If we respond properly to His rebukes, they actually become an anointing oil upon our heads.

What distinguishes rebuke and chastening? Rebuke is *verbal* correction; chastening is *nonverbal* correction. Jesus uses both. His rebukes may come to us through the Scriptures, or from another person, or through the inner voice of the Holy Spirit. Sometimes He will seek to avert the need for chastening by coming to us first with a rebuke. If we hear the verbal rebuke and respond properly, often we can preempt nonverbal chastening.

If we don't heed the rebuke, He may have to use other means to arrest our attention.

There are occasions, however, when Jesus chastens without first giving a rebuke. I once read a tweet by a prominent Christian leader who said, "God's judgment only comes after His goodness has been ignored." That statement is true some of the time but not always. Sometimes the Lord bypasses rebuke and goes directly to chastening. In such instances, His chastening doesn't necessarily mean there's compromise in our lives. Rather, it can mean He's shaping us in a profoundly deep way. For example, neither Job nor Joseph were chastened because of a refusal to respond to the Lord's rebukes. Both were living in obedience to God's word. In actuality, they were both chastened *because* of their consecration and obedience. Their obedience had qualified them for a promotion in the kingdom of God. More on that in chapter 15.

Defining Chastening

Before we progress further, let's pause and look at the meaning of the word *chastening*. The Greek word for *chastening* in Hebrews 12:5 is *paideia* (Strong's #3809). Among English Bible translations, it's usually rendered either as *chastening* (e.g., KJV) or *discipline* (e.g., NASB). The renderings of *punishment* (BBE) and *training* (MNT) are uncommon. Most agree that *chastening* or *discipline* should translate *paideia* here.

The idea of *paideia* is disciplinary correction. It derives from the Greek word for *child*, which is *pais*, pointing to the tutorage, education, and training of children. It evolved to mean chastening because the effectual training of children necessitates the inclusion of chastening and correction.

For the purposes of our study, I prefer the perspective of Spiros Zodhiates[1], who sees *nouthesia* (admonition) as primarily representing correction and instruction by verbal means, and *paideia* (chastening) as primarily representing correction by nonverbal means.

In Ephesians 6:4, Paul used both Greek words: "And you, fathers, do not provoke your children to wrath, but bring them up in the training [*paideia*] and admonition [*nouthesia*] of the Lord." Paul seemed to affirm the necessity of both nonverbal and verbal means to properly raise our children in the Lord. The Lord treats His children in the same way.

Vincent's Word Studies of the New Testament prefers discipline over chastening when translating *paideia*. Whichever English word you prefer, it points to the same reality: primarily nonverbal correction and training of children through the use of means such as corporal punishment and bodily disciplines. I am using *chastening* in this book because that's the word used in my translation of choice, the New King James Version.

The Bible uses many metaphors to describe God's formative processes in His children. Chastening is just one of those metaphors. Other helpful metaphors include pruning a vine, refining gold or silver, sharpening an arrow, breaking and shaping a potter's vessel, imprisoning, weaning a child, taking into captivity, walking through a wilderness, enduring a winter season, the crushing of grapes to make wine, the formation of pearl, crucifixion, etc. All of these metaphors overlap each other to some degree. The value of each metaphor is found in the unique way it sheds light on God's ways with His people. No single metaphor fully reveals, in itself, all the

1 See Spiros Zodhiates on Strong's numbers 3559 and 3809 in his volume, *The Complete Word Study New Testament*, Chattanooga, TN: AMG Publishers, 1992, pp. 924, 926-927.

ways of God in forming and maturing His children. But the metaphor of chastening is one of the more helpful ones.

For the purposes of our study, let me repeat this suggested definition of chastening from chapter 1:

> Chastening is the redemptive use of adverse circumstances to correct and discipline children for their progress and maturity.

Two Extreme Responses

In Hebrews 12:5-6, the writer quoted Solomon when he said, "My son, do not despise the chastening of the LORD, nor be discouraged when you are rebuked by Him" (see Prov 3:11-12). Solomon identified two undesirable responses to the Lord's chastening. On the one hand, we could be tempted to *despise* it, and on the other hand, we could become *discouraged* by it.

Let's look at those two undesirable responses.

To Despise Chastening

The first undesirable extreme is to despise the Lord's chastening. In our passage, *despise* denotes something different from the common English meaning, *to disdain or hold in contempt*. That's the meaning of *despise* back in Hebrews 12:2 where it says Jesus despised the shame of the cross. A different Greek word is used there, meaning *to disdain*. But here in Hebrews 12:5, the Greek word for *despise* means *to care little*, or *to regard lightly*, or *to make little of*. It's a failure to give due recognition, attention, or weight to the signals God is sending.

When the Lord chastens, it can be tempting to blow it off or dismiss it with a shrug, "Well, I don't think that was God trying to get my attention. The way everything happened was just a fluke. This whole situation is just a weird coincidence. I don't think I need to pay it any more attention." But God doesn't want us to dismiss His corrections.

Jeremiah described a time when Israel despised correction:

> O LORD, are not Your eyes on the truth? You have stricken them, but they have not grieved; You have consumed them, but they have refused to receive correction. They have made their faces harder than rock; they have refused to return. Therefore I said, "Surely these are poor. They are foolish; for they do not know the way of the LORD, the judgment of their God" (Jer 5:3-4).

In Jeremiah's time, the people of Israel didn't give proper heed to God's corrections. They didn't know the judgment of their God and, consequently, were invaded by Babylon—a chastening that could have been avoided had they responded soberly to His word in the first place. God wanted their full attention, but instead of trembling at His word (Isa 66:2), they shrugged off the rebukes of His mouth and brushed aside the signs around them.

Isaiah also described a time when Israel despised correction:

> And in that day the Lord GOD of hosts called for weeping and for mourning, for baldness and for girding with sackcloth. But instead, joy and gladness, slaying oxen and killing sheep, eating meat and drinking wine: "Let us eat and drink, for tomorrow we die!" Then it was revealed in my hearing by the LORD of hosts, "Surely for this iniquity there will be no atonement for you, even to your death," says the Lord GOD of hosts (Isa 22:12-14).

God wanted His people to respond to His correction with repentance, but they gave themselves to self-indulgence instead. God was so displeased with the way they despised His discipline that judgment became inevitable.

Consequently, some of the people actually died. There were false prophets in Jeremiah's day, for example, who were killed by God because their message was encouraging the people to despise God's corrections. One case in point is Hananiah in Jeremiah 28:16-17.

When the Lord cried, "Hear the rod!" in Micah 6:9, He pleaded with them to listen carefully to the message He was conveying through His correcting rod. When He disciplines, He's talking. He's after something. His corrections are not mysterious or obscure but clear and forthright. He wants us to get the message.

Let's be careful never to despise the Lord's chastening but to give careful heed to His intended message. It's wise to ask, "Lord, what are You saying to me right now through these circumstances?"

To Be Discouraged by Chastening

The other improper response, when being chastened by the Lord, is to be so overwhelmed with discouragement and despair that we become immobilized, nonfunctional, and buried by grief. Our text says it this way, "Nor be discouraged when you are rebuked by Him."

The word *discouraged* in Greek literally means *to faint*. It's the same word used when Jesus, in compassion for the multitudes who had been with Him for three days, didn't want to send them away hungry, "lest they faint on the way" (Matt 15:32). When He chastens, Jesus doesn't intend for us to faint or collapse or lose our way. Yes, we should be gripped and arrested; but we should also keep moving forward, even if the steps are halting and small.

When the Almighty God chastens us, it can really wipe us out. He has such a big hand! We can easily feel overwhelmed. When the Lord said we shouldn't be

discouraged by His chastening, He wasn't unsympa-
thetic to our frailty. Throughout Scripture, the Lord has
always shown Himself compassionate toward our afflictions and sufferings. Consider, for example, how Exodus
6:9 described the affliction of Israel while in slavery in
Egypt: "So Moses spoke thus to the children of Israel;
but they did not heed Moses, because of anguish of
spirit and cruel bondage." God acknowledged that their
bondage was "cruel" and that it produced "anguish of
spirit." God understood their pain and sympathized with
their weaknesses in suffering.

When God said, "Don't be discouraged," He didn't
mean, "Don't be gripped by the pain." He meant, "Don't
let this derail you from your divine destiny. Don't give
up. Stay in the race."

The temptation to be discouraged is strongest when
God's chastening is on the intense end of the spectrum.
I say that because there are various degrees of intensity
in chastening. Let me use my experience as a father as
an example. When I disciplined my kids, there was everything from a light cuff to "an event." Speaking of a light
cuff, I remember giving my son a swat on his diaper. My
swat made a loud smacking sound on the plastic casing
of his diaper, but the diaper was so thick that he barely
felt a thing. But because of the loud smack, he bawled
like someone who had just been mortally wounded.
Although he felt nothing, he wanted me to think it really hurt. So on one end of the spectrum were those mo-
ments of chastening that were very light.

On the other end of the spectrum were those occasions when chastening became an event. In those cases,
my children would get a spanking they didn't soon forget. In the most intense times of discipline, my desire
was to save them from death (Prov 23:14).

In a similar way, when God chastens us, it can be everything from a little swat to an event. When God stages an unforgettable event with us (a particularly strong chastening), it is so we might be changed forever. He wants to effect changes in us that will affect our inheritance both in this life and in the one to come.

Regarding tests, trials, and chastening, we see from Scripture that there is a *big one*. What I mean is that sometimes God will design a test for one of His children that is one-of-a-kind, such as we haven't seen before nor will ever see again.

In terms of Israel's history, the *big one* for Israel was the exile to Babylon. It was the most severe chastening of their biblical history. One-of-a-kind. And, by the way, so profoundly instructional to our topic of divine chastening that it will be mentioned repeatedly in this study.

In speaking of the Babylonian captivity, God said to the nation, "For this is like the waters of Noah to Me; for as I have sworn that the waters of Noah would no longer cover the earth, so have I sworn that I would not be angry with you, nor rebuke you" (Isa 54:9). Just as the flood was a unique event that would never happen again (Gen 8:21), never again would the Lord destroy Jerusalem and take His people into exile for seventy years. It was a one-of-a-kind chastening.

Here's what I want you to hear from this. If God ever takes you into a chastening "event," you will likely experience only one of those in your entire life. And although unprecedented in its intensity, it will be transformational in every holy way imaginable. If, that is, you refuse to be discouraged or stopped by it.

Isaiah then went on to address what was going on if, after the return from Babylon, another nation should come against Israel. Here's what Isaiah said about that possibility:

"Indeed they shall surely assemble, but not because of Me. Whoever assembles against you shall fall for your sake... No weapon formed against you shall prosper, and every tongue which rises against you in judgment you shall condemn" (Isa 54:15,17).

Isaiah was saying, "If you get invaded again after I restore you to the land, it will not be because of My chastening hand. It will be because of evil aggression. I will fight for you, and they will fall before you. The enemy will not prosper in his designs, but you will be victoriously triumphant." The Lord assured them that another exile would not happen. The exile was a one-of-a-kind chastening, never to be repeated again.

I mean for this principle to encourage those who have experienced a *big one* at the hand of God. Don't be so discouraged that you give up and quit. If you persevere, you'll be profoundly changed and will never again have this kind of trial at the hand of God. Should the enemy try to attack you again, there will be a new spiritual authority upon your life, and he will fail and fall for your sake.

Jesus had many trials during His three years of ministry, but He also had an event, a *big one*. The cross. Never again to be repeated. Referring to the cross, Isaiah prophesied, "He will not fail nor be discouraged" (42:4). Jesus didn't succumb to the temptation to be so overwhelmed with discouragement on the cross as to give up. No, He didn't fail in His mission.

When in the biggest trial of our lives, we are assaulted with discouragement. Our knees buckle, our arms give out, and we teeter on the verge of collapse with the urge to quit. This is why the writer of Hebrews said, "Nor be discouraged when you are rebuked by Him."

Again, there are two extreme responses to chastening that we want to avoid. When the trial is light, we don't want to despise and blow it off; and when the trial is severe, we don't want to be so discouraged that we abandon the journey.

God Doesn't Despise or Abhor

One final reason we shouldn't view His chastening too lightly or too heavily is because He doesn't view it either way. David affirmed this when he wrote, "For He has not despised nor abhorred the affliction of the afflicted" (Ps 22:24). God doesn't *despise* (view too lightly) or *abhor* (view too heavily) our affliction.

Why should we *despise* our affliction when God doesn't? He doesn't look at our trial and snort, "That's nothing. I could have made it a lot worse. Toughen up." He doesn't view our afflictions as trivial or trifling. He knows how gravely the implications impact our lives and how severely our soul feels the wound. He understands and He cares.

And why should we *abhor* our affliction when God doesn't? He doesn't look at your affliction, become disgusted by your hideous condition, and turn His face from you. No, He looks on you tenderly with great love and compassion. He is nearer to you than ever because of your trouble (Ps 91:15).

Rejoice—the Lord is for us!

If God doesn't think too lightly or too heavily of our affliction, then why should we?

How Should We Respond?

If we're not to despise or be discouraged by the trial, then how are we to respond? We will explore more of the answer later, but the most concise answer is given by Christ: "As many as I love, I rebuke and chasten: be zealous therefore, and repent" (Rev 3:19). His counsel was succinct: Be zealous and repent. Instead of despising it, repent; and instead of being discouraged, be zealous.

First, be zealous. Discouragement wants you to disconnect and check out of the whole process; Jesus wants you to enter zealously into the process and pursue God's purposes. Your soul might want to collapse, but your spirit is zealous to find out what pleases the Lord.

God wants the trial to awaken the zeal of your spirit. That's how Asaph responded, who wrote, "My spirit makes diligent search" (Ps 77:6). Because of trouble in his life, God had his attention. Asaph's spirit was on high alert, diligently searching the Spirit and the word for understanding into God's thoughts. Asaph wanted to know what God's underlying message was in the trouble he'd experienced. He was eager to repent of anything God might show him so that He might obtain God's intention in the trial.

Be zealous to pursue the heart of God in His word. The psalmist said, "Unless Your law had been my delight, I would then have perished in my affliction" (Ps 119:92). I have actually experienced this verse. I am here today only because of a zealous pursuit of God in His word. Had I not clung to His word for sheer survival, the storm would have taken me out.

Sometimes it takes trouble in our lives to make us truly zealous for God. For example, in the days of Esther, it was not until their lives were threatened with death that all the Jews joined together to fast from both food and drink for three days. God had their attention, and suddenly they were zealous to pray.

This coincides with the testimony of Psalm 78:34, "When He slew them, then they sought Him; and they returned and sought earnestly for God." The Puritans had a proverb, "Either the love of Christ will *draw* you to His breast or the wrath of God will *drive* you to His breast."

Jesus loves it when we are zealous for Him. He didn't die on the cross to gain a Bride who yawns in His face on Sunday mornings. He died for a Bride who has fire in her eyes for Him like He has in His eyes for her. He wants us to be zealously passionate for His face. Discouragement wants to extinguish our flame, but the Lord designs the trial to actually kindle our flame for Him.

First of all, then, be zealous.

Secondly, when Jesus chastens, repent. When we despise God's chastening—that is, when we don't think He's trying to get our attention—we don't change anything. But God wants us to hear His message, apply that word to every aspect of our lives, repent, and change.

Jesus delights in rapid repentance. He doesn't want to strong-arm us into repentance. In other words, He doesn't want us so defensive that He has to present an overwhelming weight of evidence before we'll capitulate and wheeze, "Okay then, I repent." No, He wants us repenting quickly and eagerly. When Jesus rebukes and chastens in your life, repent as quickly and thoroughly as you possibly can. Call every sin in its worst possible terms and own it. Identify it, confess it, turn from it, and flee from it. Change. This is the kind of repentance that moves the heart of Jesus.

Be ready for the Lord to convict you, over time, in more areas than you might have expected. You might think He is after a few issues, but He's probably thinking, "While you're in this fire, let's take advantage of the opportunity and deal with everything from A to Z." You will come out of this crucible conformed to the image of Christ!

5

He Disciplines the Ones He Loves

Hebrews 12:6 goes on to say, "For whom the LORD loves He chastens, and scourges every son whom He receives." This echoes the words of Jesus, "As many as I love, I rebuke and chasten" (Rev 3:19). Correction is not rejection. In fact, it's the opposite. It's an expression of His love. Chastening comes only to those He loves and receives.

How can *loves* and *scourges* be in the same sentence? How can a loving God scourge? Well, let's look at it. *Scourges* is the same word that described how the Romans scourged Jesus, and how the Jews would scourge people as a form of correction (Matt 10:17). They viewed corporal punishment as an effective way of teaching a lesson. When it says He "scourges every son whom He receives," it does not use the standard Greek word for *receives* (which would have been *lambano*), but a more particular word (*paradechomai*) which denotes receiving with approval or delight. The verse emphasizes the Lord's love, approval, and delight in His sons.

If He loves you, He chastens you. And if He really loves you, He really chastens you. Does anyone out there feel especially loved?

Chastening always involves some level of pain, designed by the Lord, and yet in the midst of it His love endures unceasingly. For example, see how the Lord yearned over His people whom He sent away to Babylon: "I have forsaken My house, I have left My heritage; I have given the dearly beloved of My soul into the hand of her enemies" (Jer 12:7). Even while giving them into the hand of their enemies, God called His people, "the dearly beloved of My soul." He did it for love.

Jeremiah 31:20 is yet another verse showing God's yearning heart for His people whom He sent into captivity: "Is Ephraim My dear son? Is he a pleasant child? For though I spoke against him, I earnestly remember him still; therefore My heart yearns for him; I will surely have mercy on him, says the LORD." Oh, how He loves us! He remembers us always with longing.

Job's best friend, Eliphaz, quizzed Job in the middle of his trial, "Is it because of your fear of Him that He corrects you, and enters into judgment with you?" (Job 22:4). Eliphaz thought the answer was self-evident, but in reality the surprising answer was, "Actually, yes." Job was being chastened because of his godly fear and fervent love. That possibility seemed ludicrous to Eliphaz, but it was true.

It's all about love.

There's a depth of love to be found in suffering that can't be found elsewhere. As the psalmist wrote, "Deep calls unto deep at the noise of Your waterfalls; all Your waves and billows have gone over me" (Ps 42:7). It's a time when something deeply intimate in the heart of God reaches out to the deep places in the heart of the child He is chastening. In the midst of our pain, we realize we are experiencing God at a depth never experienced when life was easy and serene. Hindsight will reveal that suffering was actually a threshold to deeper places in God's heart.

Sometimes, He chastens in order to draw us into deeper intimacy with Him. At other times, He chastens *because of* our intimacy with Him. It can be His way of saying, "I'm so pleased with your consecration and love that I have chosen you for a higher rank."

For some, a God who loves and a God who chastens is a contradiction. For others, it's a contradiction to think a God of love would send people to hell. But consider this. *God is so committed to love that He is willing to do whatever He must to confront and remove its every hindrance.* That's the purpose of His end-time judgments as recorded in Revelation 16 and other passages. His judgments proceed from His love, moving Him to drive from our planet everything that hinders holy love. His love is so fiery and consuming that any hindrance must eventually be judged and taken away. This is why He chastens His children now. He is unwavering in His resolve to bring us into perfected love.

Jacob and Esau

The Lord used Jacob and Esau to illustrate His love for the nation of Israel:

> "I have loved you," says the LORD. "Yet you say, 'In what way have You loved us?' Was not Esau Jacob's brother?" says the LORD. "Yet Jacob I have loved; but Esau I have hated, and laid waste his mountains and his heritage for the jackals of the wilderness." Even though Edom has said, "We have been impoverished, but we will return and build the desolate places," thus says the LORD of hosts: "They may build, but I will throw down; they shall be called the Territory of Wickedness, and the people against whom the LORD will have indignation forever" (Mal 1:2-4).

When the Lord told Israel, "I have loved you," they couldn't see it. This is typical of those who have been chastened of the Lord. They often struggle to feel the Lord's love in their afflictions. The Israelites were so aware of their sufferings that they asked, "In what way have You loved us?" There was an element of accusation in this question. Israel was implying, "You don't love us. Look at our circumstances! If You loved us, everything would be different. How can You say You have loved us?"

In response, the Lord used the examples of Jacob and Esau to illustrate His love for them. God wanted them to look at the nation of Edom (Esau's descendants) and consider their state. Edom had been removed from its land, and the land was now left desolate. Israel, on the other hand, was back in her land after seventy years of exile in Babylon. That Israel should be back in her land in this manner was nothing short of supernatural intervention. It was a miracle! Why? Because God's love was upon the people of Israel.

The reason the nation of Edom came under God's indignation traces back to Esau himself. How did God show His hatred for Esau? By just leaving him alone. When you look at Esau's life, it looked the way a Christian's life should look. He was married, with children, friends, security, prosperity, possessions, favor, pleasures, stability, and peace. His was the picture-perfect image of the blessed life.

In contrast, when you look at Jacob's life, you see virtually the opposite. Jacob's life was characterized by wanderings, misunderstanding, rejection, labors, exploitation, deception, wrestling, affliction, famine, and bereavement.

To all appearances, Esau was preferred and Jacob was cast off. But God said Esau was hated and Jacob loved. In what way was Esau hated? God left him alone. Without divine interference, Esau led a quiet and secure life. But the outcome in his descendants was so wicked that the entire nation came under God's judgment.

In what way was Jacob loved? God set His fiery gaze on Jacob and would not let him go in the path he would have naturally chosen for himself. God interrupted his life, chastened him severely, and because of it was able to raise up a nation that benefitted from the redemptive power and grace of God. Jacob's afflictions were the very tokens of God's love. And Esau's ease was a token of God's hatred.

The last thing you want is for God to leave you alone. If He loves you, He will interrupt your life with His chastening rod because, left to yourself, you will choose the wrong path. To get to higher places in the kingdom of God, we sometimes need help. Chastening is one way Jesus helps us reach things in the kingdom we would not have otherwise touched. This is why Psalm 94:12 says, "Blessed is the man whom thou chastenest" (KJV).

When I was in a particularly severe season of chastening, someone said to me, "This is the Lord's love for you." At the time, I was in so much pain that I couldn't conceive how that much distress could be the Lord's love. So I said in a semi-sincere way to the Lord, "If this is how You love, love somebody else." Those were words spoken out of pain, but in my innermost being I really did want His love. I just didn't want the pain.

It took me a long time to see that the chastening was, in fact, His love for me. I continued to seek the Lord in His word, in fasting and prayer, and by enduring in the word I slowly gained increasing clarity on the Lord's lovingkindness in my life. He loved me enough to interrupt the way I would have taken in my own understanding, to take me on a path I would have never chosen but which was actually taking me in the direction my heart longed to find.

Now I truly have ownership of Jesus' words, "As many as I love, I rebuke and chasten." I truly believe His chastening in my life was a tangible token of His affection.

I will give you my testimony. He wounded me, and I fell in love. I love Him now more than ever. He did it for love. As the Scripture says, "Rebuke a wise man, and he will love you" (Prov 9:8).

One of the great uncertainties, during the Lord's chastening, is whether we will continue to love Him. Paul wrote to the Corinthians, "The more abundantly I love you, the less I am loved" (2 Cor 12:15). I wonder if the Lord might feel that way, sometimes, with the sons He chastens. When He shows us extra affection by coming particular close with His refining fire, we sometimes love Him less for it. The great secret, in chastening, is to set your love upon Him. Loving Him in your darkness is one of the most powerful things you can do. Here's where we discover the blessing of Psalm 91:14, "Because he has set his love upon Me, therefore I will deliver him." As Paul wrote, "And we know that all things work together for good to those who love God" (Rom 8:28).

Is God Angry with Us?

When being chastened, we know God's love is upon us, as He said, "For whom the LORD loves He chastens" (Heb 12:6). And yet, when we're in the maelstrom of the storm, it *feels* like He's angry with us. I found myself asking, "God, are You angry with me?"

As I studied the Scriptures on this question, the answer seemed to come clear: Yes. There is an element of anger expressed in God's chastening, even though He deeply loves us.

I found this answer specifically in the book of Zechariah. In referring to the Babylonian exile, the Lord revealed His perspective to Zechariah.

> The LORD has been very angry with your fathers…"I am exceedingly angry with the nations at ease; for I was a little angry, and they helped—but with evil intent" (Zech 1:2, 15)

I want you to grasp the meaning of this passage. The Lord was "very angry" with the idolatry and sins of Israel's fathers, so He sent the nation captive to Babylon as a means of chastening. The rod that God used to judge His people was the nation of Babylon, as well as other nations who participated. These nations helped God in His cause, but they did so with evil intent. That is, they were harsher with Israel than God intended. It was this overreaching judgment by the nations at ease that made God "exceedingly angry." He said their overreaching malice against Israel would incur His judgment.

In Zechariah 1, God said He had been "very angry" with Israel. But when He contrasted that anger with the exceeding anger He now had toward Israel's enemies, His anger toward Israel paled in contrast. In actuality, with Israel He was only "a little angry" because of His exceeding anger against her enemies.

Here's the bottom line. Yes, God was angry with Israel, but only "a little angry." Isaiah confirmed this when he wrote, "With a little wrath I hid My face from you for a moment; but with everlasting kindness I will have mercy on you" (Isa 54:8). God was only a little angry with Israel, and only "for a moment." On the other side of the chastening, He was going to demonstrate "everlasting kindness" and mercy to them. What redemption!

So when God chastens in our lives, is He angry with us? Probably. But only a little bit. He is probably a little angry at such things as our presumption, pride, covetousness, envy, haste, selfish ambition, unbelief, etc. But there's something moving Him that is much larger than

His anger, and that is *His love*. He loves us so much! One day we will praise Him for the great love and mercy He showed by not leaving us to ourselves.

But just as Babylon came against Israel with malice, in the same way Satan comes against us. God might give Satan limited permission to afflict us, but Satan assaults us in the same way that Babylon afflicted Israel—he attacks us with a malice and vengeance God never intended. Like Babylon with Israel, Satan always overplays his hand. When God gives him permission to touch His saints, Satan tries to afflict them as severely as he possibly can.

But now let me reassure you with the words of David, who wrote, "Your rod and Your staff, they comfort me" (Ps 23:4). David portrayed the shepherd's rod as an instrument of comfort. When you consider how the Lord wounds with His chastening rod, you might wonder, "In what way should I feel comfort from the Lord's chastening rod? All I'm feeling right now is pain!" But the truth is, the primary function of the Shepherd's rod is not to chasten the sheep, but to ward off the wolf. His use of the rod as a chastening tool is only a secondary function. When a wolf or lion attacked the flock, *that's* when the rod came out with a vengeance!

If you have known the pain that comes from the Shepherd's chastening rod, remember this: *The Shepherd reserves the strongest blows for your adversary.* He may have been "a little angry" with you at first, but now He is "exceedingly angry" with your enemy for his overreaching (Zech 1:15). If you know what it's like when He is "a little angry," can you imagine what kind of blows He has reserved for your adversary? One day you will witness His vehement indignation when He arises with His rod to punish the arrogance of your adversary.

Yes, let His rod comfort you! He loves you!

The Strategic Significance of the Captivity

The seventy-year captivity of Israel in Babylon was a severe chastening of the Lord, and yet it was also a manifestation of the Lord's great love for His people. Let me explain.

In 586 BC, the armies of Babylon invaded Jerusalem, burned the city and temple to the ground, killed many Jews, and took the rest in captivity back to Babylon. This event, referred to as "the exile" (because God called them exiles) and called "the captivity" many places in the Bible (e.g., Matt 1:17), was one of the most significant events in the entire Bible. It isn't talked about much in the church today, but from God's perspective its implications were huge. When the captivity came onto God's radar, there came a sudden explosion of prophetic writings. Nearly a third of the Old Testament is composed of Scripture that either points to it, was written during it, or composed in its wake. The captivity was the Lord's most severe chastening of the Jewish nation in Old Testament times (Isa 26:16; Jer 2:30). Its significance can hardly be overstated, for it became the context in which much of God's heart toward His people was revealed through the prophets.

One of the books written during the captivity was Lamentations. Jerusalem fell in 586 BC and Jeremiah wrote the book of Lamentations not long after. It derives its name from the fact that it was written as a lament. In the book, Jeremiah mourned the destruction of the temple, the fall of Jerusalem, and his own personal suffering as someone who lived in Jerusalem when it was taken. Although Jeremiah spoke of his own pain, he seemed to see himself personifying the sufferings of the collective soul of the nation. He hurt in ways that all God's sons hurt when they are being chastened of the Lord (Lam 3:1).

At a cursory reading, the book of Lamentations might seem to some to be rather dismal and depressing. But when you've been chastened by the Lord, the book suddenly becomes amazingly comforting and powerfully relevant to your life.

We could take many pages to talk about the contents of Lamentations, but instead, I want to point to what I consider to be the central message of the book. The means whereby I came to identify its central message is, for me at least, both poetic and fascinating.

The Message of Lamentations

If you have a Bible nearby, I invite you to open to Lamentations right now and discover something for yourself. Go ahead, get your Bible. You'll notice that Lamentations consists of five chapters. Now look at chapter one. How many verses are in chapter one?

Actually, I'd like you to count how many verses are in each chapter. It should take you only a few seconds to do a verse count in each of Lamentation's five chapters.

Chapter one   22 verses.
Chapter two   22 verses.
Chapter three   66 verses.
Chapter four   22 verses.
Chapter five   22 verses.

Four of the chapters have the same verse count. Why are there 22 verses each in four chapters of Lamentations? The answer is very simple. There are 22 letters in the Hebrew alphabet, and each chapter is an acrostic of the Hebrew alphabet. The first verse begins with the first letter of the Hebrew alphabet, the second verse begins with the second letter, the third verse with the third letter, etc., until all 22 letters of the Hebrew alphabet are used. The fifth chapter is the only one not written in acrostic style, but it still has 22 verses, so the poetic symmetry of the book is obviously intentional.

You'll notice that chapter three is different. It has 66 verses in it—three times as many as the other chapters. And why is that? Because that chapter is written in a cadence of triplets. The first three verses begin with the first letter of the Hebrew alphabet, the next three verses begin with the second letter of the Hebrew alphabet, and so on. In the acrostic pattern of chapter three, three verses are given to each letter of the alphabet. So you have 22 letters multiplied by three verses each.

22 letters x 3 verses each = 66 verses

The following diagram shows the five chapters in relation to their verse count.

A Verse Count in the Book of Lamentations

When you look at the above diagram, which chapter in the book of Lamentations do you think was viewed by Jeremiah as the most important of the book? If you chose chapter three, then I would agree with you.

Lamentations is written as a chiasm. If that term is new to you, do an internet search on "Hebrew chiasm" or "Bible chiasm." A chiasm is a literary device used quite often by biblical writers to show that the central or most important point in a literary passage is to be found in its *center*. The ideas surrounding the central thought often mirror each other in some way, helping the reader to land upon the central thought as the author's leading message.

The thematic content of a chiasm might be diagrammed in this manner:

$$A - B - C - B - A$$

In this example, the themes in each A would mirror each other, the themes in each B would mirror each other, and then C would be the central theme. This literary device would reinforce the fact that special emphasis is placed upon the message in C.

Lamentations is written in this chiastic manner. The layout of the book is intended to draw particular attention to chapter three as the most important chapter in the book.

Since Lamentations is clearly a chiasm, I have taken it a step further. I think it's possible that chapter three was intended to be a chiasm in itself, and that the most important verse in that chapter—and hence in the entire book—is to be found in the center of chapter three. If that's true, and if chapter three contains 66 verses, then I would like to suggest that verse 33 is the central and most important idea of the entire book. What is the message of Lamentations 3:33? Here it is.

> For He does not afflict willingly, nor grieve the children of men (Lam 3:33).

God wants us to know that when He afflicts and grieves His children through chastening, He doesn't enjoy the process or delight in their sufferings. God never delights in our pain. The only thing He delights in is the good that will come out of it in the end.

This is the central thought of Lamentations. God wants us to know His motivation in chastening. It's important to Him that we realize how His heart is pained in our pains. Satan enjoys our pain, but God is grieved by it.

When Jerusalem was destroyed, God seemed to be saying, "This is not My first choice. I wish I didn't have to do this the hard way. I'm not enjoying this at all. I'm so sorry that I must correct you in such a painful way."

The pain of chastening is not God's first choice for our lives. He wishes we could mature and develop in a more peaceful, happy way. He afflicts us with chastening only because He knows it's the best way to move us forward in Christlikeness. We've never done well with ease. We've always needed discipline in order to progress in our walk with Christ.

The tenderness of God's heart toward us, in the midst of severe chastening, is the central message of Lamentations. Oh, how He loves us!

In Jeremiah 48:31-32, God said He would "wail" and "cry out" and "mourn" and "weep" for Moab, because of the judgment He was sending against them via Babylon. If God felt that way toward a Gentile nation that was at enmity with His people, how much more must He have comparable feelings for His own children?

Hosea indicated that God indeed did have similar emotions toward Israel: "How can I give you up, Ephraim? How can I hand you over, Israel? How can I make you like Admah? How can I set you like Zeboiim? My heart churns within Me; My sympathy is stirred" (Hos 11:8). It was as though God was caught between. If He didn't chasten, they backslid; if He did chasten, His heart would churn over their plight. Either way, God was pained for His people.

If you've been chastened by God, I hope the message of Lamentations will comfort you. God does not rejoice over your grief. His sympathy is stirred and His heart churns for you. If you've been chastened, it's because He *loves* you!

6

God Chastens Only His Sons

In the last chapter, we looked closely at Hebrews 12:6, "For whom the LORD loves He chastens." Let's progress now to the next verses.

> If you endure chastening, God deals with you as with sons; for what son is there whom a father does not chasten? But if you are without chastening, of which all have become partakers, then you are illegitimate and not sons (Heb 12:7-8).

It's hard to imagine a son whose father refuses to chasten him. Why? Because sons need it.

Chastening is a mark of sonship. It means the son is loved and the father is engaged and caring. The only reason a loving father wouldn't chasten his son is if he's been jaded against its wisdom.

Parents who refuse to chasten their children often replace it with yelling or verbal lashings. But the tongue can be much more harmful to a child than a rod. In reference to the tongue, Solomon said, "Death and life are in the power of the tongue" (Prov 18:21). Contrast that with what he said about the rod: "Do not withhold correction from a child, for if you beat him with a rod, he will not die" (Prov 23:13). Solomon said the rod wouldn't kill, but the tongue could. The tongue can wound and scar a child for life. Rather than slashing with his words, a wise father will use a rod in tender correction.

When the above passage says, "of which all have be-come partakers," it means that God chastens *all* His chil-dren. None are exempt or without need of it. If you're a son of God, you will get chastened somewhere along the way. As the Lord said to the nation of Israel in the wilderness, "You should know in your heart that as a man chastens his son, so the LORD your God chastens you" (Deut 8:5).

Endure the Discipline

Hebrews 12:7 says sons "endure chastening." Chastening is not over when the son wants it to be over; its duration is determined by the father. All the son can do is buckle up and endure. Until it's over.

It's common among Christians to speak of "embrac-ing" the dealings of God in our lives. We often say things like, "Embrace the cross," or "Embrace the crushing," or "Embrace the crucible," or "Embrace the chastening." When I was encouraged to embrace the discipline of the Lord, I didn't know what to do with that. How could I embrace something from which I was seeking to be healed? How can a crucified victim embrace his cross? How do you wrap your hands around your cross when they're impaled to it?

I struggled with this question for years, and then the Lord answered it for me from Hebrews 11:13, which says, "These all died in faith, not having received the promis-es, but having seen them afar off were assured of them, embraced them and confessed that they were strangers and pilgrims on the earth." This verse says the saints em-braced *promises*. They didn't embrace the Lord's disci-pline, they embraced His promises. In contrast, Hebrews 12:7 says we are to "endure discipline."

There it was. *Endure the discipline, embrace the promise.* Immediately, the question was resolved for me. I knew what to do. I knew I needed to endure the Lord's chastening with fortitude, and embrace with all my strength His promises of healing, deliverance, and a higher kingdom purpose.

God's Fathering Paradigm

The writer of Hebrews is very bold to portray God as a loving Father who chastens His children. There are some today, however, who resist painting Him in that light. Often, they claim a holy zeal to defend His reputation in the earth as being a *good* Father. But goodness and chastening are not mutually exclusive. In fact, His goodness is expressed in His chastening.

When we say the Father chastens in His goodness, we find ourselves with some pretty strong questions. For example, if the Father is always good, how can we say that the cross was His goodness expressed toward Jesus? How can a good Father crucify His Son? That question is momentous and actually takes us to the heart of the matter. Find the answer to that question and you discover how God directs His favor toward all His favorites.

Those in the Bible who were closest to God—the prophets—suffered the most. Those He loved most were given the most bitter cups. And the one He *really* loved received the most bitter cup of all—the cross. What kind of a Father is this?

While planning His Son's crucifixion, the Father said, "I will be to Him a Father, and He shall be to Me a Son" (Heb 1:5). What kind of Father crucifies His Son? How could Isaiah say, "Yet it pleased the LORD to bruise Him"? (53:10). How could the Father find pleasure in His Son's sufferings? How do we speak properly of this kind of fathering paradigm? How is *this* benevolent?

The Lamb, however, was deeply passionate about His Father's goodness (Matt 7:11; John 10:32). For Him, there was no question—Abba is good! How, then, do we reconcile His kindness with the bitter cup of suffering He gives His sons?

As soon as the question is raised, Satan is quick to jump in and malign the Father. He wants us to share his conviction that the Father is a tyrannical, heavy-handed, oppressive disciplinarian. He even tried to convince Jesus of this. At Christ's forty-day temptation, when Satan offered Jesus the kingdoms of the world, it seems to me he was inferring, "I will be a better father to You than Your own. He'll give You the kingdoms of the world if You'll do the cross. But I'll give You the kingdoms of this world without any cross. All You have to do is worship me, and I'll give You everything."

Jesus looked at Satan's offer and basically concluded, "I'll go with Abba." Jesus knew His Father's leadership in His life was perfect (Matt 5:48). He considered the cross perfect fathering.

I once heard a Christian pastor say he was offended at the suggestion that God killed Jesus, because for him it meant that at the cross God was pitted against God. Offensive as it is, I am declaring the Father crucified Jesus. Truthfully, the cross offends. The implications, of course, are obvious. If God gave Jesus His cross, He might give us one, too. And we don't want one. If we can come up with a way to say that God *didn't* crucify Jesus, we can remove some of the offense of the cross, and perhaps get a pass on enduring our own crucifixion.

But our text tells us that, if we are without chastening, we are not sons.

The goodness of God in crucifying His sons is not seen immediately in the crucifixion itself but in the resurrection that follows. Once the son is resurrected, the Father's goodness in the entire proceedings becomes apparent to all. Because of the cross, Abba is able to give His sons much more than if the suffering had never happened. The cross portends a crown.

Jesus said, "As the Father knows Me, even so I know the Father; and I lay down My life for the sheep" (John 10:15). He found the courage to lay His life down because He knew intimately His Father's beneficence. He knew the cup would be bitter, but He also knew the final outcome would be glorious. When Jesus set His face toward Calvary, He had no uncertainty about Abba's kindness.

If God fathers you in the same manner as Jesus, here's what He'll do for you: He'll send you, crucify you, bury you, resurrect you, glorify you, and seat you at His right hand. He's a fabulous Father!

Illegitimate Children

Hebrews 12:8 reads, "But if you are without chastening, of which all have become partakers, then you are illegitimate and not sons." An illegitimate child is a child born out of wedlock.

The New King James version uses the adjective *illegitimate,* but the original Greek word *nothos* is a noun. To be most accurate to the original text, therefore, we should translate *nothos* with a noun rather than an adjective.

The old King James Version does just that. Here's its rendering:

> But if ye be without chastisement, whereof all are partakers, then are ye bastards, and not sons (Heb. 12:8).

It's shocking but true—the King James Version of the Bible has the word *bastards* in it. And it's the best translation. It's the actual noun used by the writer of Hebrews.

Bastards

What is a bastard? A child born outside of lawful matrimony. The word describes a child whose parents didn't marry. Raised by a single mom, a bastard is not a legal heir to his biological father's inheritance.

A bastard would be without chastening probably because his father is not present in the home. His father loved his mother enough to get her pregnant, but not enough to marry her and be present as a husband and parent.

A bastard would be without chastening because other men in the community wouldn't bother with it, and understandably so. Men don't punish other people's children; they have their hands full with their own. They're not about to take on the other children in the neighborhood. That's for their own fathers to do.

Similarly, God doesn't chasten anyone else's children. He takes on only His own.

Let me suggest another definition of *bastard*: right mother, wrong father.

You had the right mother because she loved you enough to bring you into the world, nurse you, care for you, and rear you. But you had the wrong father because he didn't love you enough to marry your mother and provide you with a secure upbringing. Instead, he left her to raise you by herself.

This principle applies to the corporate church of Jesus Christ. There are bastards in the church. They've got the right mother (the church of Jesus Christ) but the wrong father (the devil). Whenever the church gets in bed with the devil, she births bastards.

Let me explain my meaning.

Over time, the church tends to institutionalize. In that process, she gathers into her ranks people whose loyalty is to the institution of the church but who have not been regenerated by the Spirit. Although they mouth correct phrases, they've never been born of the Spirit (John 3:5), so they're still sons of the devil. But they're devoted to their mother church. Satan encourages this loyalty because it means he has sons representing his interests within the corridors of the church he hates. The church cooperates with Satan's purposes when she fails to purge from her midst the lies of the evil one. A church that tolerates compromise is in bed with the devil and naturally produces bastards.

The religious leaders of Jesus' day were bastards. Well, Jesus didn't actually call them bastards. He didn't use such harsh language. He simply said to them, "You are of your father the devil" (John 8:44). They had the right mother (the commonwealth of Israel) but the wrong father.

They claimed God as their Father (John 8:41), but were in fact sons of the devil.

> "You are of your father the devil, and the desires of your father you want to do. He was a murderer from the beginning, and does not stand in the truth, because there is no truth in him. When he speaks a lie, he speaks from his own resources, for he is a liar and the father of it" (John 8:44).

They adamantly claimed God as their Father, but in the end their actions demonstrated they shared the murderous genes of the devil. DNA doesn't lie.

Satan has no qualms about siring sons who are

committed to the church. In fact, he is pleased when they find recognition within the church. How better to dilute and distract the church's mission than to place his sons in positions of strategic leadership?

A Distinguishing Factor

What might distinguish bastards from true sons? For starters, they're not chastened. God leaves them alone. Why? Because He doesn't chasten Satan's sons. He only disciplines His own.

When you watch a movie that depicts the crucifixion of Christ, scroll across the scene on that bleak hill. You'll see the bastards standing about and staring—clothed in their elaborate regalia, prestigious in rank, established in status, and satisfied in a nasty but necessary job finally done. The comfort and dignity of their lives appear to be tokens of divine affirmation.

And then there's the gasping figure on the middle cross. Cursed, abused, tormented, naked, forsaken, despised, twisted in spasms of agony.

Who, on that lonely mountain, had the favor of God?

Not the insulated ones. Not the bastards.

Don't mistake immunity for approbation.

While a man won't chasten the kids in his neighborhood, sometimes he may *rebuke* a neighbor's kids. And interestingly enough, we find that God sometimes rebukes the devil's sons.

For example, Jesus rebuked the bastards of His day. Why? Because He was showing them mercy. They could never say, at judgment day, that Jesus didn't warn them. His rebukes found their apex in Matthew 23. "Woe to you, scribes and Pharisees, hypocrites!" (v. 13). If you don't see His mercy in Matthew 23, you might view that chapter as an angry, blistering diatribe against the Pharisees. But

in actuality, His denunciation was the merciful sound-
ing of an alarm—in the hope that they might possibly
come to their senses and be drawn to repentance. We
see in Matthew 23, therefore, the willingness of Jesus to
rebuke bastards. But chasten them? No.

Should We Ask for It?

For years I have pondered the question, *Is it proper to
ask the Lord to chasten us?*

When Jesus taught us to pray, "And do not lead us
into temptation," (Matt 6:13), that prayer didn't sound
much like a request for chastening. But there are other
places where the tone is different.

For example, Jeremiah seemed to ask for it when he
wrote, "O LORD, correct me, but with justice; not in Your
anger, lest You bring me to nothing" (Jer 10:24). When
you look more closely, however, Jeremiah was not inviting a future correction but was speaking of a present
correction he was experiencing. He was smarting with
the sting of God's corrections upon the city of Jerusalem.
He wasn't asking God to remove His corrections, but He
was asking for a tender, rather than an angry, touch. It
was an appeal for gentleness, much like Habakkuk's appeal, "In wrath remember mercy" (Hab 3:2).

David prayed, "Search me, O God, and know my
heart; try me, and know my anxieties" (Ps 139:23; see
also Ps 26:2). He was inviting God to search and try him,
but I'm not persuaded that meant he was asking the
Lord to chasten him.

Actually, there are a couple places where David
asked the Lord *not* to chasten him:

> O LORD, do not rebuke me in Your anger, nor chasten
> me in Your hot displeasure (Ps 6:1; see also Ps 38:1).

We want the Lord to search and try us because we

want to be known by Him, we want to become more pleasing to Him, and we want Him to enjoy the integrity of our hearts. But we're not really asking to be chastened.

I don't know any children who ask for a spanking.

And yet, it's possible to pray in a way that produces God's chastening in our lives, even though that's not specifically what we were asking for or expecting. I experienced this in my own life. I prayed a passionate prayer back in 1992, "Lord, lift me to a higher place in You," and didn't realize until later that the Lord's way to answer that prayer was through chastening. He chastened me by means of a physical affliction so that I might press into Him with desperation and fervency. Through the intensity of the trial, the Lord has taken me on a journey toward a higher place in Him. I didn't ask to be chastened, but that's how the Lord chose to answer my prayer.

I see something similar in the life of Job. In the midst of his trial, Job said, "I am one mocked by his friends, who called on God, and He answered him" (Job 12:4). He was saying, "I asked God for something, He has answered my prayer, and now my friends mock me." What did Job ask for? We don't really know for sure. Whatever Job asked for, he understood his trial was the consequence of his request. He had asked God for something, and God's way of answering him was by taking him through a journey of chastening.

So should we ask to be chastened? Here's my best answer. I don't see a biblical basis for asking the Lord to chasten us. So I don't think you need to ask for it. But I do think it's biblical to ask for more of Him. Then, if your journey to the fulfillment of that prayer necessitates a walk through chastening, let the Lord be the one to decide that.

Sometimes God starves us out until we become so hungry for more of Him that we pray dangerous prayers. "Whatever it takes! I must have more of You!" I am an advocate of dangerous prayers—cries of total abandonment to God. Ask for more! Actually, there are some things in the kingdom that are not touched until you ask for them. Pray the dangerous prayer, then let Him decide the best way to answer it.

Comparisons

When you're being chastened, one of your first responses is to look around at others and wonder why they aren't writhing in pain like you. In contrast to others, your trial doesn't seem fair.

Beware the temptation to compare your trial with the way God is or isn't chastening the other sons and daughters around you. God fathers all of us individually. He doesn't chasten all His children in the same way or at the same time. This principle is seen in Isaiah 28:

> Does the plowman keep plowing all day to sow? Does he keep turning his soil and breaking the clods? When he has leveled its surface, does he not sow the black cummin and scatter the cummin, plant the wheat in rows, the barley in the appointed place, and the spelt in its place? For He instructs him in right judgment, his God teaches him. For the black cummin is not threshed with a threshing sledge, nor is a cartwheel rolled over the cummin; but the black cummin is beaten out with a stick, and the cummin with a rod. Bread flour must be ground; therefore he does not thresh it forever, break it with his cartwheel, or crush it with his horsemen (Isa 28:24-28).

Isaiah's point is that God deals uniquely with each grain in order to produce the greatest harvest within each crop. He applies that same kind of individual care to each of His sons, using unique means in each of our lives to produce the greatest spiritual harvest possible. So don't compare. While God is crushing you, He's probably promoting your neighbor. It's probably a setup— Their success is meant to test you. Remember that comparison cripples. Don't concern yourself with their exaltation; just set your focus on God's work in your own life. How Jesus is walking with your brother is of no concern to you (see John 21:22).

Ruth's Amazing Response to Naomi's Chastening

Some will disagree with me, but I believe Naomi's afflictions were a chastening of the Lord. Naomi experienced uncommon suffering: A famine dislodged her from her inheritance in Bethlehem and sent her and her family running for relief to the land of Moab. Then, her husband died in Moab. At some point in time, her two sons married Moabite women, but then both of her sons died. Naomi experienced loss of land, home, husband, sons, provision, and security. Little wonder Naomi mourned how God afflicted her:

> "The hand of the LORD has gone out against me!" (Ruth 1:13).

> But she said to them, "Do not call me Naomi; call me Mara, for the Almighty has dealt very bitterly with me. I went out full, and the LORD has brought me home again empty. Why do you call me Naomi, since the LORD has testified against me, and the Almighty has afflicted me?" (Ruth 1:20-21).

Some would say God didn't do these things to Naomi, but I agree with her angle on it. The hand of the Lord had afflicted her. Her daughter-in-law, Ruth, stood faithfully at her side and also suffered collateral damage by being so closely associated with her.

Ruth had personally watched Naomi's faith and had learned of the God of Israel when she married into the family. Faith had been awakened in her heart, and she realized that, by marrying an Israelite, she had become a partaker in the hope of Israel. When she looked at Naomi's life, all she could see was affliction, loss, and sorrow. And yet, in the midst of God's grievous chastenings, faith was awakened in her heart.

When Naomi set out to return to Bethlehem, she tried to convince Ruth to stay back in her homeland (Moab), but Ruth's response was simply fantastic:

> But Ruth said: "Entreat me not to leave you, or to turn back from following after you; for wherever you go, I will go; and wherever you lodge, I will lodge; your people shall be my people, and your God, my God" (Ruth 1:16).

What an amazing utterance of faith! Ruth was saying, "The God who has done these things to you—taken you from your home and taken your husband and sons from you—I want Him to be my God." She beheld the severe chastening of the Lord and still chose Him. Wow.

And her faith truly was rewarded. She ended up giving birth to Obed, who was King David's grandfather. Her faith brought her into the very lineage of Christ (Matt 1:5). The book of Ruth is a fabulous story of how God honored the faith of a Moabite widow. But even more than that, to be precise, the book is the redemption story of Naomi. Had God left Naomi alone, we would have never known her name. But because of God's intervention and gracious chastening, Naomi went down in the annals of redemptive history as one of the greatest mothers in Israel.

> Then Naomi took the child and laid him on her bosom, and became a nurse to him. Also the neighbor women gave him a name, saying, "There is a son born to Naomi."

And they called his name Obed. He is the father of Jesse, the father of David (Ruth 4:16-17).

The story ended with glorious redemption for Naomi. And Ruth gained a magnificent heritage in the faith because she didn't despise how the Lord chastened Naomi.

God Resurrects His Sons

If you've been chastened simply because you're a son, then I want to encourage you with this truth: As a son of God, you are also a son of the resurrection. Jesus called God's sons, "Sons of the resurrection" (Luke 20:36).

What does it mean to be a son of resurrection? It means resurrection is engraved in your destiny.

How does God treat His sons? He chastens them, and then He resurrects them. If you are a son of chastening, then be encouraged because you shall also be a son of resurrection.

God resurrects His sons. It's simply how He fathers. When you're being chastened you're in good hands.

7

Benefits of Chastening

Here's the next verses in our Hebrews 12 text:

Furthermore, we have had human fathers who corrected us, and we paid them respect. Shall we not much more readily be in subjection to the Father of spirits and live? For they indeed for a few days chastened us as seemed best to them, but He for our profit, that we may be partakers of His holiness (Heb 12:9-10).

With these verses, our focus is turned to the benefits of chastening. Two benefits of chastening are mentioned here: We enter into true spiritual life, and we become partakers of His holiness. Let's look at these two, and then widen our scope to consider benefits of chastening that are mentioned in other portions of Scripture.

Chastening Produces Life

Hebrews 12:9 asks the question, "Shall we not much more readily be in subjection to the Father of spirits and live?" I want to key on the word *live*. Chastening is designed by God to bring us into authentic spiritual *life*. It doesn't only save us from death (Prov 23:14), but also directs us into the path of everlasting life.

When we learn from the Lord's chastening and change, we are choosing life.

According to Hebrews 12:9, we respected our human

fathers for having the grit to correct us. They hazarded our misunderstanding their intentions in the moment so we might be better for it later on. For that, we honor them. They prepared us for the wisdom of living life skillfully on earth. We respected them because we knew, if we didn't honor the chastening, we could really be in trouble.

If we respected our human fathers for preparing us for natural life on earth, how much more should we respect our heavenly Father who wields a much mightier rod, and who is also willing for us to misunderstand His hand in the moment that we might later share in the riches of eternal life?

That word *live* is lively! It points to the life of God, to true life—to life that is experienced both here on earth and also in the age to come. Chastening culls from our lives all things deadly and brings us into real, experiential, spiritual life. This is the first benefit of chastening specified in our text. It brings us into abundant life in Christ.

Chastening is counterintuitive. At the time, God is killing so many things in you that you feel like you're dying. But stay in the journey because God will bring you through to His intended end. At first, you might feel like chastening is producing only death in you; but one day you will come out the other side and realize His grace has brought you through to abundant life in Christ.

Chastening Produces Holiness

The second benefit of chastening, as recorded in verse 10 of our text, is it makes us partakers of God's holiness: "For they indeed for a few days chastened us as seemed best to them, but He for our profit, that we may be partakers of His holiness" (Heb 12:10).

Our human fathers chastened us "for a few days"—
that is, for a brief span of time in our childhood. By disciplining us at the right stage of development, our fathers positioned us for a lifetime of successful living. In
a similar way, when we consider the eternal benefits of
God's chastening, His afflictions in our lives are compar-
atively brief—only for "a few days" in the grand scheme
of things. Even if they last *years* in this sojourn, they will
be seen as merely "a few days" in light of eternity.

Our human fathers chastened us "as seemed best to
them" (Heb 12:10). Their knowledge and understanding
was limited, and their motives were sometimes mixed
with clouded judgment or limited experience. They did
their best, but they chastened us imperfectly. In contrast, our heavenly Father's corrections are perfect in every respect, without error or excess, tailored for nothing
but our profit.

God chastens to grant us greater entrance into the
vast storehouses of His holiness. We'll find depths of intimacy with Jesus that were opened only through chastening. Holiness is beautiful, intimate, fiery, and highly
desirable. It bestows authority. This explains why chastening is part of the process of bringing us into higher
authority in the kingdom; the chastening is necessary
so that we might properly steward the greater authority
that comes with the higher office.

Hebrews 12:10 affirms that God has holy purpose in
chastening us. Even though there is pain for a season,
God is using it to produce a positive result. God assures
us there is purpose in the pain. The reason hell is so
hellish is because its sufferings are without purpose—
making men only more like demons. In the kingdom,
suffering always has noble purpose—making us more
like Christ. Purpose-driven suffering carries the hope of

greater holiness and a higher calling.

Someone might ask, "Are you saying God uses sickness or trouble to make us more holy?" No. Sickness or infirmity doesn't make anyone holy. In fact, it can have the opposite effect. Some people become disoriented in their infirmity and lose their way. It makes us holy only if we respond properly.

God's design is for the trouble to produce spiritual desperation, causing us to press into the word and prayer with passion and zeal. Most people don't pursue God with desperation on their own initiative. We're little children. We need parental help. The Father uses chastening to help us find dimensions of holiness we wouldn't have discovered without His intervention.

It's not the crisis that changes us, but the pursuit of God in the crisis. As we abide in the word and the Spirit, He brings us into His holiness. Calamity is simply a catalyst to get us there.

Let's Also Look at Revelation 3

As already stated, Hebrews 12:9-10 mentions two benefits of chastening. But there are more. Revelation 3:14-22 presents four additional benefits of the Lord's chastening.

> "And to the angel of the church of the Laodiceans write, 'These things says the Amen, the Faithful and True Witness, the Beginning of the creation of God: "I know your works, that you are neither cold nor hot. I could wish you were cold or hot. So then, because you are lukewarm, and neither cold nor hot, I will vomit you out of My mouth. Because you say, 'I am rich, have become wealthy, and have need of nothing'—and do not know that you are wretched, miserable, poor, blind, and naked—I counsel you to buy from Me gold refined in the fire, that you may be rich; and white garments, that you

may be clothed, that the shame of your nakedness may not be revealed; and anoint your eyes with eye salve, that you may see. As many as I love, I rebuke and chasten. Therefore be zealous and repent. Behold, I stand at the door and knock. If anyone hears My voice and opens the door, I will come in to him and dine with him, and he with Me. To him who overcomes I will grant to sit with Me on My throne, as I also overcame and sat down with My Father on His throne. He who has an ear, let him hear what the Spirit says to the churches.'"

In this passage, Jesus said, "As many as I love, I rebuke and chasten." One reason you can trust Jesus' chastening is because He Himself was chastened of the Father. You want to be chastened by someone who has experienced it themselves. That's why you can fully trust Jesus when He goes to chastening in your life. He chastens in compassion and He knows its benefits.

This letter to the Laodiceans is a sister passage to Hebrews 12, keying on the topic of chastening. When we examine this letter, I believe we can see what Jesus was seeking to accomplish in their lives. His letter conveyed four benefits He wanted them to enjoy as a result of His chastening:

- He wanted to rescue them from spiritual lukewarmness.
- He wanted them to see their true spiritual condition.
- He wanted them to be changed in His refining fire.
- He wanted to bring them into greater intimacy with Him.

Let's look at these four benefits.

Chastening Produces Spiritual Fervency

The first benefit of chastening in Revelation 3:14-22

is that it compels us to discard spiritual apathy. Either we become cold or hot in fervency for Jesus. He said, "I could wish you were cold or hot." Now, it *is* possible to be passive and neutral—until Jesus chastens. Once He chastens, though, you can no longer sit on the fence. The intensity of the trial will throw you into one of two opposite responses: Either you'll press into Him with fiery abandonment (become hot), or you'll be offended and pull back from His embrace (become cold). It will be impossible to remain lukewarm in the middle ground.

Jesus warned that in the last days, "The love of many will grow cold" (Matt 24:12). In such a spiritual climate, what could be more merciful and compassionate than for Him to visit us with His chastening rod? When you realize He has chastened to make your love fierier and more fervent, you can only bow in gratefulness for such a tender mercy.

Chastening Produces a Clearer Self-Appraisal

The second benefit of chastening in Revelation 3 is that it reveals our true spiritual condition. Historically, God's people have never done well with material prosperity (e.g., Hosea 13:6). When we're rich and comfortable, we tend to sink into spiritual poverty without even realizing it. The Laodiceans thought they were rich spiritually because God had supplied all their needs—so rich, in fact, they had need of nothing. But Jesus saw their condition differently. To Him, they were wretched, miserable, poor, blind, and naked.

To see themselves as Jesus saw them, they needed to be chastened. They needed the film to be removed from their eyes so they could see how bankrupt they really were. Chastening is God's way of going after our spiritual cataracts.

You might see yourself as full of the joy of the Lord, but when trouble hits your life and your joy disappears, you realize how shallow your joy truly is. You might think of yourself as full of faith, but when calamity hits and your faith suddenly evaporates, you are faced with the glaring poverty of your soul. You might think you have keen spiritual perception, but when God immerses you in the darkness of a deep trial, you come to realize just how blind you are.

When God uses difficulty to help us see our true spiritual condition, we realize His rod is gentle and kind. Without it, we would have continued in our self-deception.

Chastening Produces Character Change

The third benefit of chastening in the letter to the Laodiceans is that it grants an opportunity for character development. His chastening is portrayed as a refining fire. In the fiery trial, we have opportunity to "buy" from Jesus "gold refined in the fire," which in one word is *Christlikeness*. When we buy something, we're exchanging money for a product or service. To buy something, therefore, means we lose one thing in order to gain another. Buying the gold of godly character will cost us something.

Some things in the kingdom are freely *given* to us, such as forgiveness, healing, deliverance, provision, peace, joy, etc. But there are other things in the kingdom that we must *buy*. The most valuable things in the kingdom are never free. Some things, such as Christlikeness, come at a price. Like Paul, we'll suffer much loss in order to gain Christ (Phil 3:7-8). The journey will involve denying ourselves and taking up our cross. The losses in following Christ are sometimes very real, but what is gained is so enriching that we view what was lost as "rubbish" (Phil 3:8). When we buy the gold of Christlikeness, we gain treasure that goes with us into the age to come.

According to Revelation 3:18, therefore, chastening gives us the opportunity to buy the gold of godliness. That same verse also says we gain opportunity to buy white garments through good works. And through the eye salve of self-denial, our eyes are healed and we begin to see again.

Chastening Produces Deeper Intimacy with Jesus

The fourth benefit of chastening from the Laodicean letter is it brings us into fresh realms of intimacy with Jesus. Jesus pointed to this when He said, "Behold, I stand at the door and knock. If anyone hears My voice and opens the door, I will come in to him and dine with him, and he with Me" (Rev 3:20). He knocks on our door. *Our first impression is that He's thrashing us; but as it turns out, He's knocking in order to find greater entrance to our hearts.*

Our self-protective instincts might tempt us at first to close our hearts because we're so accustomed to saving and preserving our lives. But He continues to knock and wait patiently for us. As we slowly open the door and gain the courage to lose our lives, we discover He's right there, waiting to come in. He wants to sit and dine. He wants to talk. He wants the exchange to be intimate and candid and real. He even serves the meal—His own flesh and blood. For Him, the whole thing is all about intimacy.

His chastening reveals how dearly He loves us and how fervently He desires us.

Come to the next chapter for even more benefits of chastening.

8

More Benefits of Chastening

In the previous chapter, we looked at the benefits of chastening as revealed in Hebrews 12 and Revelation 3. But let's not stop there. There are other portions of Scripture that reveal even more benefits.

One of the benefits of the Lord's corrections in our lives is that we might become a resting place for the Holy Spirit (Num 11:25; Isa 11:2; Luke 3:22). We see this in Proverbs 29:17, "Correct your son, and he will give you rest." The Father corrects His sons so that our hearts might become His resting place and home (John 14:23). When our walk is rough and careless, the dove of the Holy Spirit can't find a place of rest. Through His corrections, the Father subdues our walk so that the dove of His Spirit might continually rest upon us.

Don't be discouraged if the process of becoming a resting place for the Holy Spirit takes a long time. God's not frantic or hurried. Allow the Holy Spirit to gently strive with the issues in your life that displease Him (Gen 6:3; Ps 103:9; Heb 12:4). He will give you many opportunities to surrender areas of carnal resistance to His will. The day will come when you realize His Spirit is no longer striving with you as He once was, and your heart has truly become an abode where He can rest.

The higher the calling on your life, the higher the consecration that is invited. This principle is seen in the Old Testament priesthood (see Lev 21). Levites had more stringent requirements upon them than the average Israelite because they served in the courts of the Lord. Priests had even more stringent requirements than Levites, and the high priest had the most stringent requirements of all (Lev 21:12). The higher the calling, the greater the consecration.

Someone might wonder, "Lord, why are Your corrections in my life more forceful than in the lives of my peers?" I can suppose His answer might be something like, "It's not that you have uncommon issues, but that you have an uncommon calling."

I want to walk carefully before the Lord in a way that befits my calling, so that the Holy Spirit might always rest upon me.

Chastening Addresses Foolishness

There's a connection in Scripture between chastening and foolishness. God chastens to target foolishness. The strongest verse for this is Proverbs 22:15, "Foolishness is bound up in the heart of a child; the rod of correction will drive it far from him."

There's a difference between being foolish and being a fool. A fool is someone who doesn't abandon his foolishness, even under chastening. As it says in Proverbs 27:22, "Though you grind a fool in a mortar with a pestle along with crushed grain, yet his foolishness will not depart from him." A wise son might have foolish areas in his soul, but he cooperates with God's grace so that, through the corrections, those things might be driven from his life.

Here's another passage that associates His chastening with our foolishness:

> O LORD, do not rebuke me in Your wrath, nor chasten me in Your hot displeasure! ...My wounds are foul and festering because of my foolishness (Ps 38:1, 5).

What was the nature of David's foolishness? Or to be more personal, what is the nature of my own foolishness? The answer is found, at least for me, by linking foolishness with unbelief. Notice the link between foolishness and unbelief in these verses:

> The fool has said in his heart, "There is no God" (Ps 14:1).

> Then He said to them, "O foolish ones, and slow of heart to believe in all that the prophets have spoken!" (Luke 24:25).

Unbelief is foolish. A fool is so unbelieving that he denies the very existence of God (Ps 14:1). When Jesus said to His disciples, "O foolish ones," He wasn't calling them fools, but He was saying they were playing the fool. What was their foolishness? Unbelief. They were slow of heart to believe in all that the prophets had spoken. The prophets had predicted His resurrection, but when it happened right before them they didn't believe.

Unbelief is consummate foolishness.

When we don't believe the word of God, we are playing the fool. One of God's purposes in chastening is to drive that foolishness from us and anchor us in faith.

Over and over in His ministry, Jesus rebuked His disciples for their unbelief (e.g., Matt 6:30; 8:26; 14:31; 16:8). In Matthew 17:17, Jesus seemed exasperated with the disciples' unbelief; but for the most part, His rebukes were not an expression of frustration. Rather, He wanted the strength of His rebukes to provoke and move them toward faith. His rebukes had the power to arrest unbelief and arouse faith.

Jesus doesn't discipline in annoyance and frustration, but in resolute tenderness. It's all for our betterment. In

His kindness, He seeks to drive the folly of unbelief from our souls. Be thankful for His rebukes because *with every rebuke comes power to change.*

Jesus doesn't just rebuke and leave it there. He follows it with the word of faith. Why? Because, "Faith comes by hearing, and hearing by the word of God" (Rom 10:17). For example, after rebuking the two on the road to Emmaus for their foolish unbelief (Luke 24:25), He proceeded to pour truth into them until their hearts burned with confidence toward God (Luke 24:27, 32).

If He rebukes you, therefore, get ready for Him to speak the word of faith!

Chastening and Money

Another benefit of chastening relates to money management. Jesus wants us living in obedience in the area of finances, stewardship, and giving. Sometimes He will chasten in our lives to bring this area into order. Solomon drew a line between finances and chastening by placing them both in the same context:

> Honor the LORD with your possessions, and with the firstfruits of all your increase; so your barns will be filled with plenty, and your vats will overflow with new wine. My son, do not despise the chastening of the LORD, nor detest His correction; for whom the LORD loves He corrects, just as a father the son in whom he delights (Prov 3:9-12).

It's not uncommon, therefore, for God to rebuke His children regarding their stewardship of financial resources. He has at least two things in mind.

First, He will correct us so we might become faithful and obedient in tithes and offerings. He wants us to prove Him as our Source and Provider. He desires that our "barns...be filled with plenty," so He'll target patterns of unbelief that rob us of that joy.

Second, the Lord chastens those who are called to steward above-average levels of financial resources. God empowers some of His servants to produce great wealth so they can support the work of God in the earth. When abundant resources flow through our hands, they try to wrap around our hearts. But God's not interested in using us in generosity and then losing us to covetousness. He knows financial blessing can be ruinous, so He chastens and rebukes in order to preserve our souls. Wow, He sure does love us!

Other Benefits of Chastening

To conclude our discussion on the benefits of chastening, I want to go to Solomon. The book of Proverbs has more to say about the correction of children than any other Bible book. What Solomon said in Proverbs helps complete our understanding on the biblical benefits of the Lord's chastening.

In the right column are my brief comments on each verse.

More Benefits of Rebukes and Chastening

The Lord's Rebuke	The Benefits
Turn at my rebuke; surely I will pour out my spirit on you; I will make my words known to you (Prov 1:23).	When we repent at His rebuke, He pours His Spirit upon us and reveals His words to us. Wow!
Do not correct a scoffer, lest he hate you; rebuke a wise man, and he will love you (Prov 9:8).	Rebuke increases our love for our heavenly Father.
He who keeps instruction is in the way of life, but he who refuses correction goes astray (Prov 10:17).	Correction secures our path in the way of life.
Train up a child in the way he should go, and when he is old he will not depart from it (Prov 22:6).	

The Lord's Rebuke	The Benefits
Poverty and shame will come to him who disdains correction, but he who regards a rebuke will be honored (Prov 13:18).	When we respond properly to rebuke, the Lord honors us. As Bill Johnson has said, He disciplines us so we can survive His blessings.
The ear that hears the rebukes of life will abide among the wise. He who disdains instruction despises his own soul, but he who heeds rebuke gets understanding (Prov 15:31-32). The rod and rebuke give wisdom, but a child left to himself brings shame to his mother (Prov 29:15).	Hearing the Lord's rebukes brings us into the ranks of the wise.
Chasten your son while there is hope, and do not set your heart on his destruction (Prov 19:18). Do not withhold correction from a child, for if you beat him with a rod, he will not die. You shall beat him with a rod, and deliver his soul from hell (Prov 23:13-14).	Chastening can save us from destruction. In kindness, God judges our hearts now rather than later. It's much better to put hindering issues behind us now than to face their consequences at the final judgment.
He who rebukes a man will find more favor afterward than he who flatters with the tongue (Prov 28:23).	After the whole thing is over and we have clear perspective on what transpired, we will be so grateful the Lord loved us enough to rebuke us.

When we consider all the Lord's benefits in chastening, we understand why David, in speaking of His judgments, said, "More to be desired are they than gold, yea, than much fine gold; sweeter also than honey and the honeycomb" (Ps 19:10). His judgments are intense and even fearful, but they are highly desirable because of the sweet rewards they produce in the end.

Aren't you glad you're a son or daughter and a partaker of His holiness?

Be Zealous for God's Intended Purpose

We must be zealous to reap every glorious benefit of the Lord's chastening. Why? Because it's possible to forfeit some of them. For example, Isaiah indicated that Israel's captivity in Babylon didn't produce in them all the benefits He had designed. Here's how Isaiah put it:

> We have been with child, we have been in pain; we have, as it were, brought forth wind; we have not accomplished any deliverance in the earth, nor have the inhabitants of the world fallen (Isa 26:18).

Isaiah likened their captivity to a pregnant woman bringing a baby to birth. God wanted the womb of their captivity to birth something of eternal value in the nation. They appeared to be pregnant, but when the release finally came, no baby came out. They didn't emerge with spiritual authority to accomplish deliverance in the earth; they just passed gas.

According to the above passage, God wanted to form them into ministers of His deliverance in the earth. He wanted to spread spiritual life to the Gentiles through their witness.[1] But sadly enough, they didn't enter into that intended benefit of the captivity.

My heart is zealous (Rev 3:19) to lay hold of that for which Christ has laid hold of me (Phil 3:12). I don't want to endure all the chastening but then, in the end, only blow hot air. The benefits of chastening are too rich and meaningful to forfeit.

Be zealous, therefore, to extract from the trial every benefit He is intending. May you become a deliverer in the earth!

---

1   The verb "to fall" in Isaiah 26:18 has eighteen shades of meaning, the meaning here being "to come to new life."

9

The Pain of Chastening

Now we're going to talk about the painful aspects of chastening because that's where our Hebrews 12 text takes us next.

> Now no chastening seems to be joyful for the present, but painful; nevertheless, afterward it yields the peaceable fruit of righteousness to those who have been trained by it (Heb 12:11).

The verse makes no bones about it: Chastening can be *painful*, especially if the trial is particularly intense.

Some translations (such as the New King James) render the Greek *lupe* as *painful*. *Lupe* means sadness, grief, heaviness, or sorrow, so the King James rendering of *grievous* is probably most accurate. Grief is a natural response to loss. In *grievous*, the idea of pain is inferred and assumed.

Elihu spoke of the painful side of chastening when he said, "Man is also chastened with pain on his bed, and with strong pain in many of his bones" (Job 33:19). Paul pointed to the intensity of chastening when he wrote, "As dying, and behold we live; as chastened, and yet not killed" (2 Cor 6:9).

Some Christians suppose pain is never God's will for our lives. One verse they might use to support that position is from the prayer Jesus gave us: "Your kingdom come. Your will be done on earth as it is in heaven" (Matt 6:10). They might say, "There is no pain in heaven where God's will is done in perfection. Therefore, when God's will is manifest in earth, all pain is taken away. There is no affliction in heaven, and thus His will is that we suffer no affliction on earth. There is no sickness in heaven, and when His will comes to earth all sickness leaves." They assume that if something is God's will for heaven, then it must also be His will for us on earth. I'm not sure that's totally accurate. I believe there are things that are God's will for our lives in this earthly sojourn that will no longer be His will for us when we're in heaven. Why? Because the two planes are profoundly different from each other. Earth is a war zone; heaven is not. On earth we have physical bodies on a groaning planet; it won't be like that in heaven. Therefore, when God's perfect will is done in our lives in this earthly sojourn, it will include painful things we won't experience in heaven—such as trials, persecution, infirmities, and adversity.

Some people suppose that, since Jesus is now in heaven, He no longer suffers. They imagine Him insulated from our pain. Scripture indicates, however, that He continues to feel our pains and sorrows. Our sufferings pain Him. John was referring to this when he described his sufferings on the island of Patmos as his sharing in "the tribulation and kingdom and patience of Jesus Christ" (Rev 1:9). John's tribulation gave Jesus tribulation. When the body hurts, the Head hurts. "In all their affliction He was afflicted" (Isa 63:9).

I will say it boldly. If there's no tribulation in your life, you should search to see if something is wrong. Like John, we should be living in both the tribulation and kingdom of Jesus Christ. Jesus feels the constraints of the Father's timetable as much as we do. He has delayed answers to His prayers just as we do. Like us, He feels the reproach of unfulfilled promises and the hatred of an antagonistic world. Herein is the patience of Christ. He sits with all authority and power in His hand and yet waits for the Father to release that authority. Since the wait is painful for us, it's also painful for Him.

That's a long way of saying pain is sometimes God's will for our lives—and that raises some questions.

Here's our first question.

Is It Okay to Fear the Pain?

If chastening is painful, our first instinct is avoidance and fear. Is it okay before God if we find ourselves fearing the possibility of His rod in our lives?

I believe the answer is *yes* and *no* because there is both a proper and improper fear of God. First, let's consider the appropriate fear of God.

Hebrews 5:7 shows how Jesus feared God during His prayer in the garden of Gethsemane: "Who, in the days of His flesh, when He had offered up prayers and supplications, with vehement cries and tears to Him who was able to save Him from death, and was heard because of His godly fear." Jesus anticipated the cross with godly fear because He knew He was about to endure the punishment of the sins of the whole world (Isa 53:5-6). His example demonstrated that it's fitting to fear the judgments of God. He trembled in fear, agonized in prayer, and then walked directly toward the cross. That's the right way to fear God.

It seems from Isaiah 57 that God *wanted* Israel to fear His judgments. He was speaking of their fear of false gods when He said, "And of whom have you been afraid, or feared, that you have lied and not remembered Me, nor taken it to your heart? Is it not because I have held My peace from of old that you do not fear Me?"

(Isa 57:11). The Lord had withheld His judgments—held His peace—for a long time, and consequently they no longer feared Him. Instead, they feared false gods. His desire, however, was that they fear Him and His judgments.

It's not only okay to fear the Lord's chastening, it's what He wants. But there's also a way to fear that displeases the Lord. So let's look briefly at the wrong way to fear God.

When God was using Assyria as His rod upon the nation of Israel, He told them *not* to fear.

> Therefore thus says the Lord GOD of hosts: "O My people, who dwell in Zion, do not be afraid of the Assyrian. He shall strike you with a rod and lift up his staff against you, in the manner of Egypt. For yet a very little while and the indignation will cease, as will My anger in their destruction" (Isa 10:24-25).

He was saying, "Assyria will strike you vehemently, just like the Egyptians struck your forefathers, but do not fear." When the Israelites remembered how Egypt struck their forefathers, they were gripped with terror. It was going to happen again! And yet, God said, "Do not be afraid of them."

Why not? Because God was promising to deliver His people from Assyria. Just as God had designed Assyria's rise against Israel, He would also design their fall. Therefore, even though they were under divine discipline, God told them plainly, "Do not fear."

Does God want us to fear His disciplines? The answer of Isaiah 10 is, *no*.

This coincides with Jesus' words to the church at Smyrna: "Do not fear any of those things which you are about to suffer" (Rev 2:10).

When God disciplined Paul, he refused to fear. In fact, he even took it a step further. He took pleasure in the beating! He wrote it this way, "Therefore most gladly I will rather boast in my infirmities, that the power of Christ may rest upon me. Therefore I take pleasure in infirmities, in reproaches, in needs, in persecutions, in distresses, for Christ's sake. For when I am weak, then I am strong" (2 Cor 12:9-10).

God didn't want Paul to fear his infirmities but to take pleasure in them because of the good things He was doing through them.

Should a Christian fear, therefore, what God might do if he or she abandons everything to Him? No. Anyone who fears what might come from the hand of their heavenly Father "has not been made perfect in love," because "perfect love casts out fear" (1 John 4:18). Love is perfected in us when we no longer fear God's fiery dealings, but welcome the severe mercy that redirects our lives. Perfected love is confident that everything He does in our lives is for our good and His glory.

So should we fear the chastening of the Lord? No!

But should we fear God when we're under His mighty hand? According to Hebrews 5:7 and Isaiah 57:11, yes!

It's both yes and no.[1]

One way to decipher between the true fear of the Lord and an unholy fear of God is to discern the direction in which it is taking you. If the fear you're feeling is causing you to pull away from the Lord and shrink back, then it is an unholy fear. If the fear you're feeling, however, causes you to draw closer to God and wrap your trembling arms around Him, then you are under the true fear of the Lord. We never fear the fear of the Lord, but run into it with confident love.

1 When Jesus taught on the fear of God in Luke 12:4-7, He articulated this same paradox. He said, "Yes, I say to you, fear Him!...Do not fear therefore; you are of more value than many sparrows." Jesus said, "Fear Him...Do not fear." It's a paradox. We do both.

Now to the next question about pain.

If It's Painful, Is It Always a Chastening?

No.

God is sovereign over everything. But I don't believe God's sovereignty means He is the providential architect of every trial and affliction people face. Sometimes, God has no causative involvement in certain trials and calamites. If God is involved, then we can probably call it a chastening to some extent. But if God is completely uninvolved in causing the painful trial, it's not a chastening. Chastening only describes situations in which God has at least partial involvement.

I see five possible causative elements in the difficulties of life: God, Satan, myself, people, and the broken nature of our fallen created order. For a fuller discussion of these five elements, please see chapter 18. But for now, let me make a couple brief, clarifying comments.

Not every trial is the Father's chastening. Sometimes sickness or calamity is purely demonic in its origins. Peter testified that Jesus went about "healing all who were oppressed by the devil" (Acts 10:38). Some trials come to us from the devil, and God has no part in them.

A sister once asked me, "I have brain cancer. Could that be the Lord's chastening in my life?" I didn't even stop to pray before answering her. I immediately said, "No!" There are some things that come into our lives concerning which God has no part. I don't believe God is ever behind cancer. I consider cancer to be a demonic affliction. And there are many other kinds of sickness and disease I consider to be totally demonic, such as lupus, colitis, diabetes, leukemia, manic disorders, hepatitis, chronic fatigue, gout, tumors, heart disease, emphysema, migraines, ADHD, Alzheimer's, epilepsy, multiple sclerosis, malaria, etc. If in some cases these afflictions are not demonic in origin, then they are the result of living in a broken creation. But they are not from God.

I will say it boldly: God doesn't use these foul afflictions to chasten His beloved children. The Lord wants to heal His children of these afflictions, that they might serve Him wholeheartedly. Now, can God somehow produce eternal kingdom fruit even through demonic afflictions such as those just mentioned? Yes, with God nothing is impossible. But was the sickness designed by Him to achieve redemptive purposes in our lives? My answer is *no*. (I qualify my meaning in chapters 11 and 23, because we must always make room for God's sovereignty.)

Some trials are simply the result of living in a broken world. For example, when a child suffers a lack of oxygen and is born with cerebral palsy, that is not an instance of the Father's chastening. That tragedy is the consequence of living in a broken, imperfect world. People have car accidents, motorcycle accidents, and other kinds of tragic accidents. In many accidents, neither God nor Satan are the cause. In a fallen world, sometimes accidents just happen.

My point here is that we shouldn't assume every trial in life is a chastening. Rather, we should "test the spirits, whether they are of God" (1 John 4:1). To "test the spirits" means to ask the Lord for discernment into the possible spiritual causations behind a situation. We need God's help to discern between the activities of heavenly spirits, demonic spirits, and human spirits. Understanding the causation helps us know how to respond. We know from James 4:7 that when God is chastening we submit to Him, and when Satan is assaulting we resist him. (More on that in chapter 19.)

Now to the next question.

Does God Chasten Incessantly?

Sometimes it sure feels like it! When we're in the painful crucible of the Lord's corrections, we often find ourselves crying with the psalmists, "How long, O Lord? Will this last *forever*?" But God's word assures us His disciplines are not interminable. That's the main point of this marvelous passage:

> Does the plowman keep plowing all day to sow? Does he keep turning his soil and breaking the clods? When he has leveled its surface, does he not sow the black cummin and scatter the cummin, plant the wheat in rows, the barley in the appointed place, and the spelt in its place? For He instructs him in right judgment, His God teaches him. For the black cummin is not threshed with a threshing sledge, nor is a cartwheel rolled over the cummin; but the black cummin is beaten out with a stick, and the cummin with a rod. Bread flour must be ground; therefore he does not thresh it forever, break it with his cartwheel, or crush it with his horsemen. This also comes from the LORD of hosts, who is wonderful in counsel and excellent in guidance (Isa 28:24-29).

The farmer and baker reveal the ways of God. The farmer doesn't plow the ground incessantly but eventually stops plowing so seed can be sown. And the baker doesn't grind wheat incessantly but eventually ceases grinding so he can form the flour into a loaf of bread. Similarly, God doesn't chasten interminably, but the time comes when He forms us into bread that will nourish others.

If soil is over-plowed, the right time to sow seed will be missed. If wheat is over-threshed, it can be spoiled. God is too wise for that. As David wrote, "He will not always strive with us, nor will He keep His anger forever"

(Ps 103:9). And the Lord affirmed through Isaiah, "For I will not contend forever, nor will I always be angry; for the spirit would fail before Me, and the souls which I have made" (Isa 57:16).

The point here is simple: God won't chasten forever. He will do it just long enough to get the fullest flavor from your life.

When Your Faith Isn't Working for You

When you're enduring chastening, you may feel like your faith isn't accomplishing anything for you. The Scriptures call this the testing of our faith.

> Knowing that the testing of your faith produces patience (Jas 1:3).

> In this you greatly rejoice, though now for a little while, if need be, you have been grieved by various trials, that the genuineness of your faith, being much more precious than gold that perishes, though it is tested by fire, may be found to praise, honor, and glory at the revelation of Jesus Christ (1 Pet 1:6-7).

When Peter said in the above verse, "you have been *grieved* by various trials," *grieved* is the same Greek word that is rendered *painful* in Hebrews 12:11. "Now no chastening seems to be joyful for the present, but *painful*." Perhaps Peter had the Lord's chastening in mind when he wrote about the testing of our faith. He understood the test to be *painful* or *grievous*.

Here's one way I define *the testing of your faith*. It's when Christianity isn't working for you. It's when certain things you believe about Jesus and His kingdom aren't manifesting in your life. No matter how much you exercise faith, nothing seems to change. You feel like the circuitry between you and heaven is disconnected. God's power doesn't seem to be reaching to your pain. You affirm things in faith, but don't experience them. You question your own faith. It's a faith test.

God tests our faith by not responding to it immediately.

When our faith is being tested, the lights are out and the house is dark. All we can do is affirm what we believe, even though none of it seems to be working for us. We must endure in faith—until the lights come on and the power is restored. When the answer comes, it probably indicates the test is complete.

In describing the testing of our faith, Peter uses the metaphor of gold being refined in fire. Here's what makes the fire so hot: Heaven is silent at precisely the time you're most desperate for heaven to talk. *Ouch!* This flame turns your faith into a molten state. When gold is molten, it's in its most vulnerable and volatile condition. If mishandled or spilled, it can damage other materials or be lost irretrievably. And yet it is also in its most malleable condition, easily formed into a vessel useful to the master.

Above, I quoted James 1:3, "Knowing that the testing of your faith produces endurance."[2] The next verse in James is one of the greatest promises in the Bible: "But let endurance have its perfect work, that you may be perfect and complete, lacking nothing" (Jas 1:4). James indicated that endurance has the power to do in your life what nothing else could do. Endurance is so transformative that you will emerge from this fiery trial "perfect and complete, lacking nothing." Perfect in faith, love, holiness, and the knowledge of Christ. Lacking nothing in intimacy, wisdom, power, or godliness. Yes, the season of endurance is probably painful. But the implications of the James 1:4 promise are so fantastic, They make the prospect of chastening entirely worth it!

2   I am substituting *endurance* for *patience* here in James 1, because *endurance* is a more precise translation.

10

Chastening Produces Fruit

In the last chapter, we considered how chastening is *painful*. Now, let's progress to the second part of Hebrews 12:11 that speaks of the fruit of righteousness: "Now no chastening seems to be joyful for the present, but painful; nevertheless, afterward it yields the peaceable fruit of righteousness to those who have been trained by it." Chastening produces fruit. Good fruit. *The peaceable fruit of righteousness.*

Fruit refers to the manner in which others will *eat* from your life. In other words, others will benefit from the things you've gained in your journey. Because of how you responded to God's discipline, others will now be edified and nourished by your witness. You clung to righteousness in the trial and now righteousness abounds in your life, imparting life to others.

In the Greek syntax, *righteousness* is the last word in the verse, making it the emphatic idea in the verse. The strongest emphasis is not on *painful* or *fruit* or *trained*, but *righteousness*. The eminently desirable thing here is righteousness.

Proverbs 11:30 testifies, "The fruit of the righteous is a tree of life," corroborating the Hebrews 12:11 idea that others are nourished by the fruit of your righteousness.

When you've been trained by chastening, something powerful happens in the way you impact others. After being with you, they come away with a deposit of authentic spiritual vitality. Your life actually changes and helps them. Before the chastening, you *wanted* and even *tried* to impart life to them; after the chastening, you actually do so. Righteousness abounds so richly in you that others now receive from you what you had always desired to impart.

After his chastening, Job looked back and called it *wonderful* (Job 42:3). He reflected on what he thought was utterly destructive and realized God had produced a tree of life through his story. The whole thing struck him as *wonderful*—beyond his ability to comprehend.

Peaceable Fruit

Hebrews 12:11 described the fruit of this righteousness as *peaceable*. What does that mean? Well, the Greek word for *peace* refers primarily to harmony of relationship between people. For example, that's how Paul used *peace* in Colossians 1:20, "And by Him to reconcile all things to Himself, by Him, whether things on earth or things in heaven, having made *peace* through the blood of His cross." Paul meant that, through the cross, God united to Himself men who were once estranged. That's the work of peace. Peace brings two together in harmony—which is the meaning behind *peaceable*.

The fruit of chastening is peaceable in the sense that people are drawn to it. Others see the outcome of the journey and are attracted by what they see. During the journey, they may have been repulsed or perplexed; but now that the faith test is over and the fruit of righteousness is evident, what they behold is appealing, delightful, and pleasing to them. It's fruit that's easy to swallow.

Nobody opposes the righteous fruit that chastening produces. Young, old, rich, poor, male, female, single, married, white, brown, black, yellow—it's desirable to everybody.

Meekness, gentleness, kindness, compassion, mercy, love, tenderness, selflessness, humility, joy, purity, faith, wisdom—who has a problem with such things? "Against such there is no law" (Gal 5:23).

At one time, others may have shunned you, but now they draw near and gather round. *Peaceable* means they're pulled in. David spoke of this when he wrote, "The righteous shall surround me, for You shall deal bountifully with me" (Ps 142:7). David predicted that outcome while still under the Lord's hand, sequestered in a cave. But because he responded properly, chastening produced a harvest of righteousness in his life that galvanized the nation around him. Chastening made of David Israel's greatest king. The righteous surrounded him because the fruit was peaceable.

Fruit Means Increase

When you're being chastened, you might feel as if your fruitfulness is cut off and removed. But afterward, the fruit of the chastening suddenly appears in its beauty. *Surprise!*

God predicted this kind of surprise would overtake the Babylonian exiles. He was speaking to a generation who had lost hope in a future posterity. He said through Isaiah, "Then you will say in your heart, 'Who has begotten these for me, since I have lost my children and am desolate, a captive, and wandering to and fro? And who has brought these up? There I was, left alone; but these, where were they?'" (Isa 49:21).

God was telling them that the chastening of the

exile would produce good fruit in their lives, and one day they would be surprised to see another generation of sons and daughters gathered around them. The passage is so rich with meaning that I just have to quote the entire section.

> "Lift up your eyes, look around and see; all these gather together and come to you. As I live," says the LORD, "You shall surely clothe yourselves with them all as an ornament, and bind them on you as a bride does. For your waste and desolate places, and the land of your destruction, will even now be too small for the inhabitants; and those who swallowed you up will be far away. The children you will have, after you have lost the others, will say again in your ears, 'The place is too small for me; give me a place where I may dwell.' Then you will say in your heart, 'Who has begotten these for me, since I have lost my children and am desolate, a captive, and wandering to and fro? And who has brought these up? There I was, left alone; but these, where were they?'" Thus says the Lord GOD: "Behold, I will lift My hand in an oath to the nations, and set up My standard for the peoples; they shall bring your sons in their arms, and your daughters shall be carried on their shoulders; kings shall be your foster fathers, and their queens your nursing mothers; they shall bow down to you with their faces to the earth, and lick up the dust of your feet. Then you will know that I am the LORD, for they shall not be ashamed who wait for Me" (Isa 49:18-23).

When the Lord spoke to the exiles in Babylon through Jeremiah, He commanded them to marry and have children. Why? "That you may be increased there, and not diminished" (Jer 29:6). When you're in exile, He wants you to increase so that afterwards the fruit of your life abounds.

When God puts you in captivity, your first impression is that He is cutting you off and diminishing you. But in actuality, His purpose is to multiply you. He always intends for captivity to be a place of growth.

Captivity is a cocoon. It's a place of supernatural protection and enlargement.

During the Egyptian captivity, there was a strange admixture of rigorous slave labor and vigorous childbearing. Exodus 1:12 says, "But the more [the Egyptians] afflicted [the Israelites], the more they multiplied and grew."

Oppression and fruitfulness. Intriguing combo.

Be encouraged. Whenever God chastens, He's always thinking, "More fruit!"

Trained

Let's conclude our treatment of Hebrews 12:11 by looking at the word *trained*. "Now no chastening seems to be joyful for the present, but painful; nevertheless, afterward it yields the peaceable fruit of righteousness to those who have been *trained* by it" (Heb 12:11). *Trained* by chastening.

There's a difference between being *taught* and being *trained*. We see this, for example, in the armed forces. When the army wants to *teach* its recruits something, they are taken to a classroom. But when they want to *train* them in something, they are taken to the field.

The same holds true for a sports coach with his team. He'll sit the team down and, with a board and marker, coach them verbally in principles necessary to win. But teaching alone isn't enough to prepare them for the games. Next, he'll take them onto the field and grill them in nonverbal training. Each player must be taught in mind and trained in body to develop a winning team.

God teaches and trains us in similar ways. When God wants to teach you something, He instructs you in truth until it's a permanent part of your understanding. But when He trains you, He doesn't simply impart knowledge or understanding. More than that, He takes you on a pilgrimage that will test everything you were taught in the classroom. Training may involve such things as rejection from friends, relational conflict, misunderstanding, financial collapse, physical affliction, unjust accusation, career disruption, failed goals, family pressure, disappointment, defamation of character, ostracization, anxiety, depression, etc. In training, He's not simply teaching you a lesson, He's rewriting your DNA.

When Jesus said, "As many as I love, I rebuke and chasten" (Rev 3:19), He meant for us to associate *rebuke* with *teaching*, and *chasten* with *training*. The first is primarily verbal, the second primarily nonverbal.

Teaching produces knowledge, wisdom, understanding, and discernment. Training produces skill, strength, endurance, resilience, conditioning, courage, boldness, and tenacity.

I wish everything we need in the kingdom of God could be received through teaching. If that were true, all we would need to do is listen to our teachers, take copious notes, apply the teaching to our lives, and *boom*, we'd be good to go.

But there are some things you can't be taught. Some things must be experienced. Why? Because God doesn't want you speaking merely from the archives of your *library*, but from the authority of your *life*.

When it comes to the theme of this book, it's not enough to simply be *taught* on the subject of chastening. I mean, wouldn't it be great if you could just read this book, use your highlighter, do a lot of underlining, and earn a certificate of completion simply by absorbing the content? "Chastening? I read the book and passed the class." Sorry. It's not that easy. The only route to overcoming in this area is by being *trained* yourself. You'll have to experience His rod for yourself.

When we first hit into a fiery trial, we can be tempted to think, "Come on, God, let's get on with it. Just tell me what You want me to learn, and then let's go and change the world." But this isn't a lesson He's trying to teach you; it's a qualifying mete for which He's training you. To change the world, you must be *trained*.

11

Lame but Running

We have now come to the portion in our text that instructs us in the response God desires after He has chastened:

> Therefore strengthen the hands which hang down, and the feeble knees, and make straight paths for your feet, so that what is lame may not be dislocated, but rather be healed (Heb 12:12-13).

But first, I want to focus on the word *lame*. Our text refers to *what is lame*, which indicates that a body member has been disabled. The obvious inference is that the Lord's chastening may render us lame in some fashion, especially in severe cases.

To say it bluntly, God lames us. That's a startling assertion, but it's the clear evidence of our text.

Now, Satan or people or natural causes may also be involved in the laming, and God may only have a small role. But if God is involved in even the smallest measure, He is such a large player that His 1 percent tends to overshadow everyone else's 99 percent. Therefore, even if Satan is predominantly the catalyst for the laming and God has only a secondary role, it is still fitting to ascribe it to Him.

This is why Job and others in Scripture ascribed their

adversity to the Lord. Even though Satan sent the whirl-wind that brought the house down on Job's children, and even though Satan afflicted him with boils, Job ascribed it all to God (Job 2:10). Was Job naive or ignorant? No. He accurately understood God was actively orchestrating His holy purposes in the trial.

Naomi, David, Jeremiah, Jonah, Joseph, Hezekiah—they all assigned their chastening to God. God might use the devil or people or circumstances as a rod to chasten His child, but in the end He's the main player in the drama. (See chapter 18 for a fuller discussion on the rods God uses.)

Does God Use Sickness?

If God lames us, does this mean He uses sickness to chasten us? This is a huge question and deserves a careful answer (see chapter 23 for more on this). Our text points to lameness not sickness. Both sickness and lameness need healing, but they are not necessarily the same thing.

In my personal opinion, I don't think sickness is commonly used by God to discipline His children. Why not? Because He wants us to run the race with a strong mind and clear spirit. He's not trying to shut us down but engage us in a process. The constraints might be rigorous, but they're not so debilitating as to incapacitate a sound mind. Many forms of sickness are debilitating and render the stricken so distraught and incapacitated that they are not able to make spiritual progress. In such cases, the trial isn't a chastening. It's something darker.

Migraine headaches are incapacitating, as are things like strokes, cancer, AIDS, and many other kinds of sickness. In contrast, the laming of a body part doesn't incapacitate one's ability to make spiritual progress.

Lameness places rigorous constraints on the soul and body, but the believer is still able to go deep in God and grow in Christlikeness.

I believe this is why Hebrews 12:13 uses the word *lame*. It's pointing to a physical affliction that is grievous to the soul and body but doesn't immobilize one's ability to walk spiritually toward God's intended end.

The psalmist seemed to point to a laming when he said, "He weakened my strength in the way; He shortened my days" (Ps 102:23). The lame have experienced a weakening of strength. And when he spoke of shortened days, he wasn't hinting at a premature death (for he was alive at the writing). Rather, *He shortened my days* points to his being taken out of the mainstream of life mid-stride. The laming was so severe he felt as if he lost a chunk of time right in his mid-life years.

How might the word *lame* describe Job's ordeal? Is it better to say Job was made lame, or made sick? He was afflicted with boils from head to foot. Should we call his boils a sickness? I think it may be better to label them a disease. He wasn't so sick that he couldn't think or function spiritually. How do we know that? Because he engaged very actively in conversation, throughout his ordeal, with both God and his friends. The affliction vexed him sorely, but it didn't hinder his ability to pray. This is an important distinction. The biblical pattern suggests that, in whatever way God might chasten—even if it's occasionally in the form of a sickness—He preserves His children's ability to devote themselves to the word and prayer.

I'm not trying to be nitpicking or hairsplitting here. I'm seeking to represent the Father's heart faithfully without boxing Him into a corner and announcing what He can and can't do. God can do whatever He pleases. If

He wants to use sickness, He can. He's God. Certain Bible stories make it difficult to make sweeping, categorical statements about the means God will and won't use in chastening. For example, consider the following four stories that demonstrate the complexity and paradox surrounding our topic. He struck Miriam with a demonic disease called leprosy. He gave Paul a demonically-charged thorn that hurt him in his flesh. He lamed Jacob and never healed him. The prophet Elisha died of a sickness, yet with enough power in the touch of his decaying skeleton to raise a dead man to life. There's enough mystery in this paragraph alone to keep us all humble, trembling, and leaning heavily on Jesus for more grace and clearer understanding.

We can't pigeonhole God. So I'm not going to say He never uses sickness to chasten. But if He does, it seems to be rare. And I don't believe He would remove from us the ability to pray, which some sickness does. Again, the imagery in our text is not that of making sick, but making lame.

God Looks on the Stricken

One of my favorite Bible verses, Isaiah 66:2, speaks to the issue of laming in chastening.

> "But on this one will I look: on him who is poor and of a contrite spirit, and who trembles at My word."

The Hebrew adjective for contrite, *nakeh*, literally means *smitten* or *maimed*. Figuratively, it can mean *dejected*. The word is sometimes translated *lame* in the King James Version. The Amplified Bible translates it, "a broken or wounded spirit."

The related verb *nakah* occurs in Song of Solomon 5:7 where the Shulamite is *struck* by the watchmen. Thus, in Isaiah 66:2, an accurate rendering for *a contrite spirit* would be *a stricken spirit*.

Nakah is translated *beat* in Proverbs in regards to chastening: "Do not withhold correction from a child, for if you *beat* him with a rod, he will not die. You shall *beat* him with a rod, and deliver his soul from hell" (Prov 23:13-14).

The biblical idea of chastening carries with it, therefore, the idea of being struck or beaten. The assurance of Isaiah 66:2 is that, when you are struck (lamed) by God and respond properly with a stricken spirit, He promises to set His eyes on you and look upon you—for good.

Jesus Was Lamed

When Hebrews 12 speaks of strengthening hands and knees and setting a straight course for the feet, the connection to the nail-wounds of the cross seems obvious. On the cross, Jesus summoned all the strength of His hands and knees to procure our salvation. When He descended to hell, He walked a straight course of holiness with His nail-scarred feet, preaching to the souls in prison (1 Pet 3:19). Consequently, instead of being permanently lamed by the cross, Jesus was healed and raised up. When He showed His wounds to His apostles after the resurrection, they were healed wounds.

Jesus was lamed on the cross. He did not die of a sickness; He died of laming wounds. Yes, He bore our sicknesses and diseases on the cross (Isa 53:5; Matt 8:16-17; 1 Pet 2:24), but He didn't die from sickness. He was maimed, stricken, and impaled. If Jesus was lamed by the Father, might we experience something similar? And if He was resurrected, might we experience the same?

The Lame Running a Race

Hebrews 11 trumpets the examples of men and women of faith who went before us. Hebrews 12 deals with the practical manner in which we follow them. We want to find what they found—a place in the great cloud of witnesses (Heb 12:1).

Hebrews 11 depicts our journey as a *pilgrimage* (v. 13). Hebrews 12 depicts it as a *race:* "Let us run with endurance the race that is set before us" (v. 1). We are running the same course yesterday's heroes ran, and the race is on for the prize.

When the writer comes to Hebrews 12:12-13, he still seems to have the idea of a race in mind.

> Therefore strengthen the hands which hang down, and the feeble knees, and make straight paths for your feet, so that what is lame may not be dislocated, but rather be healed.

The stricken saint is often prone to abandon the race, which is why we're enjoined to strengthen the hands, knees, and feet, and stay in the race.

Chastening knocks the wind out of you. Your hands collapse and fall to your side, your knees buckle, and you're stopped dead in your tracks. If you park there and capitulate to the compulsion to quit, you'll never complete the race. Even though the challenge is great, we must strengthen our hands and knees, and resolve to keep moving forward on the highway of holiness. As we stay in the race, lame feet and all, we are healed in the way.

Strengthening the Weak Hands and Knees

How are we to respond to chastening? The answer comes clear when we look more closely at the word *strengthen* in this phrase, "Therefore strengthen the hands which hang down, and the feeble knees" (Heb. 12:12). The New King James Version uses *strengthen* to translate the Greek word *anorthoo*, which means, *to straighten up.* To compare its usage elsewhere, we see that *anorthoo* is also used of the bent-over woman whom Jesus raised upright: "And He laid His hands on her, and immediately she was made straight, and glorified God" (Luke 13:13). It would be inadequate to say, "She was made strong." Rather, to translate the word properly, we must say, "She was made straight." Therefore, I would suggest it's not adequate to translate *anorthoo* in Hebrews 12:12 with *strengthen*, as does the New King James Version.

God wants us to *anorthoo* our hands and knees, but what does that mean? Many translators render it, "Lift up." For example, the King James says, "Wherefore lift up the hands which hang down, and the feeble knees." The problem with that rendering is that *anorthoo* is something we are to do to *both* our hands and knees. You can *lift up* hands that hang down, but how do you *lift up* feeble knees? *Lift up* just doesn't quite fit.

Zodhiates provides a solution with his definition: *to make straight or upright again.*[1] You can do that to both hands and knees, so it fits the hands and knees context. Vincent's says medical writers used *anorthoo* to describe the setting of a dislocated body part. Thus, Vincent's well defines it as *set right; brace.*[2]

The idea of bracing up or shoring up is implicit to *anorthoo.* Use a wrap or a brace if need be. Don't let the lamed member just hang and atrophy. Wrap a brace around the thing, gather your strength, and continue to hobble your way forward.

How does God want us to respond to chastening? He wants us to keep moving, even if it's with a hobbling

1   Spiros Zodhiates, *The Complete Word Study New Testament*, Chattanooga, TN: AMG Publishers, 1992, p. 883.
2   Marvin R. Vincent, *Vincent's Word Studies of the New Testament*, McLean, VA: MacDonald Publishing Co, Volume IV, p. 546.

limp. We'll be healed as we stay in the race.

Isaiah 35 and Hebrews 12

Hebrews 12:12-13 is referencing Isaiah 35:3, which says, "Strengthen the weak hands, and make firm the feeble knees." Isaiah 35 was describing the glorious return to Jerusalem of God's people from captivity. As Israel returned from captivity, they were urged to strengthen the hands and knees that were enfeebled from God's chastening. God wanted to heal them so they could lay hold of their inheritance in Jerusalem.

The parallels between Isaiah 35 and Hebrews 12:12-13 are gripping when placed side by side. Both passages describe the saint who is recovering from chastening and walking into God's realized promises and purposes. Beyond doubt, the author of Hebrews had Isaiah 35 in mind.

Parallels Between Isaiah 35 and Hebrews 12

There's a mutual exhortation to the hands and knees.	Isaiah 35:3, Strengthen the weak hands and feeble knees. Hebrews 12:12, Strengthen the weak hands and feeble knees.
Feet are walking a straight highway.	Isaiah 35:8, A highway shall be there, and a road, and it shall be called the Highway of Holiness. Hebrews 12:13, Make straight paths for your feet.

There's entrance into God's holiness.	Isaiah 35:8, It shall be called the Highway of Holiness. Hebrews 12:10, That we may be partakers of His holiness.
The lame are healed.	Isaiah 35:5-6, Then the eyes of the blind shall be opened, and the ears of the deaf shall be unstopped. Then the lame shall leap like a deer, and the tongue of the dumb sing. Hebrews 12:13, So that what is lame may not be dislocated, but rather be healed.

When these passages are paired up, the confirming voice of Scripture crescendos to a veritable *roar*: Don't give up! God has a purpose. Get back in there, and finish the race! You'll be healed as you run.

12

The Necessity of Healing

Our primary text for this book is Hebrews 12:1-13, and now we see that, according to verse 13, the final word on the Lord's chastening is healing.

> Therefore strengthen the hands which hang down, and the feeble knees, and make straight paths for your feet, so that what is lame may not be dislocated, but rather be healed (Heb 12:12-13).

The chastening process can be so intense, in its most severe cases, that the child of God is lamed. But it's not God's will for the lame part to be *dislocated* or be a permanent handicap. God wants to leave His children lame no more than a parent, who has sent a child to their room in punishment, wants that child to stay in their room for the rest of their lives. The parent always intended for the child to be released at the right time. In the same way, God wants you released at the right time. He wants to heal.

Jeremiah confirmed this truth. When he spoke of Zion's chastening in Babylon, he prophesied that God would heal their wounds: "For I will restore health to you and heal you of your wounds," says the LORD, "Because they called you an outcast saying: 'This is Zion; no one seeks her'" (Jer 30:17).

Never accept the chastened condition as God's intended end.

Any discussion of this doctrine that doesn't end with healing is incomplete. To properly represent God's heart, we must emphasize the necessity of healing to the chastening process. Without this truth, the entire doctrine loses its credibility. If we don't realize He intends to heal, we lose heart to endure; but, even more tragically, God is mistakenly viewed as a strict, harsh, even sadistic disciplinarian.

Without healing in the mix, the doctrine of chastening becomes oppressive and depressing. But when healing completes the picture, suddenly the entire journey bursts to life with glorious, eternal purpose.

Does God always heal all His chastened children? No. Some don't attain to healing. But that doesn't change the truth of our text, that it was God intention for them to be healed. (For those who might ask why Jacob wasn't healed of his limp, I attempt to answer that exception in chapter 23.)

He chastened you because of His great love for you (Heb 12:6), and then He healed you because He delighted in you (Ps 18:19). In the end, you realize how much you are loved and how good He really is!

Your healing is not a nicety or a luxurious add-on, in the way that a sunroof might be optional to a car. (A sunroof may be nice to have, but it's not really necessary to driving around.) Some people view healing like a luxury—something that's nice to have but not essential to the journey. Big mistake! Not only is healing necessary, it's absolutely *crucial*. Why? Because without it, the Father's goodness comes into question. People wonder, *What kind of a Father does this to His beloved children*? The Father's reputation in the earth is at stake.

The cross proved He is a good Father who orchestrates the crucifixion of His sons but then raises them in glory and honor. How the world views our Father is so important that we are always praying, "Hallowed be Your name." When healing follows wounding, suddenly the goodness of the Father comes into full light. People see He was kind enough to interrupt our lives so He might write a story that rivets a generation. His reputation is exonerated—and *that* isn't optional. Therefore, neither is healing optional.

The Temptation to Give Up

Healing is predicated, as discussed in the previous chapter, on shoring up hands that want to fall into disuse, bracing knees that easily buckle, and setting straight paths for feet that want to quit. Everything in the soul wants to collapse and quit; but the hope of healing motivates us to press forward toward the prize.

When you've been lamed, all of heaven watches with bated breath. Satan participated in the chastening because he had an agenda to turn you into a casualty, but God's agenda is to make you a mighty end-time weapon in His hand. Your first response is to collapse. But when you move one finger, even slightly, and make the smallest movement with your hand, heaven gets excited. When I say you move a finger, I mean you do something as small as reach out to someone who is hurting. Perhaps you whisper a sentence of encouragement to them. Your wounds are fresh, and yet you rise above your own pain to invest in someone else. To heaven, this is *huge*.

I can imagine the angels wondering to one another, "Perhaps we have another one!" When you refuse to crumple to the ground, but brace up your knees and shakily stand again to your feet, heaven watches with even more excitement. "Look at her! She's still standing. We just might have another one!"

When you refuse the temptation to quit walking with Christ, but take the smallest step forward on the highway of holiness, heaven breaks into applause. The angels marvel, "I think we've got another saint like Job, or like Jacob, or like Joseph—someone who won't collapse but will lay hold of God's purpose in their trial. This just may be another mighty one in the earth that God will raise up."

Satan participates in the chastening because his intention is to steal, kill, and destroy. But your Good Shepherd intends that you have life and have it more abundantly (John 10:10). The trial opens the way to that more abundant life.

The text says that God doesn't want the lame body part to become *dislocated*. The Greek word, *ektrepo*, means "to turn aside." It's pointing to a body part that is put out of joint, and if not properly bound up and healed, will become a permanent disability. Vine's says that *ektrepo* is often used to describe medical situations, and prefers the Revised Version margin rendering, "to put out of joint."[1] God doesn't lame us in order to render us permanently handicapped, but that we might eventually be healed and come out of the trial much stronger for it.

When I was a youngster, I broke a bone in my left thumb by catching a baseball incorrectly. After the doctor set the bone, it healed in a manner that left that thumb stronger than my unbroken thumb. I'm told that kind of thing is not uncommon. Broken bones, once reset, are often stronger than their original condition. That

---

1   W.E. Vine, *Vine's Expository Dictionary of New Testament Words*, Iowa Falls, IA: Riverside Book and Bible House, 1952, p. 1174.

same dynamic can happen in our spiritual lives. When the Lord heals what was once lame in our lives, we are stronger than ever.

Never collapse! Brace up the hands and knees that you may be healed.

An Incurable Wound

When God was using Babylon to chasten the nation of Israel, Jeremiah suffered collateral damage simply by living in Jerusalem at the time. He took some hits personally from the Jews who rejected his message, and bemoaned his wound, calling it *incurable*.

> Why is my pain perpetual and my wound incurable, which refuses to be healed? Will You surely be to me like an unreliable stream, as waters that fail? (Jer 15:18).

Jeremiah expressed two feelings that are common to the chastened: There is no human cure for the malady; and the suffering seems interminable. Jeremiah wondered if the Lord's deliverance was like *an unreliable stream*—that is, like a desert wadi. Desert wadis are creeks or rivers that flow only briefly during the rainy season. In the heat of summer, the streambed shows all the promising marks of water but lo—the bed is hard-baked in the summer sun. When will water flow again—if ever?

Micah also said of Jerusalem's sorrows that "her wounds are incurable" (Mic 1:9). Job used the same language regarding his ordeal, saying, "My wound is incurable, though I am without transgression" (Job 34:6).

Sometimes, when God chastens, there is no human solution. But what is incurable with man is curable with God. Nothing shall be impossible with God! For healing to come, therefore, there must be supernatural intervention. This is where the doctrine of chastening gets glorious—God steps in!

I will say it again: Wounding without healing was never God's intention. If you've been wounded by God, then healing is implicit to your divine destiny. Hear Christ's assurance, "Nothing will be impossible for you" (Matt 17:20).

Is It Contradictory to Ask for Healing?

Someone might ask, "If God is the one who wounded me, isn't it contradictory to ask Him to heal me?"

No. There are several places in Scripture where people asked God to deliver them from a trial that had come from Him. For example, David asked the Lord to save him from adversity He had originated:

> Help me, O LORD my God! Oh, save me according to Your mercy, that they may know that this is Your hand— that You, LORD, have done it! (Ps 109:26-27).

David viewed the Lord's deliverance as proof to his enemies that He was involved in the trial from the start. He knew God had orchestrated the trial but he didn't resign himself to it as though the chastened condition was now his lot in life. No, he contended for deliverance.

Psalm 107 also speaks of men crying to God for deliverance from God-induced calamities. For example, verses 23 through 32 picture traders in ships on the sea when God commands a windy storm to assail them. At their wits' end, they cry out to the Lord and He answers by calming the storm. In response, they are glad and give thanks to God.

We see, therefore, that it's not a contradiction to pray for deliverance from a calamity that has come from God. In actuality, God intended all along for the trial to motivate us to call on His name. He wanted us to cry out to Him so that He might deliver us.

Here's the point. When you know you are being chastened by God, cry out for healing. Don't back away from faith but contend for the miraculous more than ever. Pray bold prayers! Be assured that God wants to bring you through to healing.

The Faith/Sovereignty Paradox

Many teachers who emphasize the doctrine of healing have little room in their theology for the chastening of the Lord. And many teachers who maintain a strong position on the Lord's chastening are rather weak when it comes to the doctrine of divine healing. To put faith for healing in the same pot with the chastening of the Lord is not common, even though our text does so (Heb 12:13).

The tension or paradox between the doctrine of divine healing and the doctrine of the chastening of the Lord is not like a gently rocking teeter-totter; it's more like a raucous bull ride. We're about to grapple with the tumultuous turbulence between faith and sovereignty.

Someone once characterized faith as *me getting from God what I want* (see Matt 15:28) and sovereignty as *God getting from me what He wants*. The tension between the two can be mighty powerful.

Those in "the faith camp" tend to emphasize our human role in exercising faith to bring the kingdom of heaven to earth. Those in "the sovereignty camp" tend to emphasize God's resolve to bring His kingdom to earth regardless of how people might disregard, resist, or respond to it.

The following diagram is my attempt to represent visually how these two theological camps relate to each other. Everyone seeks to find the proper balance between the two, but most of us naturally favor one side of the spectrum.

The Faith/Sovereignty Balance

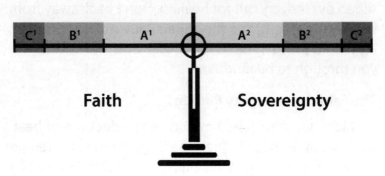

Let me explain what this diagram is depicting.

Sections A1 and A2: These two portions of the diagram represent those truths on both sides of the paradox that both camps espouse and agree upon. When it comes to truths about faith and sovereignty, most believers are able to agree with each other on the fundamentals of both doctrines.

Section B1: This section represents teachings of the faith camp that are true, accurate, and necessary, but which are dismissed, resisted, and even rejected by the sovereignty camp.

Section B2: This section represents teachings of the sovereignty camp that are true, accurate, and necessary, but which are dismissed, resisted, and even rejected by the faith camp.

Section C1: This portion of the diagram represents teachings in the faith camp that are reactionary to the sovereignty camp. When the sovereignty camp resists the truths in B1, the faith camp sometimes reacts and over-reaches, claiming things that are extreme, imbalanced, and erroneous.

Section C2: This portion of the diagram represents teachings in the sovereignty camp that are reactionary to the faith camp. When the faith camp resists the truths in B2, the sovereignty camp sometimes reacts and over-reaches, claiming things that are extreme, imbalanced, and erroneous.

The most balanced understanding in this paradox is that which subscribes to the truths of A and B while rejecting the excesses of C. It's challenging and rare to find those who are able to say *yes* to all the truths in both B1 and B2. Most of us tend to favor one side of the fulcrum.

The excesses of C1 and C2 produce theological quarrels in the body of Christ. Those on either side of the paradox accuse the other of being deceived and extreme in their views. The things taught in C1 and C2 cause each camp to feel justified in their antagonism toward the other.

As an illustration, let me show how the topic of divine healing might fit into this diagram.

Divine Healing in the Diagram

A1: This part of the diagram represents faith statements about healing that virtually everyone agrees with. For example, the faith camp will say that divine healing is available to those who have faith to be healed. The sovereignty camp will usually agree with that statement.

A2: This part of the diagram represents sovereignty statements about healing that virtually everyone will agree with. For example, the sovereignty camp will say that authentic trust surrenders one's health fully to the hands of God and believes in His providential goodness. The faith camp will usually agree with that statement.

B1: This part of the diagram represents things the faith camp will say about divine healing which are true, but which are resisted by the sovereignty camp. For example, the faith camp will sometimes say believers suffer foolishly in their bodies because they have submitted to sickness and infirmity that has been laid on them by the devil. The sovereignty camp will resist that statement because they don't want to think they're submitting to the devil. They will argue that they're submitting to God. They would do well, however, to receive what the faith camp has to say in section B1.

B2: This part of the diagram represents things the sovereignty camp will say about divine healing which are true, but which are resisted by the faith camp. For example, the sovereignty camp will say that God sometimes purposes to use sickness and infirmity redemptively in the lives of His children to conform them to the image of Christ. The faith camp will resist that statement because they perceive it to undermine faith for healing. They may respond cynically with comments such as, "Well then, ask God for even more sickness!" They would do well, however, to receive what the sovereignty camp has to say in section B2.

C1: This part of the diagram represents excessive positions in the faith camp. When the sovereignty camp resists the truths in section B1 of the diagram, the faith camp tends to react and make extreme statements to try to make a point. For example, some in the faith camp might say that all sickness, infirmity, and affliction is only from the devil and is never God's will for our lives. But that's not true. It's an extreme position that has stepped over into error, and it only makes the sovereignty camp feel justified in their opposition.

C2: This part of the diagram represents excessive positions in the sovereignty camp. When the faith camp resists the truths in section B2 of the diagram, the sovereignty camp tends to react and make extreme statements to try to make a point. For example, some in the sovereignty camp might say something like, "Believers who truly trust God will ask to be healed only if it's God's will, and then will relinquish to God whether He chooses to heal them." The faith camp becomes indignant over statements like that, concluding the saint in that posture will never be healed. And they're probably right. It's not biblical to pray, *If it be Thy will*, in an area where God has revealed His will. God has already revealed His will to forgive all our iniquities and heal all our diseases (Ps 103:3). The excessive positions represented by C2 in the diagram have stepped over into error, making the faith camp feel justified in their opposition.

My illustrations here may not be worded 100 percent perfectly, but they are an attempt to show how the paradox between faith and sovereignty sometimes tears and divides the body of Christ.

Supporting Scriptures

Perhaps I can illustrate the differences between the two camps by listing some of the Scriptures each camp would likely gravitate toward.

When it comes to divine healing, the faith camp would tend to cling to verses such as these:

"I am the LORD who heals you" (Exod 15:26).

"Most assuredly, I say to you, he who believes in Me, the works that I do he will do also; and greater works than these he will do, because I go to My Father" (John 14:12).

So Jesus said to them, "Because of your unbelief; for assuredly, I say to you, if you have faith as a mustard seed, you will say to this mountain, 'Move from here to there,' and it will move; and nothing will be impossible for you" (Matt 17:20).

Jesus said to him, "If you can believe, all things are possible to him who believes" (Mark 9:23).

"For assuredly, I say to you, whoever says to this mountain, 'Be removed and be cast into the sea,' and does not
doubt in his heart, but believes that those things he says
will be done, he will have whatever he says. Therefore
I say to you, whatever things you ask when you pray,
believe that you receive them, and you will have them"
(Mark 11:23-24).

Now this is the confidence that we have in Him, that if
we ask anything according to His will, He hears us. And
if we know that He hears us, whatever we ask, we know
that we have the petitions that we have asked of Him
(1 John 5:14-15).

On the other hand, when it comes to divine healing,
the sovereignty camp would tend to cling to verses such
as these:

And he said: "Naked I came from my mother's womb,
and naked shall I return there. The LORD gave, and
the LORD has taken away; blessed be the name of the
LORD" (Job 1:21).

"Though He slay me, yet will I trust Him" (Job 13:15).

"Father, if it is Your will, take this cup away from Me; nevertheless not My will, but Yours, be done" (Luke 22:42).

For You, O God, have tested us; You have refined us as
silver is refined. You brought us into the net; You laid affliction on our backs (Ps 66:10-11).

Be still, and know that I am God (Ps 46:10).

Therefore humble yourselves under the mighty hand of
God, that He may exalt you in due time (1 Pet 5:6).

It is good for a man to bear the yoke in his youth. Let
him sit alone and keep silent, because God has laid it on
him; let him put his mouth in the dust—there may yet
be hope. Let him give his cheek to the one who strikes
him, and be full of reproach (Lam 3:27-30).

"If that is the case, our God whom we serve is able to
deliver us from the burning fiery furnace, and He will

deliver us from your hand, O king. But if not, let it be known to you, O king, that we do not serve your gods, nor will we worship the gold image which you have set up" (Dan 3:17-18).

My heart says *Yes!* to both lists of verses. I want to be someone who is able to embrace truth fully from both sides of the paradox.

In my observation, some people tend to receive more from God when they lean into the faith side of the spectrum, while others seem to receive more from God when they set their hearts on the sovereignty side of the spectrum. Perhaps the differences have to do with personality, or with theological bent, or with how God chooses to walk uniquely with each person. The important thing is that each of us finds our own way to connect with the life and power of God. Wise leaders will recognize that within most congregations are some who are "faith people" and others who are "sovereignty people," and we are called to feed all the flock of God. So let's cover both sides in our teachings.

Before we move on, let me mention the verse that neither camp likes: "Many are the afflictions of the righteous, but the LORD delivers him out of them all" (Ps 34:19).

The faith camp *loves* the second half of that verse. They will preach passionately and powerfully about how the Lord delivers the righteous from all their afflictions. They just don't like the first part of the verse, which says the righteous have many afflictions. For the faith camp, if you had walked in righteousness you wouldn't have all your afflictions. The fact that you have all these afflictions is evidence, for them, that there is compromise in your righteousness. Some in the faith camp believe that righteousness gives you immunity from affliction.

The sovereignty camp *loves* the first half of that verse. They are so aware of how many afflictions assault the godly as they stand righteously in their generation. They just don't like the second half of the verse. They don't like to teach that it's God will to deliver you from "all" your afflictions. For them, that kind of teaching lays a yoke of expectation upon saints already burdened with affliction, and sets them up for further heartbreak.

So it's the verse that nobody likes.

But my heart wants to say *yes* to the entire verse. I agree that many afflictions come to the righteous for no fault of their own, and I also agree that it's God's will to deliver the righteous from them *all*.

When it comes to paradox, our natural tendency is to buy into one side of the equation and then look askance at the other side. To say *yes* to both is much more difficult because it requires a robust engagement with all of God's truth. But this is precisely what the mature believer pursues—the full embrace of both God's sovereignty and the exercise of our faith when it comes to the extension of God's kingdom in the earth.

The Lord's chastening thrusts us into the vortex of this paradox. We'll likely wonder whether we should be still and rest in God's plan and timing, or whether we should rise up in faith and lay hold of His promise to deliver. The paradox is in the fact that sometimes we need to do both. How do you rest and lay hold at the same time? It's a paradox. But in the end, God desires that the lame part *rather be healed*.

God Prefers Healing

Before we move to the next chapter, I want to point to a single word in Hebrews 12:13. It's a word that's easy to gloss over, but it's massive in our discussion. It's the word *rather*. "Make straight paths for your feet, so that what is lame may not be dislocated, but *rather* be healed." While *healed* is the last word in our English translation of the verse, *rather* is the last word in the original Greek text. Its placement makes it the most emphatic word in the verse.

Rather is the Greek word *mallon*. *Mallon* is translated in the New Testament as *better, more, much more,* or *rather*. The word indicates better in terms of preference. *To be preferred over*. Healing is to be preferred.

Here's what *mallon* signifies in our text: God values and appreciates the brokenness and character development that has come with your chastening, but He *prefers* your healing even more. Yes, He esteems all the good that is coming from your trial, but *mallon*—even more than that—He values your deliverance.

The same implication of *mallon* is found in Romans 8:34, where it is translated *furthermore*: "Who is he who condemns? It is Christ who died, and *furthermore* is also risen, who is even at the right hand of God, who also makes intercession for us." Let me explain the implications of *mallon (furthermore)* in that verse.

Paul asserts that Christ died for us—which is tremendous all in itself. But *furthermore*, or *even better than that (mallon)*, He is also risen. Christ's resurrection was *better* than His crucifixion. God valued Christ's death on the cross because of what it accomplished, but He valued His resurrection even more. Here's the compelling *mallon* principle of Romans 8:34: *God values crucifixion, but He prefers resurrection.* This is also true in your life. He values your crucifixion, but He prefers your resurrection.

Mallon is translated *more* in Hebrews 9:14.

> For if the blood of bulls and goats and the ashes of a heifer, sprinkling the unclean, sanctifies for the purifying

of the flesh, how much *more* shall the blood of Christ, who through the eternal Spirit offered Himself without spot to God, cleanse your conscience from dead works to serve the living God? (Heb 9:13-14).

I have a question. If the blood of bulls and goats could cleanse the flesh, how much *more* can the blood of Christ cleanse the conscience? Can you quantify the difference? How much *more* is the blood of Christ to be preferred over the blood of bulls?

The answer is, the blood of Christ is infinitely *more (mallon)* effectual than the blood of bulls and goats.

Come back to Hebrews 12:13 now, and let's allow those other occurrences of *mallon* to inform its meaning here: "Make straight paths for your feet, so that what is lame may not be dislocated, but *rather [mallon]* be healed." Let's ask the same question here that we asked of Hebrews 9:14. How much *more (mallon)* is your healing to be preferred over a permanent laming? I think the answer is the same: infinitely *more (mallon)*. Infinitely *rather*.

Mallon—it's a *huge* word!

God values your chastening, but He *prefers (mallon)* your healing.

13

Journey Toward Healing

That huge, little word *mallon* in the previous chapter is provoking me to say, I love literal Bible translations. I like to read and use a translation that is as close to the original manuscripts as possible, while maintaining readability and integrity in English. To say it from the opposite angle, I don't personally enjoy Bible paraphrases. (Paraphrases are loose Bible translations that represent the meanings of phrases rather than the specific words in those phrases. They're sometimes more of a commentary than a translation.) Paraphrases are fine for supplemental reading, but I want my primary reading Bible to be a literal translation.

Why? Because when you've been chastened, every word of Scripture becomes intensely important to you. A single word, rightly understood, can open the doors of understanding and produce great faith, hope, and love in the heart. When you're being chastened, you become desperate to know precisely what God is saying to you in His every word.

Here's why the word *mallon* in our text is prompting me to write like this. If I had been using a paraphrase in my Bible reading, chances are I wouldn't have even realized *mallon* existed. For example, *rather* is not even mentioned in the verse in the following paraphrases or translations: New English Translation, New Living Translation, Contemporary English Version, Good News Translation, J.B. Phillips translation, The Living Bible, The Message, and New Life Version. I came upon an understanding of that word because I was using a literal Bible translation (in my case, the New King James Version, although it's not the only option) that actually said *rather*. Faith is based on absorbing the actual words of God (Rom 10:17). When I saw the word *rather* in my Bible and searched it out, it produced great faith in my heart. I realized, *He actually said that word. God prefers my healing.*

If your experience is like mine, you'll find the only way to endure the discipline is by hearing and clinging to every word that comes from His mouth.

I believe, based on Hebrews 12:13, the Father wants to heal every child that has been lamed by His rod. Even if not all attain to that healing, I believe healing is always the Father's ultimate intention for those He disciplines. Those who object to my position often use Hebrews 11:35-40 as a basis for their objection. I'd like to respond to their objection. Let me explain.

The Objection of Hebrews 11:35-40

Those who object to my position might express it this way: "*Some* may be healed, but not *all*. It's not God's will to heal all." They often support their position with Hebrews 11:35-40, so let's take a look at that passage.

In the verses preceding Hebrews 11:35-40, it speaks of the conquests and exploits of faith-filled saints in Bible times. It says they quenched fire, escaped death, were victorious in battle, "who through faith subdued kingdoms, worked righteousness, obtained promises, stopped the mouths of lions" (Heb. 11:33). But then, in verse 35b, the tone of the passage suddenly switches and describes men and women of faith who, instead of gaining deliverance, suffered grievously:

> Others were tortured, not accepting deliverance, that they might obtain a better resurrection. Still others had trial of mockings and scourgings, yes, and of chains and imprisonment. They were stoned, they were sawn in two, were tempted, were slain with the sword. They wandered about in sheepskins and goatskins, being destitute, afflicted, tormented—of whom the world was not worthy. They wandered in deserts and mountains, in dens and caves of the earth. And all these, having obtained a good testimony through faith, did not receive the promise, God having provided something better for us, that they should not be made perfect apart from us (Heb 11:35b-40).

Based on this passage, my objectors might say, "The men and women of faith described in these verses didn't receive deliverance from their afflictions, even though they were commended as people of faith. Therefore, people of faith are not always healed. Just as these believers 'did not receive the promise' (11:39), there are people of faith today who will be chastened of the Lord but will not always receive the promise of healing."

Allow me to answer this objection.

There's a paradox in Hebrews 11 that isn't always properly understood. In Hebrews 11:33, it says that people of faith "obtained promises," and then in Hebrews 11:39 it says they "did not receive the promise." The paradox lies in this question: Do people of faith obtain promises, or not?

The answer lies in understanding that verses 33 and 39 are describing two different groups of faith. The first group of faith (11:32-35a) saw mighty deliverances whereas the second group of faith (11:35b-38) didn't.

Here's the difference between the two groups. The first group had promises of deliverances, and through faith they obtained them; the second group didn't have promises of deliverance, and through their faith they endured through suffering. God has not promised to deliver us from every instance of suffering on earth. The sufferings of the second group were the consequence of persecution, and God has not promised to deliver us from all instances of persecution and oppression from wicked people. Some persecutions must be endured. That doesn't make us lesser in faith. It simply means we weren't promised deliverance from all evil human oppression in this life.

When you're suffering something from which you have no promise for deliverance, what do you do? You persevere in faith, knowing you have a reward in heaven.

When it says in verse 39, to this second group, that they "did not receive the promise," it's referring to the promise given to Abraham—the promise that the people of faith would inherit all of heaven and earth. Saints of all history have died while fighting to obtain that promise. It hasn't been given yet. We will all enter into that promise together in the last day.

How can you know whether you are in the first group and can expect to obtain promises in this life, or are in the second group and may die without obtaining the promise? Here's the answer. *You know it's your destiny to obtain promises*, according to Hebrews 11:33, *if He's given you promises*. Have you received a promise from God? Never let go until you obtain that promise.

If you've been chastened of the Lord and made lame, you have a promise. God has promised to heal those He has lamed (Heb 12:13). So if you've been chastened by God, it's your destiny to press all the way through to healing. Never relent until you obtain the intended end of the Lord.

Chastening Is a Process

If chastening is light, it may be over in a couple minutes. Swat, repentance, forgiveness, restored intimacy—the small incidents can happen just that fast. But if it's a moderate or severe chastening, then get ready for a journey. This will not be over in a just a few minutes. You're walking something out with God.

One example of a severe chastening would be Joseph's prison. Joseph prayed strenuously for deliverance, but he was not delivered from prison with his first prayer. Nor his second or third. In fact, it seems he was almost ten years in prison before his cry for deliverance was answered. Why so long? Because it was a severe chastening. When you're in that kind of a situation, healing is not likely to come with the first prayer you offer. Like Joseph, you may need to walk a journey with God before you're healed.

Not every theological position in the body of Christ will agree with me here. Some believe that, if you have faith for healing, you will be healed immediately. For example, I have read authors who use the first three words of Hebrews 11:1, "Now faith is," to say, "Faith always operates in the *now*." What they mean is, if you truly have faith, you will receive the object of your faith *now*. And if you don't receive your answer now, then that means, according to their understanding, your faith is weak and lacking.

There is a measure of truth to that teaching. But I am suggesting there are unique contexts in which you can have *now* faith and yet not be healed until the journey of chastening is complete. You may be a child of faith, but the journey will require that you endure until the object of your faith can be realized. Caleb, for example, went into the wilderness with faith to enter the Promised Land, but he didn't actually enter Canaan until forty-five years later. Why not? Because God was using the wilderness to bestow upon Caleb an uncommon level of spiritual authority—mountain-taking authority.

Let me say the same thing from a different angle. When you're newly into a journey of chastening, it's not possible to have *now* faith for your healing. Why not? Because God's timing for your healing is further on down the road. You have enduring faith that will carry you in this journey, but not catalytic *now* faith that apprehends its object in the moment. You may need to wait for that releasing word of faith until you get to the trysting place His heart has designed for you. If He's not ready to take you into the next chapter of the story yet, it's not possible to generate faith for healing from your own resources. That kind of faith can't be manufactured but can only be received from above.

Perhaps this is what Peter meant with his term, *due time*: "Therefore humble yourselves under the mighty hand of God, that He may exalt you in *due time*" (1 Pet 5:6). When you are being chastened, you are "under the mighty hand of God." You feel the weight of His hand heavily upon you. What is Peter's advice? Humble yourself. Get low, that God *may exalt you in due time*. The term *due time* seems to imply that God has a timetable for the chastening, and you will not be exalted before His timing is fulfilled.

Don't be disheartened if your prayer isn't answered immediately. Rather, humble yourself and wait on God for His due time. Keep asking, keep seeking, keep knocking. Never relent. In due time, God will lift you up.

Hebrews 12 was placed immediately after Hebrews 11 to assure us there is no contradiction between the life of faith (Heb 11) and enduring the chastening of the Lord (Heb 12). *Faith endures!*

Someone might ask, "If I don't have enough faith yet for healing, what should I do?" Follow the counsel of 1 Timothy 6:11 and 2 Timothy 2:22, "Pursue...faith." Go after faith with all your heart, until He fills you with mountain-moving faith. One reason for chastening is to remove pseudo-faith from your soul and take you on a journey in God that culminates in mountain-moving faith.

We don't seek healing so we can circumvent the training; we seek healing so we can graduate.

If someone says, "I believe I will be healed at the time God has designed," there are critics who will say, "That's not true faith. If you had true faith, you would know that now is the accepted time and today is the day of salvation" (2 Cor 6:2). And yet, Jesus also said, "My time has not yet come, but your time is always ready" (John 7:6). I agree that most of the time faith operates in the now. But when it comes to chastening, faith endures in the spirit of James 1:3-4.

> Knowing that the testing of your faith produces patience. But let patience have its perfect work, that you may be perfect and complete, lacking nothing.

When you're being chastened, God isn't only after perfecting your faith. He's after perfecting you in *every* area, so that you come through the trial *perfect and complete, lacking nothing.*

Those who persevere through the chastening all the way to the healing of their wound will experience sevenfold light.

Moreover the light of the moon will be as the light of the sun, and the light of the sun will be sevenfold, as the light of seven days, in the day that the LORD binds up the bruise of His people and heals the stroke of their wound (Isa 30:26).

The Cry to Be Healed Early

In Psalm 90, Moses deals with our human lifespan in light of the Lord's disciplines. First, he extols the eternity of God. "Even from everlasting to everlasting, You are God" (v. 2). "For a thousand years in Your sight are like yesterday when it is past" (v. 4).

Then in contrast, Moses points to the ephemerality of man's fleeting days.

"For all our days have passed away in Your wrath; we finish our years like a sigh. The days of our lives are seventy years; and if by reason of strength they are eighty years, yet their boast is only labor and sorrow; for it is soon cut off, and we fly away...So teach us to number our days, that we may gain a heart of wisdom" (Ps 90:9-12).

When you're under the weight of God's hand, you feel the transience of human life—it's but a breath. And when you're being chastened, you can feel like your brief span of years is being swallowed up by God's dealings in your life.

I believe this is why Moses, in the context of grappling with these realities, cried to the Lord, "Oh, satisfy us early with Your mercy, that we may rejoice and be glad all our days!" (Ps 90:14). He was basically saying, "Please don't take forever!" God is in eternity, but we are frail and have only a few years to live. Therefore, he cried to God for mercy, that He might come to us early in the chastening, deliver us, and graciously grant us many years of gladness and rejoicing.

Asking God for an early release is a biblical prayer.

Overcoming Chastening

I'm going to continue my dance with controversy and say it boldly: Chastening is something to overcome. Since chastening comes from the hand of God, I am suggesting we are invited to overcome the hand of God. I realize that sounds arrogant, so let me explain my meaning.

In the letters to the seven churches (Rev 2 and 3), Jesus repeats this line to each church: "To him who overcomes." We are called to overcome the world, the flesh, the devil, and temptation. But there is something even greater and more challenging to overcome, and that is the judgments of God. Jesus said there are "many" who will overcome the devil by casting out demons and doing wonders, but will not overcome the judgment, because the Lord will cast them away from His presence. Here's the Scripture I have in view: "Many will say to Me in that day, 'Lord, Lord, have we not prophesied in Your name, cast out demons in Your name, and done many wonders in Your name?' And then I will declare to them, 'I never knew you; depart from Me, you who practice lawlessness!'" (Matt 7:22-23).

The greatest challenge you will ever face in your existence is to overcome the judgments of God.

In the letter to Laodicea, Jesus said, "As many as I love, I rebuke and chasten" (Rev 3:19). Then He said to them, "To him who overcomes I will grant to sit with Me on My throne, as I also overcame and sat down with My Father on His throne" (Rev 3:21). The question is, to him who overcomes *what*? What is Jesus inviting the Laodiceans to overcome? When you look at the letter to Laodicea (Rev 3:14-21), you realize He was calling them to *overcome chastening* (v. 19). It was a call to overcome the judgments of God—to prevail in the wrestling match with God.

To the one who overcomes chastening comes the greatest promise of all seven letters: to sit with Jesus on His throne.

Jesus called on the Laodiceans to overcome "as I also overcame." He was referring to the cross. As Jesus overcame His cross, we must overcome ours. If we do, we will share His throne.

When Jesus prevailed over the cross, He earned the right to open the scroll in the Father's hand (see Rev 5:1-7). That scroll represented His destiny for leading our planet into the next epoch of God's purposes for the earth. Prevailing over the cross qualified Jesus for the role the Father wanted to give Him. The same is true for us. When we overcome chastening, we qualify to open the scroll of our eternal destiny in God. We will look more fully at this qualifying dynamic in the next two chapters. Overcoming the Father's discipline will place an authority on your life that you will carry into the age to come.

Please come to the next chapter because now we're coming to the heart of this book.

14

Three Purposes of Chastening

I consider the next two chapters the most important and helpful of this book. When you understand the three purposes of chastening, the whole subject comes into focus.

I can't overemphasize the importance of understanding these three purposes of chastening. Understanding enables us to cooperate with God's purposes and enter into the fullness of the holy destiny He designs for us.

Before we look at the three purposes of chastening, though, let me give one reason why this area is sometimes shrouded in mystery for some. Some folks make the mistake of evaluating what's happening in chastening by analyzing external circumstances. Externals can really throw us off course, however, and we can end up totally misdiagnosing what's going on.

Sometimes we try to discern situations according to our eyes rather than our ears. But Jesus said, "As I hear, I judge" (John 5:30). He meant that He didn't judge people's circumstances based upon what He could see externally but based upon what He heard internally from the Father.

One of the main reasons people often misinterpret what God is doing in someone's life is because they haven't always grasped this important principle: *The means God uses to discipline the obedient and punish the disobedient are often identical.*

Let me explain this important principle, and then we will come immediately to the three purposes of chastening.

The Means of Punishment and Promotion

The means God uses to punish the rebellious and to promote the consecrated are sometimes identical. As an example, I'd like to compare Deuteronomy 28:30-35 with the story of Job.

In Deuteronomy 28:30-35, the Lord spoke of the consequences that would befall His people if they backslid and turned away from Him. He said,

> You shall build a house, but you shall not dwell in it... your donkey shall be violently taken away from before you, and shall not be restored to you...your eyes shall look and fail with longing for [your sons and your daughters] all day long...there shall be no strength in your hand...The LORD will strike you in the knees and on the legs with severe boils which cannot be healed, and from the sole of your foot to the top of your head.

All these things would befall the disobedient.

When you come to the story of Job, you realize that everything mentioned in the above passage happened to him. His son's house was destroyed by a tornado, his donkeys and livestock were violently taken from him, all ten of his children were killed, and then he was covered with boils from head to foot. An undiscerning eye could look at Job's calamities and think, "Job experienced everything that God said in Deuteronomy 28:30-35 would come upon the disobedient. Therefore, Job must be living in great disobedience. He is clearly under the wrath of God."

But that conclusion would be totally wrong. Because the means God uses to punish sinners (Deut 28) are sometimes the very same means He uses to promote His favorites. It's usually impossible to look at the external circumstances and know whether the person experiencing the trial is being punished or promoted. The only way to know if the person is a sinner being punished or a saint being promoted is by receiving divine information on the situation.

I'll say it again. The means God uses to punish transgressors are often identical to the means He uses to promote those whose hearts were perfect toward Him. The following chart gives some examples of people in the Bible whose lives illustrate this principle.

Means God Used	Punishment	Promotion
Sickness/disease	Miriam, Uzziah, Herod	Job, Hezekiah
Infirmity/handicap	Nabal, Nebuchadnezzar	Zacharias, Jacob
Prison	Zedekiah, Samson	Joseph, Paul
Exile/captivity	Judah exiled to Babylon	David, John
Wilderness/isolation	Cain, Jonah	Moses, John the Baptist, Jesus
Bereavement	David & Bathsheba	Job, Naomi, Anna
Financial loss	Jehoram	Job, Naomi
Barrenness	Michal, Abimelech's house	Hannah, Elizabeth

The means God uses to discipline the obedient and punish the disobedient are sometimes identical.

To help us understand what this graph is depicting, let me explain two of the above examples.

Example number one: Look at the first line in the graph, related to sickness and disease. God used the disease of leprosy as a means to punish Miriam and Uzziah for their disobedience, and He struck Herod with worms because of his arrogance. With these three people, He used disease or sickness to punish them. However, in the cases of Job and Hezekiah, God used sickness (with Hezekiah) and disease (with Job) as the means to promote and advance them to a higher place in Him. We see, therefore, that God will use sickness and disease both to punish the disobedient and promote the obedient to something higher. An undiscerning mind might conclude, "God must have been punishing Job, because He uses disease only for punishment." But rather than punishing Job, God was actually promoting him to a higher office in the kingdom.

Example number two: Look at the Prison category— the third means listed in the graph. God used prison to punish King Zedekiah and Samson for their disobedience. But God also used prison to promote Joseph and Paul because of their exceptional consecration. Prison was a means God used with both the rebellious and the submitted. So when you see someone in prison, you can't automatically assume the prison is a punishment. It might be—but it could also be a promotion. The only way to know God's intent is to receive divine information on the situation. Without supernatural discernment, it's easy to misdiagnose what God's doing in someone's prison.

You can even have a Bible verse to substantiate your opinion on someone's life and be totally wrong. For example, the chief priests could have cited Proverbs 15:10 at the cross, "Harsh discipline is for him who forsakes the way, and he who hates correction will die." They could have used that Scripture to say, "Jesus is dying on the cross because He has forsaken the way and He hates correction." But they would have been wrong. It's not enough to use a Bible verse in discerning God's heart; we must have the Spirit of discernment.

Again, the point here is that it's easy to look at someone going through difficult circumstances and automatically conclude, "God must be punishing them for an area of compromise and disobedience in their life." That might be true. But it's also possible He is promoting them, in His pleasure, to a higher rank in the kingdom. This is the meaning behind the above graph, that the means God uses in punishment and promotion are often identical.

When we think of chastening, the first association that often comes to mind is *punishment*—God is punishing us for something we did wrong. Now, it's true that punishment is often operative in chastening to some measure, but it's not the only element at work. There are actually three elements involved in chastening, and until we understand all three we will have an incomplete or skewed view of God's chastening. Let's start by looking at the first.

Punishment

The first purpose of chastening is punishment. In most cases of chastening, there's an element of punishment involved. In such cases, God's basic message is, "I want to teach you not to do that again." In other words, *punishment* is God responding to the ways in which we blew it. All of us sin to some degree in everyday life, so punishment is a common element in discipline, even if it's fractional.

That's why, whenever you're being chastened, it's wise to stop and ask the Lord, "Is there anything in my life that is displeasing to You?" If He shows you something, then repent. If He doesn't, then turn your focus to the next two purposes of chastening. But at least ask the question.

Eliphaz saw punishment operative in Job's chastening: "Behold, happy is the man whom God corrects; therefore do not despise the chastening of the Almighty" (Job 5:17). Eliphaz claimed that God was correcting Job for ways in which he had sinned, and that God wanted him to repent and get back on track. Was it true that Job had sinned? Certainly, in the sense that all of us fall short of God's glory in various ways. But was Job's chastening because of a sin in his life? No. Contrary to Eliphaz's diagnosis, God wasn't trying to correct a sin in Job's life.

When we sin, occasionally the Lord's chastening can follow. Psalm 99:8 shows that it's possible to be forgiven by God for a certain sin and still suffer some punishment for it. Why? Because some sins carry consequences. One example of this is when David numbered the people of Israel without divine permission (2 Sam 24:10-15). Even though God accepted David's repentance, He still punished the nation for David's transgression.

I agree with RT Kendall, that "Chastening is not God getting even. He got even at the cross." When being punished, we are not atoning for our sins. But the consequences of sin are sometimes unavoidable. We should learn from them so that we never repeat the same mistake.

The cross satisfied God's wrath against sin, but when His children sin willfully and presumptuously, they can still face painful consequences.

It's rare for punishment to be the *only* element operative in chastening. In the vast majority of cases, God uses chastening to produce something positive and of eternal value in our lives. However, there are rare instances in which God's chastening is 100 percent punishment.

In the words of Graham Cooke, "Discipline without development is punishment."[1] One example would be the deaths of Ananias and Sapphira (Acts 5:1-11), who knew better but presumptuously lied to the Holy Spirit. I believe they went to heaven when they died, but they were given no further opportunity to cultivate eternal treasure in their earthly walk.

Another tragic example of 100 percent punishment is seen in the life of King Uzziah. When God prospered and strengthened him, his heart got lifted up in pride. He became so confident in his sphere he presumed to step into a sphere not his. He felt so favored of God that, as if being king was not enough, he thought he could function as a priest in the temple. Success had gone to his head. So he entered the house of the Lord and began to burn incense on the altar of incense. God punished his presumption by striking him with leprosy on the spot. He remained a leper until his death. I consider his chastening totally punitive because of this verse:

> King Uzziah was a leper until the day of his death. He dwelt in an isolated house, because he was a leper; for he was cut off from the house of the LORD (2 Chron 26:21).

The most devastating consequence of his leprosy was that Moses' law forbade any leper to enter the Lord's house (Lev 13:46). There was nothing redemptive about being cut off from the Lord's house. It was totally punitive and terribly devastating. I'm sure God forgave him, but still he paid an exorbitant price for assuming the role of a priest in the temple. Uzziah's story demonstrates that it's better to be chastened by the Lord *before* we get lifted up in pride than *after*.

Someone once asked me, "Are all consequences of

---

1   Graham Cooke, Qualities Of A Spiritual Warrior, Vacaville, CA: Brilliant Book House, 2008, p. 32.

sin irreversible? How do you know if certain parts of your destiny are actually lost forever out of your disobedience?" Uzziah's story illustrates that, in some cases, we may live with consequences from our sin for the rest of our lives—especially sins committed knowingly in blatant presumption. But I consider such instances to be rare. In most cases, the Lord restores and redeems us from sins for which we are completely repentant. He is the God of the second chance.

I have said that punishment is rarely the only thing happening in chastening. I will add this: Punishment is not an element in every instance of chastening. For example, God used prison to chasten Joseph—not for what he had done wrong, but right. God used prison to correct Joseph's youthful propensity to talk too freely about his dreams, but that was God *purifying* him, not *punishing* him. I am not aware of any sense in which Joseph's prison was punitive.

We should not assume, therefore, that just because someone is under the chastening hand of the Lord that he or she is being punished by God for something. Those with a "punishment paradigm" of chastening automatically assume people in trouble are being punished for their wrongs. Such a narrow view of chastening simply doesn't answer how God works in most believers' lives.

The chief priests in Jesus' day seemed to have a punishment paradigm of chastening. Isaiah indicated that when they looked at Christ on the cross, they thought He was "stricken, smitten by God, and afflicted" (Isa 53:4). They thought the cross proved He was under divine displeasure. Clearly, they misinterpreted the cross.

Yes, punishment is the first purpose of chastening. But it's often the least significant element of the three purposes. And in some cases (such as Joseph's prison), it's not a factor at all.

The next two purposes of chastening really take us to the substance of what's going on.

Purification

The second purpose of chastening is our purification. God chastens in order to transform us into the image of Christ. Chastening is like a refining fire that serves to burn away the dross of un-Christlikeness so that we are changed in the process and progress toward complete obedience.

I realize not everyone agrees with me here. Some don't believe God chastens in order to purify or refine our lives. But I believe He does, in accordance with Hebrews 12:10, "For they indeed for a few days chastened us as seemed best to them, but He for our profit, that we may be partakers of His holiness." Jesus chastens in order to change us and bring us into His holiness. I understand that to mean He uses the intensity of His refining to purify things in us that won't readily change apart from His fire. God's refining fires reach places in our hearts that not even we ourselves can reach. His leadership in our lives is so effective and wise!

The punishment element is designed to persuade us to avoid that same compromise in the future, and the purifying element is designed to makes us fuller partakers of His holiness.

The Lord will refine us until righteousness and holiness resonate throughout our entire being. He has ways to reach deep and deal with our iniquities at the source. What a glorious kindness, when He loves us enough to subdue our iniquities! This is what Micah celebrated when he wrote, "He will again have compassion on us, and will subdue our iniquities. You will cast all our sins into the depths of the sea" (Mic 7:19).

Peter made the stunning statement that, when we endure suffering in our bodies in a redemptive way, we are cleansed from sin.

> For he who has suffered in the flesh has ceased from sin, that he no longer should live the rest of his time in the flesh for the lusts of men, but for the will of God (1 Pet 4:1-2).

Suffering can be a detergent.

Paul was someone who suffered in the flesh in a way that kept him from sin. God used Paul's thorn in the flesh as a means of purification in his life. Here's how Paul explained the purpose of the thorn:

> And lest I should be exalted above measure by the abundance of the revelations, a thorn in the flesh was given to me, a messenger of Satan to buffet me, lest I be exalted above measure (2 Cor 12:7).

God used the thorn to keep Paul in a place of humility, brokenness, and dependence on Him. I deal with Paul's thorn separately in chapter 20, but my point here is that God used the thorn to deal with potential pride. It was a means of purification for Paul.

Purification, therefore, is the second purpose of chastening. God's using it to change us for the better.

A Third Purpose

When I say that God chastens to punish and purify in our lives, many believers readily agree. But for some, those two things represent the complete purpose of chastening. But I have something very important to say in this book: There's a third purpose for chastening.

This third reason is the least understood of the three, and yet it's the most encouraging and empowering of all. And it's the most compelling principle of this book.

Before I come out and identify the third purpose of

chastening, I want to set the stage for it by asking the million-dollar question.

I'm about to ask the question that splits the body of Christ into two general theological camps. It's a question of paramount importance, and our tendency, when we read the question, might be to offer a snap, knee-jerk answer. But I ask you to slow down and process the question carefully with me.

The Million-Dollar Question

Here it is:

Was the cross in any respect an instance of the Father chastening His Son?

Let's analyze that question critically by looking at the purposes of chastening discussed so far.

The first purpose of chastening is punishment. Was the cross, therefore, an instance of the Father *punishing* His Son, the Lord Jesus, for sins He had committed on earth? Clearly, our answer must be a firm, *No!* Even though Jesus was tempted in all ways as we are, He was "yet without sin" (Heb 4:15). Paul said that Christ "knew no sin" (2 Cor 5:21). On the cross, He "offered Himself without spot to God" (Heb 9:14). We conclude, therefore, that Christ was not chastened on the cross as punishment for sins He had committed.[2] He died as "a lamb without blemish and without spot" (1 Pet 1:19).

The second purpose of chastening is purification. How about the matter of purifying, then? Was the cross an instance of the Father *purifying* His Son from imperfections so He might be made completely perfect and pure through His sufferings?

2 I should point out the testimony of Isaiah who said, "The chastisement for our peace was upon Him" (Isa 53:5). Some translations render it, "The *punishment* for our peace was upon Him." Isaiah's meaning, however, is not that Jesus was punished for sins He had committed; rather, He was punished for the sins *we* had committed.

Again, our answer must be a resounding, *No!* The cross did not change Jesus Christ! It didn't make Him into a better or more complete person. Rather, "Jesus Christ is the same yesterday, today, and forever" (Heb 13:8). He was as perfect in wisdom and virtue before the cross as He was after.

If our concept of divine chastening is limited only to punishment and purification, then, we would categorically rule that the cross was *not* a chastening of Christ.

But there's a third purpose of chastening.

15

The Third Purpose of Chastening

Before I present the third and most significant purpose of chastening, I want to point to a difficult verse in Hebrews. The answer is intricate because the problem in the verse is very strong. Here's the problem verse:

> For it was fitting for Him, for whom are all things and by whom are all things, in bringing many sons to glory, to make the captain of their salvation *perfect* through sufferings (Heb 2:10).

Referring to the cross, this verse says that through His sufferings Jesus was made *perfect*. (The same idea is reiterated in Hebrews 5:9 and 7:28.) What did Hebrews mean when it said the cross made Jesus perfect? Was He imperfect before the cross?

The Greek word for perfect, *teleios*, has three primary meanings: to be made perfect, complete, or mature.

Applying those meanings of *teleios*, does Hebrews 2:10 mean, therefore, that Jesus was *imperfect* in character before the cross? Or does it mean that He was *incomplete*, but that the cross made Him a complete person? Or does it mean that He was *immature* beforehand, but the cross completed His maturity process?

To all three questions we answer an unequivocal, *No!* Prior to the cross, Jesus was eternally perfect, complete, and mature.

What, then, does Hebrews 2:10 mean? How did the cross make Jesus, the captain of our salvation, "perfect through sufferings"?

To answer that question, let's look again at the Greek word, *teleios*. Its primary meanings are perfect, complete, and mature. But there is a secondary, subtler meaning to *teleios*, and it's this secondary meaning that answers our enigma.

Teleios also carries the meaning of *qualified*. This meaning is widely supported by noted authorities. For example, Matthew Poole says the Greek word signifies "the consecrating or accomplishing of a person for office by sacrifice."[1] Matthew Henry writes, "He perfected the work of our redemption by shedding his blood, and was thereby perfectly *qualified* to be a Mediator between God and man."[2] Albert Barnes puts it, "To render him wholly *qualified* for his work."[3] To interpret *teleios* as *qualified* is consistent with how Christ Himself used the word when He said, "Go, tell that fox, 'Behold, I cast out demons and perform cures today and tomorrow, and the third day I shall be *perfected*'" (Luke 13:32).

We conclude, therefore, that Hebrews 2:10 means this: Through the sufferings of the cross, Jesus *qualified* to become the "High Priest of our confession" (Heb 3:1). The suffering of death gave Him the necessary experience to become the Captain of our salvation (Heb 2:10).

There are some ranks and stations in the kingdom of God for which one must qualify. This principle is true in the natural order as well. For example, for a pilot to

1   Matthew Poole, A Commentary on the Bible, McLean, VA: MacDonald Publishing Company, Vol. III, p. 816.

2   Matthew Henry, A Commentary on the Whole Bible, Old Tappan, NJ: Fleming H. Revell Company, Vol. VI, p. 897.

3   Albert Barnes, Notes on the New Testament, Grand Rapids, MI: Baker Book House, 1983, Vol. XII, p.64.

become a flight instructor, he would have to have certain course work completed and so many hours of logged flying time in order to qualify for the rank of instructor. In another example, in order for a student to qualify for a PhD or diploma, he must satisfy a rigorous regimen of academic study and related work. In yet another example, a Private would have many years of strenuous labor and dutiful faithfulness in front of her before she could qualify as a Sergeant Major of the Army. This principle of qualification runs through all of life. Some ranks can't be reached until a candidate has properly qualified for the higher position.

The same is true of Christ as Captain of our salvation. Although He was eternally perfect and complete, He could not serve as our High Priest until He had come to earth as a Man, died on the cross, and resurrected.

Now, because of the sufferings of death, He is qualified as the Captain of our salvation to lead every believing saint through the valley of our own death into the resurrection life He purchased for us.

Was the cross a chastening, then? *Yes!* Not in the sense of punishment or purification, but in the sense of *qualification*. Through the chastening of the cross, Jesus qualified to become our Apostle and High Priest.

Revelation 5 confirms that the cross qualified Jesus as our Redeemer.

> Then I saw a strong angel proclaiming with a loud voice, "Who is *worthy* to open the scroll and to loose its seals?" And no one in heaven or on the earth or under the earth was *able* to open the scroll, or to look at it (Rev 5:2-3).

According to this passage, Jesus was both *worthy* and *able* to take and open the scroll in the Father's hand. What qualified Him to be worthy and able to open it? The cross. Prior to the cross, Jesus was neither worthy nor able to open that scroll; He had to endure the cross in order to qualify to open it.

Before Jesus became a Man, He was fully God and limitless in power. Nevertheless, in His pre-human state, He was not *able* to open this scroll. Why not? Because He lacked strength? No. He lacked the necessary life experience. The cross was a qualifier. By enduring it, Jesus gained the authority to open the scroll of the Father's blueprint for the earth and the human race in the age to come. Jesus alone is qualified to lead us into our eternal destiny in God.

Connecting the Cross with Chastening

I would like to take you to three significant verses that corroborate the assertion that the cross was a chastening of God.

> Then Jesus said to them, "All of you will be made to stumble because of Me this night, for it is written: 'I will *strike* the Shepherd, and the sheep of the flock will be scattered'" (Matt 26:31).

The fact that God said He would "strike" His Son carries a clear association with chastening.

Here's a second verse.

> And you have forgotten the exhortation which speaks to you as to sons: "My son, do not despise the chastening of the LORD, nor be discouraged when you are rebuked by Him; for whom the LORD loves He chastens, and *scourges* every son whom He receives" (Heb 12:5-6).

Scourges is the same word that is used for the scourging of Jesus at His crucifixion. Not only did the Father scourge Jesus at the hands of the Romans, He scourges *"every* son whom He receives." The link between the cross and chastening is clear. Christ was chastened by the Father upon the cross.

Thirdly, Isaiah strengthens the connection between the cross and chastening.

> Just as many were astonished at you, so His visage was marred more than any man, and His form more than the sons of men (Isa 52:14).

When Isaiah says, "Just as many were astonished at you," he is speaking of the Babylonian captivity. When the Israelites were exiled to Babylon, they suffered such humiliation and abuse at the hands of the Babylonians that people in other nations were astonished at how severely Israel was chastened in the captivity. Isaiah's point is that, just as other nations were astonished at how God had chastened Israel, in the same way men will look at how God chastens Jesus upon the cross and be astonished at the extremity of Christ's suffering. Thus, Isaiah draws an undeniable connection between the chastening of the Babylonian captivity and the cross of Jesus. The captivity prefigured Christ's death. Just as the Father used the Babylonians to chasten Israel, He used the Romans to chasten Jesus on the cross.

The Scriptures substantiate our conclusion, therefore, that the cross was an instance of the Father chastening His Son. But again, He wasn't *punished* or *purified*; rather, He was *qualified* to serve as our Redeemer.

Our Chastening Is Qualifying

Just as Jesus' chastening qualified Him as our Captain, our chastening can also be qualifying. This truth infuses our times of distress with great hope and significance.

Until you see the significance of qualification in the chastening process, the entire subject remains unclear and perplexing. For example, if your only template for chastening is punishment and purification, then Job's story is bewildering. Some have supposed that God was punishing Job for fear in his life because of what he said in Job 3:25, "For the thing I greatly feared has come upon me, and what I dreaded has happened to me." If God was punishing or purifying Job because of a stronghold of fear that had developed in his heart, we could understand Job going through a difficult season. But when you look at the intensity of his crucible, it seems like overkill. Why would a stronghold of fear incur such extreme, intense suffering? The punishment seems grossly excessive. The whole story remains inexplicable. What sin was so great that he needed to be purified with such extreme measures? If all we see in chastening is punishment and purification, therefore, we simply can't make sense of Job's story.

But what if Job was qualifying for a higher office in the kingdom? With that possibility, suddenly the book of Job becomes a sparkling, life-giving jewel. His trial qualified him to write the first book of the Bible, to become a mentor and spiritual father to every generation, to prefigure the cross of Christ, and to behold the glory of God with his physical eyes. The trial made him a General in God's army!

Just as God chastened Job to qualify him for a higher office, God chastened Jesus to qualify Him as the Captain of our salvation. It's the same operation at work in both Job and Jesus. While some see no connection between Job and Jesus, I find the connection between their lives absolutely stunning.

Here is the great hope within chastening. If He loves you, He will chasten you—that you might qualify for greater servant leadership. The higher rank comes with the grace to lose your life even more for the sake of others.

God's discipline doesn't mean He's angry with you,

even if He was "a little angry" (Zech 1:15). It means He delights in you! He is so pleased with your consecration and fervency He invites you to a journey that leads to greater intimacy and greater effectiveness in the harvest.

The Hope of Qualification

Think of it! God is chastening you—just as He did Jesus—so that you might have the authority to accomplish greater exploits in the kingdom and produce greater fruit.

This is why your trial is so intense. It may seem even doubly intense in its extremity, but God is using it to qualify you for the scroll of your own destiny in God. Once again, let me quote Isaiah 40:2.

> "Speak comfort to Jerusalem, and cry out to her, that her warfare is ended, that her iniquity is pardoned; for she has received from the LORD'S hand double for all her sins."

If your chastening is doubly intense, then pay attention. God may be qualifying you to behold His glory.

Job's trial was not the only one in the Bible that seemed doubly intense. Consider the stories of Jacob, Joseph, Naomi, David, Jesus, and others. All their stories suddenly make sense when we realize they were qualifying for a higher entrustment in the kingdom.

One reason Jesus' sufferings were so intense was because He was qualifying for an *eternal* office. When God is qualifying us for something eternal, we might find the process doubly intense.

"The LORD is a God of justice" (Isa 30:18). If you suffer double for your sins, God's justice considers that you now qualify for twice the promotion. It would not satisfy His justice to take you through a double trial and then abandon His purpose in your life.

Equity, justice, judgment—these are very important to God. It's important to God that due price be paid for things. That's why the fuss over weights and measures in the Old Testament (see Deut 25:13-16); God's justice demands that full price be paid for what is purchased. This sense of justice affects how He trains His sons. When the price has been paid, the rank must be given.

Does your suffering seem unfair? It just may be. But here's the thing: God is Master of the payback for unjust suffering. His great sense of justice demands that the unjust suffering of His chosen ones be answered. Double suffering can qualify you for the double honor of a higher rank.

Resurrection Qualifies Us

Again, the cross and resurrection qualified Jesus to serve as the Captain of our salvation. Had He endured the cross only, but not been resurrected, He wouldn't have qualified as our High Priest. Paul attested to this:

> And if Christ is not risen, your faith is futile; you are still in your sins! (1 Cor 15:17).

The implications of this statement are astounding. Paul said that if Christ had died on the cross but not resurrected, nothing that He accomplished on the cross would be ours. We would still be dead in our sins.

I will say it again for emphasis. If Jesus had been mocked, beaten, spat upon, scourged, crowned with thorns, impaled to the cross, had writhed in torments for six hours, died, and descended to hell—but not been resurrected—nothing that He labored to purchase on Calvary would be ours. To qualify as our Redeemer, He *had* to be resurrected.

The same is true for you. In order for your chastening to qualify you for your next assignment, you must be raised up. Resurrection is not simply desirable, it's *essential*.

When God heals and raises you up, everything you labored for in your years of chastening will become available to the body of Christ, and you will qualify for an even greater abandonment in servanthood.

The DNA of Your New Assignment

Inherent to the nature of your trial is the DNA of your greater assignment. Let me explain.

When you are being chastened by the Lord, consider carefully the nature of your trial. Is it related to finances? Then your next assignment will likely involve helping others overcome in their financial challenges. Is it related to physical infirmity? Then when you are healed, you will likely help others gain their healing in God. Is it related to mental health? When you overcome, you will help others with mental distresses come into peace and wholeness. Is your crisis related to your children? Your trial will give you the authority and understanding to help other parents with their children. Is your trial related to your marriage? Then God will likely equip you to help other marriages in due time.

The challenge before you is like a qualifying mete. Once you accomplish this exploit or feat, it will qualify you with greater authority and understanding to lay your life down in greater servanthood for others facing similar challenges.

The Example of Zacharias

God chastened Zacharias so that he might qualify to serve as an effective father to John the Baptist. I want to talk about his story because I believe it will fill your heart with hope.

When Gabriel appeared to Zacharias to tell him that his wife, Elizabeth, was going to have a son, Zacharias couldn't believe it. Not only was his wife barren, but she was also elderly. A double negative. Gabriel's message seemed surreal to him. So Gabriel said, "But behold, you will be mute and not able to speak until the day these things take place, because you did not believe my words which will be fulfilled in their own time" (Luke 1:20).

God lamed Zacharias in his voice for ten months by making him mute. It was a chastening.

Some people might look at Zacharias's muteness as punishment, as though God were saying, "You didn't believe Me, Zacharias, so I'm slapping you with a fine. Your punishment will be the frustration of not being able to talk until your son is born. I'm going to teach you how displeasing your unbelief is to Me."

While there may have been an element of punishment in his muteness, I really don't think that was the main substance of the trial. Rather, I think it had to do with qualifying Zacharias for spiritual fatherhood. Let me explain.

As a faithful priest of God, Zacharias was godly, blameless, and devout. He was not living in compromise but was humbly serving God to his best ability. His problem was not rebellion, but unbelief. How did he fall into that unbelief? Through deep disappointment and heartsickness. For decades, Zacharias cried out to God for a son, but his prayer had gone unanswered. As the years turned, his soul calcified and his heart became like an old, hardened wineskin. When the mighty angel Gabriel came with great news, Zacharias' heart was so hardened by disappointment that he simply couldn't respond in faith. He couldn't make the leap to God's ways. Too many had been the years of dashed dreams and unfulfilled hopes. Life had been too hard. After fifty-some years of deferred hope, this heartsick man was incapable of responding in faith to Gabriel's fabulous announcement.

I can imagine God thinking something like, "Zacharias, we've got to do some fast work here. John the Baptist needs a prophetic father, and we've only got around ten months to make you into that man. Your old wineskin needs serious renewal. I'm going to have to put you into My accelerated program. I'm going to put you into a prison of infirmity. In the same way that Joseph's dungeon accelerated his growth curve, this affliction will force you to find a new walk with Me. The intensity of the trial will cause you to press into Me like never before. In my mercy, I am granting you an opportunity to be changed. So buckle up. You're going to endure a very trying ordeal. I'm making you deaf[4] and mute."

The chastening was effective in Zacharias's life. Around ten months later, after John was born, Zacharias wrote those famous words, "His name is John," and his tongue was immediately loosed. Rather than doubt and unbelief coming out of his mouth, a fiery stream of prophetic declarations erupted from this man. Zacharias burst into a prophecy that rang with clear insight and courageous faith.

Zacharias! Who are you? You're nothing like the man of ten months ago. What happened to you?

In one word, chastening. God used a prison of muteness to effect powerful changes in his heart. The old wineskin of his crusty heart was totally renewed, and he emerged from the trial with prophetic understanding into God's redemptive purposes. If you have time for it, marvel at the glory of his prophecy after his chastening:

4 Luke 1:62 indicates that Zacharias was not only mute, but also deaf, for they made signs to communicate with him.

Now his father Zacharias was filled with the Holy Spirit, and prophesied, saying: "Blessed is the Lord God of Israel, for He has visited and redeemed His people, and has raised up a horn of salvation for us in the house of His servant David, as He spoke by the mouth of His holy prophets, who have been since the world began, that we should be saved from our enemies and from the hand of all who hate us, to perform the mercy promised to our fathers and to remember His holy covenant, the oath which He swore to our father Abraham: To grant us that we, being delivered from the hand of our enemies, might serve Him without fear, in holiness and righteousness before Him all the days of our life. And you, child, will be called the prophet of the Highest; for you will go before the face of the Lord to prepare His ways, to give knowledge of salvation to His people by the remission of their sins, through the tender mercy of our God, with which the Dayspring from on high has visited us; to give light to those who sit in darkness and the shadow of death, to guide our feet into the way of peace" (Luke 1:67-79).

God chastened Zacharias to purify and change him, but even more than that, to qualify him. Through his faithfulness in the trial, he was made *able* to serve as a spiritual father to John the Baptist.

What an encouraging story! God is qualifying us for something greater in the kingdom.

16

Brother Yun's Prison Break

Therefore strengthen the hands which hang down, and
the feeble knees, and make straight paths for your feet,
so that what is lame may not be dislocated, but rather
be healed (Heb 12:12-13).

We have come to the end of our exposition of
Hebrews 12:1-13. In Part 2, we will examine issues and
questions related to the Lord's chastening, some of
which are rather controversial. But before we progress
to Part 2, I want to share a powerful story related to
Hebrews 12:12-13. It's the story of a Chinese believer
named Brother Yun who experienced a miraculous escape from prison. I'm telling the story as it was told in his
book, *The Heavenly Man*.[1]

In March 1997, eleven house church leaders gathered
in Zhengzhou City to meet together. Brother Yun was
one of the leaders attending this gathering. Unknown
to them, government agents had followed someone to
the meeting house and arrested all the leaders. Public
Security officers were hiding in the apartment when
Brother Yun arrived. When he stepped in the door, they
met him and announced his arrest.

---

1   *The Heavenly Man*, with Paul Hattaway, pp. 241-262. London, England:
    Monarch Books, 2002.

He tried to avoid arrest by turning around immediately and jumping out the window. He badly injured
his feet in the long fall, only to realize that several officers were outside. They immediately rushed him and
proceeded to beat and kick him. They stomped on him,
pistol-whipped him, and tortured him with an electric
baton until he lost consciousness. Amazingly, he wasn't
killed.

All the leaders who were arrested were tortured hor-
rendously. Furthermore, authorities were sent to Brother
Yun's home town of Nanyang to arrest his wife and other
believers in the church.

At his court hearing, the judge rebuked Yun for his
witnessing activities and his several escapes from custo-
dy. "Tell me Yun," he asked, "If you have the opportunity
to escape again, will you take it?"

Yun decided to answer truthfully and said he would.
He was called to preach the Good News all over China
and wanted to fulfill that calling.

All the officials were furious at his answer. The judge
said, "I'm going to break your legs permanently so you'll
never escape again!"

He was taken to a room where a certain man with
a baton began to beat his legs from the knees down.
He destroyed his legs, breaking them in multiple places
until Yun was screaming on the floor. His legs below his
knees turned completely black.

Then he was placed in solitary confinement in
Zhengzhou Number One Maximum Security Prison,
where some of the other leaders were also held. For
the first thirty-six hours he was beaten and interrogat-
ed nonstop. Then interrogations were every other day,
with torture. They especially beat their heads, hands,
and legs.

Yun said he would shout out Bible verses at the top of his lungs, clinging to God's promises. He would also sing loudly, both day and night.

Because he couldn't walk, three other Christian leaders were charged with carrying him between his cell, the torture room, and the toilet. One of those brothers was a prominent Christian leader in China named Brother Xu.

An informant was placed in Brother Xu's cell to spy on them. One day he became gravely ill, and Brother Yun asked to be carried to him so he could give him a "massage." In actuality, Yun prayed for him, and the man was healed and recovered quickly.

Brother Xu hinted to Yun that he should try to escape if he had an opportunity.

As the weeks continued, Yun's depression grew. Each night, he would prop his crippled legs up against the wall to try to lessen the pain a bit. His wife was in a women's prison, and he had no idea what had become of his two children. At the time, Yun was thirty-nine years old, and it was the lowest point in his life.

Brother Xu continued to suggest he try to escape. Yun complained, "My legs are smashed, and I am locked in my own cell with an iron door. I can't even walk! How can I escape?"

On May 4, 1997, like every evening in the previous six weeks, Yun painfully propped his legs against the wall. By diverting the blood, his legs would become numb and the agony would be lessened a little bit.

Yun felt abandoned by the Lord and thought he would rot in prison. The next morning the Lord encouraged him from passages in Jeremiah 14 and 15, and Hebrews 10:35. Yun sobbed as he identified with Jeremiah's words, and as the Holy Spirit whispered assurances to his heart.

Suddenly, Yun had a vision in which he was with his wife and she was treating his wounds. She asked him, "Why don't you open the iron door?" Then the Lord said to him, "This is the hour of your salvation." Immediately he knew he was to attempt an escape.

Yun knocked a signal on the wall to Xu in the adjacent cell, asking him to pray. Then he called to the guard, "I need to go to the toilet right now." The guard opened the door to Xu's cell and told him to carry Yun to the bathroom.

Whenever prisoners were outside their cells, an iron gate in the corridor was locked to prevent escape. Each floor was protected by a guarded iron gate. For Yun to escape, he would have to go through three iron gates and pass six armed guards.

When Brother Xu came to his door, he said, "You must escape!" Yun pulled on a pair of trousers and placed as a belt around his waist a string of toilet paper upon which he had written some Scriptures. He prayed, "Lord, You have shown me that I must try to leave this prison. I will obey You now and will try to escape. But when the guards shoot me, please receive my soul into Your heavenly dwelling."

It was almost 8:00 a.m. on May 5, 1997. To the natural mind, this seemed the worst time of day to attempt an escape, with so much activity everywhere and all the guards at their posts. Yun chose blind obedience.

He shuffled out of his cell and walked toward the iron gate in the hallway. He just looked straight ahead and prayed. At the precise moment he reached the gate, it opened to allow another believing inmate, Brother Musheng, access to the cell block after completing his chores outside. He said to Brother Musheng, "Don't close the gate," and without breaking stride he walked straight through the gate.

The guard accompanying Brother Musheng heard a phone ring down the hall, and he ran to answer the phone, so he never saw Yun. Yun picked up a broom leaning against a wall, and walked down the stairs to the second floor. An armed guard sat at a desk, facing the second iron gate. The gate was sometimes left open because it was watched constantly by the guard. The Holy Spirit spoke, "Go now! The God of Peter is your God."

The guard seemed to be blinded. He looked directly at Yun with a blank stare. Yun just looked ahead and kept walking. He knew he could be shot in the back at any moment, but no shot came.

He walked down the stairs but nobody stopped him and none of the guards said a word to him. When he arrived at the main iron gate leading to the courtyard, he discovered it was already open. This was very strange because usually it was the most secure gate of all. The two guards normally stationed there were not present. Yun discarded the broom he was carrying and walked through the gate into the courtyard. The bright morning light made him squint. He walked past several guards, but no one said a word to him. He then strolled through the main gate of the prison, which for some inexplicable reason was also ajar.

Adrenalin pumped through his system. He was now standing on the street outside the Number One Maximum Security Prison in Zhengzhou. Nobody before had ever escaped from that prison!

Immediately, a taxi pulled up next to him, and the young driver opened the passenger door to him. "Where are you heading?" Yun got in and said, "I need to go to my office as quickly as possible, so please drive fast." He gave him the address of a Christian family he knew. Upon arrival, Yun ascended the three flights of stairs to the family's apartment to get the fare to pay the taxi driver. One of the family daughters gave him the taxi fare, and Yun quickly ran down the stairs and paid the driver.

Back in the apartment, one of the daughters told him, "The whole church has been fasting and praying for you and your coworkers for more than a week. Yesterday the Holy Spirit told my mother, 'I will release Yun, and the first place he will stop will be your home.'"

They had arranged a place for Yun to hide. After prayer, Yun left on a bicycle they had provided for him. A family member rode behind him on the bike to direct him to the hiding place.

The moment Yun began to pedal the bicycle was when he suddenly realized he had been healed in his legs and feet. He had been so distracted with the unexpected escape that he hadn't noticed until that moment. Brother Musheng later told him that as he passed him on the third floor he was walking normally, so it seems the Lord healed him as he stepped out of his cell.

As Yun rode on the bicycle, the Scripture that came to mind was Hebrews 12:13, "And make straight paths for your feet, so that what is lame may not be dislocated, but rather be healed." His heart rejoiced because he was experiencing the fulfillment of that verse.

Brother Xu later wrote, "I believe one reason why God chose to release Yun in such a manner was because the prison authorities had mocked the Lord and Yun when they smashed his legs. They said, 'We'd like to see you escape now!' The Lord is always up to meeting a challenge."

PART TWO

Paul's Thorn and Other Questions

17

Is God Capable of Evil?

God is good—all the time! Everything He does springs from infinite goodness. And so now we ask a profound question: Is He capable of evil? Some of the means used in chastening seem to be evil, so how can they be said to come from God?

This is a controversial question. But as you've seen, we're not shying from controversy in this book.

Before articulating my understanding on this question, I want to quote at length from someone who strongly disagreed with my position. I quote him verbatim because I want to represent his viewpoint accurately. It's important to ponder what others have to say on both sides of an issue.

The below quotation is a transcript from a sermon by John Alexander Dowie, the founder of the city of Zion, Illinois. He lived over a century ago and was a mighty man of faith—used powerfully by God in signs, wonders, miracles, and healings. I *love* that aspect of his ministry. Any time I come across someone with a passion for divine healing, I feel a strong affinity and team spirit with them.

When it comes to the topic of chastening, however, Dowie (as well as others God has used powerfully to minister divine healing) disagreed with me strongly, which is painful to my soul because of our mutual passion for the demonstration of God's miraculous power. Please excuse the length of the following quotation. I hope you find it helpful. I want to emphasize that I agree with some of the things he says, while I disagree with other things. The mentions of "amen" reflect the affirming response of the audience while he preached.

The greatest lie that ever was uttered concerning the Word of God since the reformation is to be found in Christian theology—a lie that has been the abomination of the Church and its pollution; a lie which has made it incapable of sustaining its position; a lie which asserts that God worked in such a way as to be the author of or the willing permitter of sin or disease; the Calvinistic lie, which made God—what shall I say?

There are words which leap to my lips which are bitter, for it is bitter to me to think of the infernal lie to which in my boyhood days I had to listen, that God had foreordained the damnation of the wicked and therefore had created them "vessels of wrath" to be subjects for His vengeance, and made them incapable of virtue or holiness. O what a lie! And that second lie that came after the first, namely, that God the Father in His infinite wisdom has consented that His children should be a prey to disease, to all kinds of sicknesses and infirmities, because by means of this God purifies the hearts of His children, and brings them to Himself. That is an infernal lie! (Amen. Amen.)

When did Christ say that? Where did Christ say that? If He should say it I should say to Him, Why did you say it? But He never did. When did He say, looking into the faces of suffering men, "Do not ask me to heal you; your Heavenly Father knows what is good for you, and therefore in His infinite love and mercy He has allowed His hand of affliction to fall upon you and has made you sick in your body that He might make you pure in your spirit"? Never! (Amen.) But the Son of God was made manifest that He might destroy the works of the Devil. What works did He destroy? In the house of Cornelius the Centurion, Peter the Apostle, in describing Christ's earthly life, said, "God anointed Him with the Holy Ghost and with power: who went about doing good, and healing all that were oppressed"—of God? No.

Of the Devil? Yes. Why? "For God was with Him." Do you see it? In Matthew 4:23, which I quoted last Lord's Day afternoon, it says, "And Jesus went about in all Galilee teaching in their synagogues, and preaching the Gospel of the Kingdom, and healing all manner of disease and all manner of sickness among the people."

Nineteen centuries ago every kind of sickness and every kind of disease was healed by Jesus. Peter declares that all whom He healed were oppressed of the Devil; if that is true, then nineteen centuries ago every kind of disease was the work of the Devil. Can it be God's work today? "No." Whose? "The Devil's." It must be so unless you are going to prove that God is doing the work today which the Devil used to do nineteen centuries ago. Now the lie that God wills diseases has crept into the churches, is embalmed in their songs, and taught from their pulpits, that God blesses humanity by laying His hand, full of corruption, upon it and making the people sick. I tell you this, as God's minister today, there are things that God cannot do.

I tell you today there are a good many things impossible with God because they are evil. It is impossible for God to make a man sick. It is impossible for God's hand to communicate disease.

Impossible! And why? For this good reason. That God is incorruptible and pure and incapable of communicating evil. Hence it is impossible for an incorruptible thing to communicate corruption. (Amen.) It is impossible for a being who is without disease to communicate disease. It is impossible for God to make people sinful or sick or unclean or miserable, for if He did He would then be a fountain of sin and disease. It is impossible for any disease to come from heaven, for in heaven there is no sin, no disease, no death, and no power of hell, and, therefore, it is impossible for any of these things to come from heaven. No possibility exists that God can be the Author of disease.

"Ah," say some, "wait! Have you not read, Dr. Dowie, in God's Word, 'Whom the Lord loveth He chasteneth, and scourgeth every son whom He receiveth'? Do you not know that these words mean that God chastens men with disease?" I do not: for Satan is the Defiler and Christ is the Healer. But I do know that this is the construction put upon this verse, even by clergymen who ought to know better. They evidently are not aware of the word "paideia," the Greek word for chastisement. It comes from the word, "pais," child, and that word is the basis for the word pedagogue in our own language, which means an instructor of children.

And so the word "paideia" means instruction, education, the training of a child, the education of its faculties, of spirit, of soul, of body. It means the careful bringing up of the child, keeping it healthy and separating the child from everything that is evil and making the child clean and wholesome, pure, holy, strong in every way. "Whom the Lord loveth He nourishes, He educates, strengthens, brings up as a father does a child," is the fair meaning of the original words. It has nothing to do with making sick, but the opposite. Do you for a moment imagine that education is imperfect unless the child is made sick? When you send your child to college do you say, "Now, Mr. Jones, I send you my son; educate him; but see that he gets a regular dose of sickness every quarter; knock out an eye if you think it necessary; give him tuberculosis, typhoid fever, or any suitable disease, at frequent intervals; or break a leg—love him, Mr. Jones, and chasten him as the Lord does His children: for whom the Lord loveth He maketh sick." If that were so I would say, "Lord, don't love me."

Disease is the result of sin and would not have been in the world but for sin. To make disease a part of the plan or purpose of God is to make God the Father of sin, and that would be to transform God into the Devil. Now this lie has been embalmed in song, prayer and preaching long enough. "Oh, but," says somebody, "don't you know that disease makes men better sometimes? That people are brought to God by sickness?" Are they? I deny it. I say there never was a statement made that had less of truth in it than that. I have some acquaintance with sickness. Last year I laid these hands more than fifty thousand times upon the sick. I know what I am talking about. I see often from one thousand to fifteen hundred sick persons in a week in Zion Tabernacle and in the Homes, etc., and I pray definitely for thousands whom I never see. I have visited hospitals and have worked among the suffering in many lands, and have for nearly twenty years been used in the ministry of healing through faith in Jesus. Shall I tell you what I know?

Disease does not bring people nearer to God; it drives them further away from Him. It is the Holy Spirit that brings people to God, whether sick or well. I ask you who are sitting here today, is that not so? "Yes." If you say that sickness and disease will bring you nearer to God, then suppose, for a moment, that I have a choice stock of diseases here, and I say, come up here and let me give you typhoid fever, or consumption, or cholera; let me knock out an eye or break a leg for you—I will do all this as God's minister to bring you nearer to God and to show you that He loves you. My experience is directly opposite to the teaching that diseases, the corruptions born of father Satan and mother Sin, ever brought people to God. Those who have lived nearest to God find that disease lessens their faith, depresses their spirits and leaves them in the shadows and darkness; and when their loved ones have passed away it often leaves a shadow behind that is never effaced so long as they think God sent the disease.[1]

1   John Alexander Dowie, *Jesus the Healer*, Tucson, AZ: Zion Restorationists, pp. 20-23.

I agree with much Dowie said here. I agree that sickness incarcerates the vast majority of people in bondage rather than making them better. Satan is the one who imprisons the human race with sickness, infirmity, and disease, and Jesus "went about doing good and healing all who were oppressed by the devil, for God was with Him" (Acts 10:38). Sickness is the result of man's disobedience, and Satan makes it his business to promote the horrific consequences of sin throughout the human race. The devil is always laboring to tempt us to sin because then we bring upon our own heads all its hideous consequences, which include infirmity, sickness, and disease. Jesus came to release us from sin's consequences, as it says in 1 John 3:8, "For this purpose the Son of God was manifested, that He might destroy the works of the devil." On these things Dowie and I agree.

But Dowie disagreed with me in a few regards. He said God never uses infirmity to purify His children. In the same regard, he said, "There are things that God cannot do." He insisted, "It is impossible for God to make a man sick." And I see these things differently.

How would I answer Dowie's objections? My answers will be found more fully in chapter 23, which is devoted to answering questions and objections. For now, I want to tackle just one question this subject raises, namely this: Is God capable of evil? I will present some Scriptures here, and then leave it with you to study and determine what the Bible says on these things.

I begin with this emphatic declaration: God is good, and there is no darkness in Him at all (1 John 1:5). James 1:16-17 clearly states that, if you receive something good, it has come to you from heaven. "Every good gift...is from above." However, James 1:16-17 does *not* say that, if it's evil, it comes from Satan. Why? Because, as we're about to see, sometimes evil comes from God.

Sometimes God's judgments, which proceed from His presence, are evil. God Himself described them as such:

> "For thus says the Lord GOD: 'How much more it shall be when I send My four severe judgments on Jerusalem— the sword and famine and wild beasts and pestilence— to cut off man and beast from it?'" (Ezek 14:21).

Severe is translating the Hebrew adjective, *rag*. *Rag* means *evil*. It's the most common Hebrew word for evil, going back to Genesis 2:9, which speaks of "the tree of the knowledge of good and evil."

I find it intriguing that very few translators render Ezekiel 14:21 as *evil judgments,* even though that's the actual wording. Evidently, *rag* has various shades of emphasis based upon the context in which it's used. Instead of evil, most translations use adjectives like sore, severe, dreadful, fearsome, deadly, calamitous, grievous, disastrous, bitter, and terrible. Why do they choose almost anything but *evil*? Perhaps because of the awkward theological implications of ascribing *rag* (*evil*) judgments to God. But make no mistake, that's what God Himself called them. God claimed to be the perpetrator of evil judgments.

Here are some other Scriptures that show God as the perpetrator of *rag*.

> "I form the light and create darkness, I make peace and create calamity [*rag*]; I, the LORD, do all these things" (Isa 45:7).

> "Is it not from the mouth of the Most High that woe [rag] and well-being proceed?" (Lam 3:38).

> "Hear, O earth! Behold, I will certainly bring calamity [*rag*] on this people—the fruit of their thoughts, because they have not heeded My words, nor My law, but rejected it" (Jer 6:19).

> For the LORD of hosts, who planted you, has pro-
> nounced doom [*rag*] against you for the evil [*rag*] of the
> house of Israel and of the house of Judah, which they
> have done against themselves to provoke Me to anger
> in offering incense to Baal (Jer 11:17).

> "Now therefore, speak to the men of Judah and to the
> inhabitants of Jerusalem, saying, 'Thus says the LORD:
> "Behold, I am fashioning a disaster [*rag*] and devising
> a plan against you. Return now every one from his evil
> [*rag*] way, and make your ways and your doings good"'"
> (Jer 18:11).

> Hear the word of the LORD, O kings of Judah and in-
> habitants of Jerusalem. Thus says the LORD of hosts, the
> God of Israel: "Behold, I will bring such a catastrophe
> [*rag*] on this place, that whoever hears of it, his ears will
> tingle" (Jer 19:3).

> (See *rag* also in Jer 11:11, 23; 19:15; 23:12; 26:19; 36:3;
> Ezek 14:22; Dan 9:12; Mic 1:12.)

Why would God describe His judgments as *evil*?
Because things like sword, famine, and pestilence are
evil to those who experience them. We know that God
created hell for the ultimate good of His kingdom, but
those in hell consider it the greatest evil in the universe.
Since the mentions of *rag* indicate that God sometimes
inflicts harm on people, I affirm that God is capable of
evil (*rag*).

But while His judgments—of which chastening is
a part—are experienced as evil by those under them,
His works never proceed from an evil heart, for there
is no evil in God. God is altogether good, and all His
judgments are motivated by His goodness. To say it
another way, *while God is capable of evil acts, He is incapable of evil motives*. Goodness pervades all His evil
judgments (Ps 119:39). For example, when Israel had
experienced the evil chastening of Babylon's invasion

and had been exiled to the land of Babylon, Jeremiah revealed God's motives in the exile when he wrote, "For I know the thoughts that I think toward you, says the LORD, thoughts of peace and not of evil [*rag*], to give you a future and a hope" (Jer 29:11). The destruction of Jerusalem was evil for the Israelites, but God's intentions in it were good. Three chapters later the Lord said, "Just as I have brought all this great calamity [*rag*] on this people, so I will bring on them all the good that I have promised them" (Jer 32:42).

While most evil in the world is demonic in origin, we should not suppose—and here I am disagreeing with John Alexander Dowie—that evil calamities are outside the power of God's sovereignty. He is God, and He reserves the right to do evil, terrible things. He is dreadful in judgment and to be feared.

When we understand that He is capable of inflicting harm (*rag*) upon people, it will produce a healthy fear of Him. "It is a fearful thing to fall into the hands of the living God" (Heb 10:31). Sinners should fear Him because He punishes unrepentant unbelievers; saints should fear Him because He disciplines His children (Heb 12:6).

Scripture assumes that true gods, if they truly are gods, would be capable of perpetrating both good and evil. For example, God taunted the false gods of the Israelites by saying to them, "'Show the things that are to come hereafter, that we may know that you are gods; yes, do good or do evil {*rag*}, that we may be dismayed and see it together'" (Isa 41:23). God reinforced the same point when he spoke to Israel through Jeremiah concerning their false gods, "'They are upright, like a palm tree, and they cannot speak; they must be carried, because they cannot go by themselves. Do not be afraid of them, for they cannot do evil {*rag*}, nor can they do any good'" (Jer 10:5).

By inference, God was implying that He is capable of both good and evil. Thus, He alone should be worshiped and feared.

Is God Ever the Author of Sickness?

Although John Alexander Dowie disagreed, I see Scripture indicating that God is sometimes the perpetrator of sickness.

In Exodus 4:11, God said He makes people mute, deaf, seeing, or blind: "So the LORD said to him, 'Who has made man's mouth? Or who makes the mute, the deaf, the seeing, or the blind? Have not I, the LORD?'"

In Micah 6:13, God said He would make His people sick: "Therefore I will also make you sick by striking you, by making you desolate because of your sins."

Habakkuk wrote, "Before Him went pestilence, and fever followed at His feet" (Hab 3:5).

Again, allow me to quote Ezekiel 14:21, which spoke of pestilence coming from God. "For thus says the Lord GOD: 'How much more it shall be when I send My four severe [rag] judgments on Jerusalem—the sword and famine and wild beasts and pestilence—to cut off man and beast from it?'" The dictionary defines pestilence as, "an epidemic of a highly contagious or infectious disease such as bubonic plague."[2] God claimed He was capable of inflicting such pestilences.

My unrenewed mind finds it unsavory to think that the good God whom I love and serve is capable of inflicting disease and infirmity, but I can't deny the witness of God Himself who said, "Now see that I, even I, am He, and there is no God besides Me; I kill and I make alive; I wound and I heal; nor is there any who can deliver from My hand" (Deut 32:39).

2 *Encarta® World English Dictionary* © 1999 Microsoft Corporation. All rights reserved. Developed for Microsoft by Bloomsbury Publishing Plc.

I agree with John Alexander Dowie that sickness and disease come from the devil. But I don't agree that they *always* come from the devil. Dowie said God was incapable of such things but God claimed He could do them.

Is God the Author of Natural Disasters?

According to one source, natural disasters occur on our planet at the rate of around one a day. Is God responsible for this?

I did an internet search on "God's sovereignty over weather," and around fifty Scriptures popped onto my screen. Here are three examples that show God directs the weather.

> "Have you entered the treasury of snow, or have you seen the treasury of hail, which I have reserved for the time of trouble, for the day of battle and war?" (Job 38:22-23).

> Fire and hail, snow and clouds; stormy wind, fulfilling His word (Ps 148:8).

> He causes the vapors to ascend from the ends of the earth; He makes lightning for the rain; He brings the wind out of His treasuries (Ps 135:7).

Storms, floods, droughts, cyclones, typhoons, hurricanes, tornadoes, tsunamis, earthquakes—God orchestrates all these. Insurance companies will sometimes categorize a natural disaster as "an act of God," and in many cases they're probably right.

But we also see that Satan had limited power to trigger storms, specifically in the story of Job. Satan sent the lightning that burned up Job's sheep and servants (Job 1:16), and he sent the tornado that brought the house down on Job's children, killing all ten of them (Job 1:19). This power had been specifically delegated to Satan by God, however, so it appears unlikely Satan could have controlled the weather like that without divine permission (Job 1:12). Some suggest that the storm of Mark 4:35-41 was instigated by Satan to resist Jesus' advance toward new territory. We see, therefore, that sometimes Satan is able to exert limited power over weather.

Does that mean he can instigate natural disasters? The biblical evidence suggests it's unlikely. The consistent witness of Scripture is that God holds the reins on the forces of nature. "For He commands and raises the stormy wind, which lifts up the waves of the sea" (Ps 107:25). Satan's ability to affect weather patterns seems very limited. It seems he must procure God's permission to affect the weather. It's my personal conclusion, therefore, that natural disasters are under the authority of God.

When Hurricane Katrina devastated the city of New Orleans, Louisiana, in August of 2005, the words of Amos 3:6 seemed especially sobering, "If a trumpet is blown in a city, will not the people be afraid? If there is calamity in a city, will not the LORD have done it?"

It seems to me that natural disasters can be caused by three agencies: God, Satan (if God specifically allows it), and natural causes. By natural causes, I mean that some weather patterns seem to be the natural result of changes in the earth's winds. Our planet groans because things in the natural order are affected adversely by the curse of mankind's sin (Rom 8:22). My personal conclusion, therefore, is that while God doesn't cause all natural disasters, He orchestrates some of them, and they are experienced by people as evil [rag] and grievous.

The book of Revelation says that God Himself will release the end-time judgments on this planet, which include many natural disasters such as earthquakes (Rev 6:12), cosmic disturbances (6:12), collisions with heavenly masses such as meteorites (8:10), scorching heat (16:8-9), massive hailstones (16:21), and other calamities. These judgments will be not merely *allowed* by God, but *executed* by Him and His angels. And they will be *evil* in the eyes of those against whom they are directed—the antichrist and his empire's armies. And yet we affirm with David, "The judgments of the LORD are true and righteous altogether" (Ps 19:9).

My point in this chapter is simply this: When we experience evil circumstances in our lives, we should not automatically assume they're always from the devil. Sometimes, they're from God. If God's involved in the difficult circumstances we're facing, then we might want to consider the possibility that God is chastening us.

18

Five Causations of Trouble

Hebrews 12:11 describes the Lord's chastening in our lives as "painful." When something painful happens to us, however, it doesn't always mean we're being chastened. Trouble can come to our lives for many reasons. To understand all the possible reasons, it's helpful to identify the five possible causative elements behind painful circumstances: God, Satan, people, ourselves, and a fallen creation. I touched on this earlier, but now I want to expand upon it and explore how these five causative elements interrelate.

Here's a summary statement on each of them.

1. God Can Cause Calamity

Sometimes, the trouble people experience comes from God. As stated in the previous chapter, anything troubling that comes from God is motivated by goodness and kindness. So even when God sends calamities, they issue from the infinite goodness of His heart.

If someone says, "Sometimes God *allows* calamity to happen to us," most Christians would probably agree with that, and rightly so. But if someone says, "Sometimes God *causes* the calamities that we experience," then the discussion becomes more intense and controversial. Not all Christians believe that God would actually *cause* a painful calamity or crisis to happen to us. They can probably see God *allowing* Satan to do something evil against us, but they struggle to see painful circumstances *originating* from God.

But, as we said in the last chapter, the Lord's testimony seems quite clear: "'I kill and I make alive; I wound and I heal; nor is there any who can deliver from My hand'" (Deut 32:39). God told the exiles that He *caused* them to be taken to Babylon: "Thus says the LORD of hosts, the God of Israel, to all who were carried away captive, whom I have caused to be carried away from Jerusalem to Babylon" (Jer 29:4). God did not merely *allow* them to be taken captive, He *caused* it. "I form the light and create darkness, I make peace and create calamity; I, the LORD, do all these things" (Isa 45:7). The Lord did not merely say that He *allows* calamity, but that He actually *creates* calamity. Sometimes calamity on the earth has a heavenly Designer. Some might find that offensive, or reprehensible, or baffling, but it's true. Again, I handled this more fully back in chapter 17, "Is God Capable of Evil?"

Even when calamity comes our way from God, we still declare, "The Lord is good, and His mercies endure forever." Jesus is perfect in leadership, perfect in love, and infallible in wisdom. So even when others are enraged at His leadership, we affirm the perfection of His plans and ways for our lives.

The first possible causation of calamity, therefore, is God.

2. Satan Causes Trouble

Some of the evil things we experience come straight from the devil.

Satan is our enemy, adversary, and accuser. He is

always laboring to do everything in his power to resist God's people and to afflict the human race with pain and calamity. Jesus described his works this way: "The thief does not come except to steal, and to kill, and to destroy. I have come that they may have life, and that they may have it more abundantly" (John 10:10).

When evil things happen in the world, let your first suspicions fall on Satan and his hosts. As Paul testified, "For we do not wrestle against flesh and blood, but against principalities, against powers, against the rulers of the darkness of this age, against spiritual hosts of wickedness in the heavenly places" (Eph 6:12).

Peter also warned us about the devil: "Be sober, be vigilant; because your adversary the devil walks about like a roaring lion, seeking whom he may devour. Resist him, steadfast in the faith, knowing that the same sufferings are experienced by your brotherhood in the world" (1 Pet 5:8-9).

3. People Cause Problems

Sometimes bad things happen to us because of people. In some cases, the negligence of others hurts us, even when they meant us no harm. In some cases, people accidentally hurt us, as might happen when a drunk driver causes a car accident. In some cases, people hurt us intentionally—by lying about us, forcing us out of our job, defaming us, or rejecting us, etc. And then in extreme cases, evil people can hurt us in malicious ways, such as robbery, rape, kidnapping, suicide bombing, war, etc.

We're part of a sinful human race, and it's inevitable we'll experience pain at the hand of our fellow human beings.

4. We Can Bring Trouble on Ourselves

Some of the painful ordeals we suffer are because of our own personal negligence, bad choices, mistakes, or sins. Sin comes with consequences: "Be sure your sin will find you out" (Num 32:23). "For the wages of sin is death" (Rom 6:23).

There are many ways we can bring trouble upon ourselves. For example, if we cheat on our taxes, we will likely suffer for it. Even if our mistake is unintentional, we can still suffer for it. And if we do something "human" such as fall asleep at the wheel while driving, we may really suffer for it.

There are hundreds of ways we can bring trouble upon ourselves and, in the end, may have only ourselves to blame.

But not everything bad that happens to us is because of something we did wrong. There's a Bible story that helps us with this. On one occasion, Jesus saw a man blind from birth, and His disciples asked, "Rabbi, who sinned, this man or his parents, that he was born blind?" Jesus answered, "Neither this man nor his parents sinned, but that the works of God should be revealed in him" (John 9:2-3). Jesus made it clear that the man was not blind because of his or anyone else's sin. We must not assume, therefore, that trouble in someone's life automatically means they've sinned.

Not every trial we face has been brought on by ourselves. But when we face one, we should at least ask the question, "Did I do something to bring this on?" because we ourselves are one of the five possible causations of trouble in our lives.

5. Creation is Broken

Sometimes the trouble we experience in life is

caused simply by living on a planet broken by sin.

Suppose it's winter. You step onto a sidewalk but don't notice it's icy. Your feet go out from under you and down you go. You fall back and bang your head on the cement. It happens so fast you don't realize what's happening until it's too late. We call that an accident because it was unplanned and unexpected. If you could have prevented it, you would have. But you didn't expect it to happen. It's an accident. When accidents happen, they can produce incredible pain in our lives.

We live in a fallen, broken world that was "subjected to futility" (Rom 8:20) when Adam and Eve sinned. The whole creation "groans and labors" (Rom 8:22) because of the negative impact sin had on our world. Now, everything seems to be flawed to some extent. Electronics malfunction, parts break, buildings deteriorate, accidents happen, animals attack, diseases spread, the weather turns rogue, food spoils, etc. Stuff goes wrong all the time.

Sometimes we suffer trouble simply by living in a broken world.

So these are the five possible causations when we are hurt: God, Satan, people, ourselves, and a broken creation. Occasionally, something happens that is caused by just one of those elements, but in many cases there is a mix of two to five of these causes at work. Some people have a tendency to oversimplify their trials and ascribe everything to just one source, such as the devil. But some trials more complex than that, caused by multiple factors.

A Mix of Factors

When more than one causation is behind a calamity or trial, each causative element is probably contributing to the situation at differing percentages. I speak of *percentages* because of the "in measure" principle found in Isaiah 27:8, "In measure, by sending it away, You contended with it. He removes it by His rough wind in the day of the east wind." Let me explain the verse.

God sent Israel into captivity because He was contending with the rebellion of the nation. But He was not the only contributing element to their captivity. He was a causative element only *in measure*, that is, to only a certain degree or percentage. Other causative elements were also involved, at various percentages.

Isaiah 27 was not referring to any specific invasion, so the principle of Isaiah 27:8 applies to any occasion when an enemy invades and takes God's people captive. Whenever trouble invades our lives, there can be a mix of percentages among the causative elements. For example, when we're blindsided by trouble, God might be involved 5 percent in the causation, Satan might be 50 percent to blame, people may have been involved at 35 percent, and we ourselves might be 10 percent to blame because we didn't handle everything perfectly. It's the mix of percentages, *in measure*, that can make the discerning and diagnosing of the causation intricate and complex.

Discerning the cause of calamities is such a thorny proposition that it's virtually impossible to identify the causative percentages precisely and accurately—unless you are given divine information. Much of the time, we're mostly puzzled. But God isn't. As David said to the Lord, "My adversaries are all before You" (Psa 69:19). In his perplexity, David recognized that God knew the causations of everything coming against him. He knew God was able, therefore, to defend his cause.

If our trial is a chastening, that means God is involved

in the trial because He's the only one who chastens His children. However, many times He's not the only one involved. Take for example the invasion of Israel by Assyria, as mentioned in Isaiah 10. God was involved because He was chastening His people; Satan was involved because he was inciting Assyria with demonic rage; the people of Assyria were involved because they were the ones actually invading Israel; and the nation of Israel had brought it on themselves, in one sense, because of their rebellion and sin. So at least four of the five possible causative elements were involved in Assyria's invasion of Israel. And none of us knows the percentages of each element's involvement.

In the case of Paul's thorn in the flesh, it was a chastening of the Lord, which means God was directly involved. If Paul thought the thorn was simply a demonic attack, he probably would have said something like, "I was hindered by Satan with a thorn in the flesh." But instead he wrote, "a thorn in the flesh was given to me" (2 Cor 12:7). Satan *attacks* apostles; God *gives* to apostles. By saying the thorn "was given to me," Paul was acknowledging a divine source. God had given him the thorn. Then he went on to clarify that it was, "a messenger of Satan to buffet me," which meant the physical affliction he endured was instigated and incited directly by a demon. It's enigmatic, but God gave Paul a demonic thorn. So with Paul's thorn, two causative elements were involved: God and Satan. And we don't know the percentages. Was it 50/50? When God and Satan are both behind your affliction, it becomes very difficult to identify precisely the source of everything that's coming at you.

There were a few instances of chastening in the Bible which were caused 100 percent by God, with no other causative elements. The first I have in mind is Jacob's limp. He got the limp at the hand of Jesus while wrestling with Him. To say it bluntly, Jesus lamed Jacob's hip. Neither the devil nor any human was involved at all. The second example is Zacharias's muteness. That came from no other source but God (administered personally by the angel, Gabriel). The blindness Paul experienced on the road to Damascus came from no other source but God. We add to this list those in the Bible who were judged by God for a specific sin. God (and God alone) struck Miriam and Uzziah and Gehazi with leprosy, withered Jeroboam's hand, made Elymas blind, struck with blindness the men attacking Lot's house, and also struck blind the Syrian army that had come to Dothan to arrest Elisha. And the list goes on. Sometimes, therefore, God is chastening with no other agents involved.

And then there are times when all five causative elements are involved. Such was the case in Job's chastening. God, Satan, and people were involved. So was nature (in the lightning and whirlwind that came against his family). And he himself was partly responsible because he had asked God for something (Job 12:4). Interestingly though, the last chapter ascribed the whole ordeal to God. "They consoled him and comforted him for all the adversity that the LORD had brought upon him" (Job 42:11). Why would the adversity be ascribed to the Lord, when all five causations were clearly involved? Here's my answer: God is such a huge player that, if He is involved in even the smallest way, His 1 percent looms larger than the 99 percent of all the other active agencies.

The Lord cried out through the prophet Micah, "Hear the rod! Who has appointed it?" (Mic 6:9). When He said, "Hear the rod," He meant He was using a rod to get their attention, and He wanted them to discern and comprehend His message. And when He said, "Who has appointed it?" God meant that He wanted them to use spiritual discernment to decipher the cause of their calamity. He knew it would be helpful if they could discern which of the five causative agents were at work in their situation. Accurate discernment would help them cooperate with God's purposes.

In other words, God wants us to ask, "Why has this happened? Father, why did You allow this to happen? Are You trying to get my attention?"

"Don't Blame God"

Some people are concerned that we not ascribe to the hand of God that which comes from the devil. They say things like, "God is good, and Satan is evil—so do not ascribe evil things to our good God!"

I've looked, but I can't find this concern in Scripture. I can't find anywhere in the Bible where God said something like, "I am indignant that you should ascribe that trouble to Me, when in fact I had nothing to do with it." Many people in the Bible ascribed their affliction or trouble to God, and not once did God reply by saying, "I didn't do that. Don't blame Me for that kind of thing."

For example, Naomi mourned, "I went out full, and the LORD has brought me home again empty. Why do you call me Naomi, since the LORD has testified against me, and the Almighty has afflicted me?" (Ruth 1:21). God didn't correct her, as though to say, "I'm not the one who has afflicted you." His silence seems to affirm her perspective. His silence seems to suggest, "Actually, Naomi, you're right. I have had a certain role in your distress. I'm orchestrating something here. So for you to cast the causation at My feet is not altogether inappropriate."

God never expressed dismay when trouble was

ascribed to Him. However, He did express dismay when people failed to ascribe to Him the chastening He was executing. The clearest example is in Jeremiah: "They have lied about the LORD, and said, 'It is not He. Neither will evil come upon us, nor shall we see sword or famine'" (Jer 5:12). In context, the people of Israel were saying that God was not sending the Babylonians to chasten them. When they said, "God is not doing this," God was troubled and displeased. He didn't want them blowing off and despising His chastening; He wanted them gripped with trembling and repentance.

We don't do wrong, then, in ascribing chastening trials to God's hand. We do wrong in not recognizing His involvement.

There are some who claim, "God would never use the devil to accomplish His purposes." This is the very objection God addressed with the people of Israel through His prophet, Habakkuk, when He said:

> "Look among the nations and watch—be utterly astounded! For I will work a work in your days which you would not believe, though it were told you. For indeed I am raising up the Chaldeans, a bitter and hasty nation which marches through the breadth of the earth, to possess dwelling places that are not theirs" (Hab 1:5-6).

God claimed that He Himself raised up the Chaldeans to invade Jerusalem. God was saying, "I am going to use a means to correct My people that you will not believe, even when I tell you. I am the one raising up the Chaldeans against Jerusalem, but even as I tell you this, you won't believe it."

The same unbelief continues today in the church. There are some who insist that God never uses evil, demonic powers for His purposes, but I am maintaining in this book that He does, in fact, do so.

Various Trials

James wrote at the beginning of his epistle:

My brethren, count it all joy when you fall into various trials, knowing that the testing of your faith produces patience. But let patience have its perfect work, that you may be perfect and complete, lacking nothing (Jas 1:2-4).

When James said we *fall* into various trials, he didn't mean falling to temptation or sin such as in a moral failure. Rather, he meant falling to unforeseen calamity. If we could have avoided it or stopped it, we would have. But it blindsided us. It was beyond our control. We took a hard fall, and now we're suffering for it.

By using the term *various trials*, James was implicitly pointing to the many possible causes of trouble. In this chapter, I have reduced the *various* possible causations to five: God, the devil, people, ourselves, and a malfunctioning world. *Various* trials have *various* causations to *various* degrees.

James was saying we should count it all joy, regardless of the source. If God is chastening you, count it all joy. If a horrible accident has happened, count it all joy. Even if Satan is attacking you, count it all joy!

Why? Because as we endure in faith through the trial, the Lord will work in our lives so powerfully that we'll emerge from the crucible entirely transformed. When endurance has had its perfect work in our lives, we'll come through the trial "perfect and complete, lacking nothing."

God Uses Rods

Sometimes God uses a rod to chasten His children—that is, He uses means other than His own hand. This is reminiscent of the manner in which Solomon, in

Proverbs, advised parents to use a rod (a means other than their hands) when spanking their children (e.g., Prov 22:15; 23:13-14; 29:15).

What kinds of rods does God use? I see three primary rods at His disposal: people, Satan, and circumstances.

First, God uses people as a rod. For example, in 2 Samuel 7:14 the Lord called Solomon His son and said, "If he commits iniquity, I will chasten him with the rod of men and with the blows of the sons of men." He said He would use maliciously minded people as a rod against Solomon, if necessary, to bring him to repentance. Another example is in Isaiah 10, where God spoke of using the nation of Assyria as a rod to discipline His people. He said, "Woe to Assyria, the rod of My anger" (Isa 10:5). He spoke woe to Assyria because, even though He had appointed them as a rod to attack and discipline His children, they fulfilled that mandate maliciously and attacked more severely than God had intended, thus bringing judgment on themselves. In both these instances, God used people as a rod to discipline His children.

When God used heathen nations to chasten Israel, the prophet Micah said of those nations, "But they do not know the thoughts of the LORD, nor do they understand His counsel; for He will gather them like sheaves to the threshing floor" (Mic 4:12). The nations didn't understand that permission to attack didn't mean permission to obliterate. God meant to chasten, but they sought to demolish. As a result, God said He would thresh those nations in judgment. He used them as a rod and then discarded them in judgment.

When God uses people to chasten you, your first impulse is to get your eyes on the people involved, see them as your antagonists, and grow resistant toward them. Rather, adopt the posture of Joseph who saw the hand of God in all that his brothers did to him. Because he saw God as the primary causative element (even though his brothers were also causative agents), he kept free of bitterness and emerged from the trial a refined vessel that God could use for noble purposes.

First of all, then, God uses people as a rod.

Second, God uses Satan as a rod. The Lord individualizes the invasion by Assyria in the person of their king, Sennacherib. He said of Sennacherib, "Shall the ax boast itself against him who chops with it? Or shall the saw exalt itself against him who saws with it? As if a rod could wield itself against those who lift it up, or as if a staff could lift up, as if it were not wood!" (Isa 10:15). God spoke of Sennacherib as a rod in His hand. In this passage, Sennacherib represented Satan as the primary enemy of God's people. By way of spiritual application, we could say that God uses the devil as a piece of wood in His hand to accomplish His purposes in the earth. Colossians 2:10 says Jesus is "the head of all principality and power" which means He has complete jurisdiction over all demonic powers. Jesus is head over Satan and uses him as He wills. The devil is a rod in His hand.

A clear biblical example of God using Satan as a tool is the manner in which Satan attacked Job. Satan stole Job's livelihood, killed his children, and afflicted him with boils—and yet we know from the story that God was orchestrating it all, using Satan as a rod. Satan likes to think of himself as a free agent, but to his chagrin, he often looks back in retrospect and realizes he was a pawn in God's hand. If Satan is like a wooden tool in God's hand, then who is the real instigator of the calamity—Satan or God? As Job asked, "If it is not He, who else could it be?" (Job 9:24). Even though Satan had risen against him, Job correctly ascribed the calamity to God. Because God's 1 percent outweighs Satan's 99 percent.

If you struggle with the idea that God and Satan would ever be involved together in a trial, perhaps it will help to see how Jesus taught this. Jesus taught us to pray, "And do not lead us into temptation, but deliver us from the evil one" (Matt 6:13). Did Jesus mean that God tempts us to do evil? Certainly not, for James 1:13 says, "Let no one say when he is tempted, 'I am tempted by God'; for God cannot be tempted by evil, nor does He Himself tempt anyone." Temptation comes, therefore, from the devil as he seeks to trap us by the evil desires of our hearts (Jas 1:14). What did Jesus mean, then, in the prayer of Matthew 6:13? He meant the Father is able to lead us in a path that exposes us to Satan's temptations, and He can also lead us in a path which is protected from them. We are to ask the Father for the latter. A biblical example of the Father allowing Satan to tempt is found in the story of Hezekiah: "However, regarding the ambassadors of the princes of Babylon, whom they sent to him to inquire about the wonder that was done in the land, God withdrew from him, in order to test him, that He might know all that was in his heart" (2 Chron 32:31). God withdrew His protection from Hezekiah, which enabled Satan to tempt him so that the true desires of his heart might be manifest. In giving us the prayer of Matthew 6:13, Jesus affirmed that the Father sometimes leads people on a path in which Satan attacks with temptation, and that we should pray in humility for the Father to spare us such a path. Hezekiah's story illustrates what Jesus taught in Matthew 6:13, that the Father and the devil can both be involved in someone's test.

The point is, God uses the devil as a rod.

Third, God uses circumstances as a rod to chasten us.

Joseph's prison, David's cave, Sarah's and Hannah's bar-
renness, Jonah's fish, Paul's thorn, Jacob's limp, Moses'
wilderness—all these are examples of the many ways
God can use circumstances redemptively in our lives.

God isn't limited in the means by which He may chasten His children. I said earlier that He doesn't use diseases like cancer. I didn't say that to limit God, as though He
can't; I said that to describe His ways—that He *doesn't*.
Am I saying it as accurately as I should? Maybe not. But
this I know: We must not limit God. He can use whatever means He wants to chasten His children, whether
it be infirmity, pestilence, financial distress, relational
tension, or accidents. When Micah predicted disaster for
the house of Jacob, he asked them, "Is the Spirit of the
LORD restricted? Are these His doings?" (Mic 2:7). With
this rhetorical question, Micah affirmed that the Spirit of
God is not restricted by the means He might use to discipline His people with disaster. He upheld the absolute
sovereignty of God. As the psalmist wrote, "But our God
is in heaven; He does whatever He pleases" (Ps 115:3).

Whether God uses people, the devil, or circumstances, they are only a rod; He's the one wielding them.
Therefore, we should look to God as the one with whom
we deal. This accords with Psalm 119:75, "I know, O LORD,
that Your judgments are right, and that in faithfulness
You have afflicted me." The psalmist's affliction might
have come from any mix of the five possible causations,
but he ascribed the affliction to God. Satan or people
might have had a role to play, but the psalmist was seeing God as the primary player who was in charge of the
trial. He kept his eyes on God, believing for His purposes
to be accomplished.

19

Is this God or the Devil?

When calamity strikes, we often wonder, "Is this from God, or is the devil coming after us?" This question is important because the answer determines our response. How we respond to things that come from God is much different than how we respond to things from the devil. James addressed this:

> Therefore submit to God. Resist the devil and he will flee from you (Jas 4:7).

If God is the cause of the trial, we submit to Him and His purposes. If the devil is the cause, we resist him and all his evil schemes. The last thing we want to do is get it inverted and submit to the devil or resist God. But in order to respond properly, we need discernment on what is God's hand and what is Satan's instigation.

Some trials come straight from the devil, and God has no part in them. For example, while Jesus taught in a certain synagogue, a woman was present "who had a spirit of infirmity eighteen years, and was bent over and could in no way raise herself up" (Luke 13:11). Here's what Jesus said about the causation of her infirmity: "So ought not this woman, being a daughter of Abraham, whom Satan has bound—think of it—for eighteen years, be loosed from this bond on the Sabbath?" (Luke 13:16). As a daughter of Abraham, Jesus acknowledged her as a woman of faith. And yet she was bound by Satan. Her infirmity was not something God was using to enlarge her heart, but Satan was using to bind her. So Jesus delivered her from the bondage of the devil, just as Peter testified, "How God anointed Jesus of Nazareth with the Holy Spirit and with power, who went about doing good and healing all who were oppressed by the devil, for God was with Him" (Acts 10:38). This story teaches us that some afflictions come from the devil and are to be resisted.

What are we to do, though, in instances of chastening in which both God *and* the devil are involved? What if God is chastening and using the devil as a rod in our lives? In such cases, we often find ourselves perplexed to know what to do. We don't want to submit to the trial because we don't want to submit to the devil; but neither do we want to resist it because we don't want to resist God. We can't submit and we can't resist. We're stymied by the perplexity of the thing.

When God and Satan are both involved in your trial, it's not that they're in *partnership*; it's better to see God, in the words of Bill Johnson, using Satan as a pawn on a chess board. In such cases, when you don't know whether to submit or resist, you may need a key from heaven to unlock the situation. Thankfully, Jesus promised that He would give us the keys of the kingdom (Matt 16:19).

To discern between God's hand and the devil's hand, we need discernment every single time. On round one of a trial, one thing can be going on, and on round two something totally different. We see this dynamic through something Isaiah said:

> "Indeed they shall surely assemble, but not because of Me. Whoever assembles against you shall fall for your sake. Behold, I have created the blacksmith who blows the coals in the fire, who brings forth an instrument

for his work; and I have created the spoiler to destroy. No weapon formed against you shall prosper, and every tongue which rises against you in judgment you shall condemn. This is the heritage of the servants of the LORD, and their righteousness is from Me," says the LORD (Isa 54:15-17).

Let me explain the passage.

Prior to these verses, Isaiah spoke of God using foreign invaders to chasten Israel. After Israel was purified, restored, and established, however, Isaiah said the enemy would rise up a second time against them. Unlike the first attack, the second attack wasn't a chastening of the Lord. This is what God meant when He said, "They shall surely assemble, but not because of Me." The second time around, God wasn't involved at all. First time, yes; second time, no. Therefore, God assured them that, when this second wave of animosity came against them, He would defend them mightily and their enemies would fall before them.

Sometimes the enemy will attempt a second shot at you. In the first round, God used the situation to transform and enlarge your heart. But the enemy wasn't satisfied to leave it there. He decided to come at you a second time. This time around, the Lord wasn't chastening, it was an outright demonic attack. God wants you to go after the powers of darkness and vigorously engage the enemy. He will enable you to quickly and decisively overcome the adversary.

When both God and Satan are at work in your circumstances, be ready for other believers to misinterpret the signals, just as Peter misinterpreted the signals at Christ's arrest. It was God's will for evil men to arrest Jesus and take Him to Caiaphas. In his zeal, Peter got out his sword and began to swing, trying to save Jesus from the Father's cup. So Jesus said to Peter, "Put your sword into the sheath. Shall I not drink the cup which My Father has given Me?" (John 18:11). Peter tried to spare Jesus from the Father's cup. In a similar way, don't be surprised if other believers try, with zeal like Peter, to spare you from your Father's cup. They will swing their sword (Bible), wielding verses that say you shouldn't suffer in this way. In their undiscerning zeal, they will actually complicate the situation and make the trial more grievous. They will rebuke what God has purposed, or quote promises that have a later fulfillment. They get so distracted with the adversary's role in your crucifixion that they don't understand how the Father's hand is also involved. Be ready for it. Some believers will try to save you from the Father's cup.

Fight!

Some are concerned that if we ascribe our trial to God, when Satan is also involved in the thing, we could end up submitting to Satan's hand. Is such a thing possible? Actually, yes. Some Christians, under the banner of "submitting to the sovereignty of God," have just lain down and allowed the devil to stomp all over them. But I don't believe that an acknowledgement of God's sovereignty means we should become passive in warfare. Instead, here's how I see it.

When we acknowledge that God, in His sovereignty, is actively involved in our trial, we are recognizing that He's the one who put us in the ring with Satan. Even though we're wrestling with demonic forces, God's the one who set the whole thing up. Through the cross, He's given us everything we need to overcome. Now it's time to fight!

Our template here is the cross of Christ. Isaiah 53:10 showed that God orchestrated Christ's death,[1] and Luke

---

1   "Yet it pleased the LORD to bruise Him; He has put Him to grief" (Isa 53:10).

22:3 showed that Satan schemed to kill Jesus.[2] Both God and Satan were involved, therefore, in the crucifixion of Christ. Jesus submitted to the cross because He knew it was His Father's will. However, He also resisted Satan because He knew He was fighting in a cosmic battle.

That the cross was a cosmic battle between Jesus and Satan is seen in Genesis 3:15. God said to Satan, "He shall bruise your head, and you shall bruise His heel." In that verse, the Father predicted Jesus would bruise Satan's head on the cross.

At the cross, Jesus and Satan went at it. Each was aiming for the head. Satan hit Jesus' heel, but Jesus made His mark. At the cross, Jesus was wounded but Satan was destroyed.

Even though the Father sovereignly designed the cross, He didn't mean for Jesus to passively submit to everything Satan was throwing at Him. No, He meant for Jesus to fight! The Father wanted Jesus to use the seven horns of the Spirit to prevail over the powers of darkness (Rev 5:5-6). On the cross, therefore, we see Jesus both submitting to God and resisting the devil.

Christ's cross is your example. Are you being chastened by the Lord? Then *fight*! Take on the powers of hell, overcome in the trial, and arise to your intended destiny in God.

Why Does God's Chastening Sometimes Seem Excessive?

The intensity of God's chastening can be anything from very light to severe, depending on the instance. When God's hand is especially severe, it can appear to us to be excessive. Its intensity can be perplexing,

---

2 "Then Satan entered Judas, surnamed Iscariot, who was numbered among the twelve" (Luke 22:3).

especially when the severity of the trial seems dispro-
portionate to the issues in our lives that need to be perfected. It can feel as though we're under His wrath rather
than His mercy.

God Himself acknowledged that sometimes the
severity of the trial appears excessive, when He said,
"Speak comfort to Jerusalem, and cry out to her, that her
warfare is ended, that her iniquity is pardoned; for she
has received from the LORD'S hand double for all her
sins" (Isa 40:2). It seems that the Lord is speaking of the
destruction of Jerusalem and the Babylonian exile. Why
would God have Israel receive *double* for her sins?

That level of suffering seems unfair and unjust. And,
in fact, it's *not* fair. Because Satan never plays fair. But
keep this in mind: God is a God of justice. Where injus-
tice has waylaid His children, He designs to answer that
with restoration, restitution, and retribution to the enemy. God is masterful at getting a payback from injus-
tice. It's one of His specialties. His great sense of justice
doesn't allow the unjust suffering of His chosen ones to
remain unanswered.[3]

What was God's answer to Israel's double chastening?

> Instead of your shame you shall have double honor, and
> instead of confusion they shall rejoice in their portion.
> Therefore in their land they shall possess double; ever-
> lasting joy shall be theirs (Isa 61:7).

Because Israel had received double for her sins,
God's justice demanded that she receive double honor,
double possessions, and everlasting joy.

The same thing happened at Christ's crucifixion. The
cross was excessive—an extravagant overpayment for
sin. Jesus didn't suffer just barely enough to purchase
our redemption and healing. He suffered double. He

---

3 I deal with this at length in my book, *Unrelenting Prayer*.

paid more than enough. The Father is right now in the process of using the excessiveness of the cross to gather to Himself His children from all nations, and in the end He will glorify the name of Jesus above every other name. I promise you, the Son shall receive double honor for His double payment!

The same is true for you. If God causes you to receive double for your sins, it's so that He might crown you with double honor. As Paul wrote, "For our light affliction, which is but for a moment, is working for us a far more exceeding and eternal weight of glory" (2 Cor 4:17). Sometimes we experience some of that glory in this life, but the greatest weight of glory will be that which He lavishes on us in the eternal city. When you see your chastening from a heavenly vantage, you realize it really is "light affliction" in contrast to the weight of glory God will receive from it.

Satan Overplays His Hand

Here's another reason why God's chastening sometimes seems excessive: Satan always tends to overplay his hand. He uses God's "permission slip" to cause more trouble than God intended. He overreaches because of his malicious hatred for God and His people. His aggression makes it appear as though God's discipline in our lives is excessive.

Satan's overreaching is illustrated, metaphorically, in the way enemies of old came against Israel. The prophets (such as Isaiah and Habakkuk) spoke of how God chastened His people by allowing evil nations to invade the land of Israel (e.g., 2 Kgs 18:25). But those nations maliciously assaulted and destroyed Israel more than God's assignment had ordained.

What was God's answer? He executed judgment on the evil nations He had used as a rod on Israel. This is why the nations that oppressed Israel—Egypt, Assyria, and Babylon—came under divine judgment. And the same is true for Satan and his kingdom. God will use Satan as a rod to chasten His people, Satan will overreach, and then God will judge Satan. How will God judge Satan? By giving His people great victory over the powers of darkness. The church will arise victoriously!

Place your hope on the double honor God will require for Satan's vicious overreaching.

Intercession Without Accusation

I have labored to show that God and Satan can both have a role in our chastening. This leads, however, to a very important question: *How can we keep our hearts free of accusation when God is partly responsible for the fiery trial we're facing?* This question is very important because Satan wants us to become bitter against God, accuse Him of afflicting us unjustly, and forfeit our spiritual inheritance.

Here's another way to ask the same question: *How should we relate to God when we realize He's partially responsible for the great suffering we're enduring?*

The answer is revealed, elegantly and allegorically, in the book of Esther. In the story that follows, I would like to suggest the following symbolism: the king of Persia represents God, Haman represents Satan, and Esther (the bride) represents the individual believer.

Here's the background to our story.

Haman had an evil hatred for the Jews and decided he wanted to wipe them all off the earth. He incited the Persian king against them, and craftily convinced him to pass a law ordering the Jews to be exterminated on a certain day. Haman himself funded the initiative and executed all the plans. The real enemy of the Jews, in the story, was not the king but Haman.

Esther was a Jew and also the queen (although the king didn't know she was a Jew). She sought to find a way to overturn that horrible legislation, but the situation was complicated. For starters, her husband (the king) was a co-conspirator in the plot. She wanted to overturn legislation that her own husband had signed against the Jews.

Here's why the situation was complicated: Because of Vashti. Vashti was the former queen who had been banished from her place because of her negative attitude toward the king. Vashti was an embittered queen who had resisted the king, and the last thing Esther wanted to do was come across as just another embittered queen who was resisting the king. Since the king himself had ratified the law to exterminate the Jews, how could she possibly show him the evil nature of his own law without coming across in an accusatory way?

Esther's strategy to win the king's heart was magnificent. She decided to throw him a banquet and invite Haman as well. She spared no expense, but fed him the most savory meats and served the finest of wines. With her gestures, facial expressions, words, and food, she was conveying to the king, "I love you. You're amazing. You're so wise. Your leadership is brilliant. I feel so honored to be your wife. There's nobody like you in all the earth. You deserve the best." She wanted the king to feel the authenticity of her admiration, devotion, and fidelity.

How did she pay for the feast? Well, the king gave his queen a monthly subsidy. Vashti—the former queen whom Esther replaced—had used the king's subsidy to lavish gifts on her friends (Esth 1:9); in contrast, Esther used her subsidy to lavish gifts and honor on the king. The king was probably thinking to himself, "I never got anything like this from Vashti. Esther is the opposite of

Vashti!" And that's exactly what Esther wanted him to realize.

At the close of the banquet, the king wanted to know what Esther's request was. But Esther wasn't sure the king was fully persuaded of her devotion. It was essential when she appealed to the king that he not interpret her challenge as just a repeat of what Vashti had done to him earlier. He must not perceive from her a spirit of accusation. To secure his heart, she decided to do a second banquet. There must be no doubt that she adored him. So she said, "Come tomorrow with Haman to a second banquet, and I will tell you my request."

So the following evening she did the whole thing all over again. Everything she lavished on the king communicated, "I trust you. You're the best. You are worthy of my devotion, and the devotion of the entire empire. You are such a wise leader. I love you!" Rather than attacking him with accusation, she showered him with praise.

Finally, at the second banquet, the moment came when she told the king her request. The text itself says it best.

> And on the second day, at the banquet of wine, the king again said to Esther, "What is your petition, Queen Esther? It shall be granted you. And what is your request, up to half the kingdom? It shall be done!" Then Queen Esther answered and said, "If I have found favor in your sight, O king, and if it pleases the king, let my life be given me at my petition, and my people at my request. For we have been sold, my people and I, to be destroyed, to be killed, and to be annihilated. Had we been sold as male and female slaves, I would have held my tongue, although the enemy could never compensate for the king's loss." So King Ahasuerus answered and said to Queen Esther, "Who is he, and where is he, who would dare presume in his heart to do such a thing?" And Esther said, "The adversary and enemy is this wicked Haman!" So Haman was terrified before the

king and queen. Then the king arose in his wrath from
the banquet of wine and went into the palace garden;
but Haman stood before Queen Esther, pleading for his
life, for he saw that evil was determined against him by
the king (Esth 7:2-7).

Can you see the brilliance of Esther's strategy? Even
though the king was partly responsible for the law to exterminate the Jews, by the time Esther finally presented
her petition to the king, she had elevated the king as
magnificently good and pinned Haman as the bad guy.
All her praise was on the king and Haman stood alone as
the sole conspirator against her people.

She had no accusation against the king, but put
all the blame for the evil legislation exclusively upon
Haman, the enemy of the Jews.

When the king pondered the whole situation while
in the palace garden, he must have wondered how he
had allowed himself to go along with Haman's plot. He
was probably kicking himself for being such a dolt! And
he was stunned by the fact that Esther had not implicat-
ed him in the least. She had placed the full blame upon
Haman.

The absence of accusation in her approach enabled
the king to direct the fullness of his anger at the adversary. Because she adored him, the king executed Haman
and overturned his evil legislation.

So what should you do when God is one of the causative agents in your trial? Follow Esther's example. Pour
your love upon your Lord, praise Him for His wisdom
and goodness, worship Him in the beauty of holiness,
and then ask Him to render judgment against your
adversary.

He'll do everything you ask—for love!

20

Paul's Thorn in the Flesh

Few things in Scripture have been more controversial among Christians than Paul's thorn in the flesh. I realize from the start, therefore, that some readers will disagree with my perspective on this topic. A sound theology of the Lord's discipline, however, must account for Paul's thorn because it was a chastening. Here's the passage in which Paul spoke of it.

> And lest I should be exalted above measure by the abundance of the revelations, a thorn in the flesh was given to me, a messenger of Satan to buffet me, lest I be exalted above measure. Concerning this thing I pleaded with the Lord three times that it might depart from me. And He said to me, "My grace is sufficient for you, for My strength is made perfect in weakness." Therefore most gladly I will rather boast in my infirmities, that the power of Christ may rest upon me. Therefore I take pleasure in infirmities, in reproaches, in needs, in persecutions, in distresses, for Christ's sake. For when I am weak, then I am strong (2 Cor 12:7-10).

Paul began by giving the reason for his discipline. To emphasize the importance of this point, he gave the reason twice: *lest I be exalted above measure.*

There are two possible meanings to that phrase. First, Paul could mean that the thorn was intended to safeguard him from becoming proud over his abundant revelations. If Paul succumbed to pride and got into the same kind of self-exaltation that seduced Lucifer, he would enter into an adversarial relationship with God—because God resists the proud (Jas 4:6). The thorn could have served to keep Paul tenderly leaning in dependent intimacy on Jesus, even in the midst of great power and revelation.

And second, Paul could mean that the thorn was designed to keep others from putting him on a pedestal and thinking of him more highly than they ought. If people were to exalt Paul, their eyes would be lowered from God to a man, carnal comparisons would ensue, and glory would be diverted from God to a human vessel.

I believe both meanings are intended. *God chastened Paul in order to keep him humble; and He also chastened him in order to keep people from giving him excessive honor.* In my opinion, the second meaning is the primary reason for Paul's thorn. I say this because Paul, in his grammatical wording, didn't use the active voice (e.g., *lest I exalt myself*) but the passive voice (*lest I be exalted*). The passive tense would suggest that the exalting was being done to him by others. God did not want others to view Paul more highly than they ought, so He designed a thorn for Paul's flesh that would make him appear not so impressive to others. To say it bluntly, God hurt Paul so he would look bad.

Crucifixion is always public. And ugly.

We could view Paul's thorn almost like a vaccine—a preventative that in a small dose was able to save him from devastating possibilities. As Mike Bickle has said, God protects power with problems. He used the "problem" of a thorn in Paul's flesh so that the power and revelations flowing through him didn't have negative consequences for either him or his friends.

Why do I view Paul's thorn as a chastening? Because it was used by God for redemptive purposes, doing something in him that no amount of verbal correction could accomplish. Furthermore, the language of the passage evokes images of chastening: *in the flesh, buffet, weakness, infirmities.*

Sometimes, God has to crack the earthen vessel (the body of a saint) so that the excellence of the power might be recognized as coming from God and not that person (see 2 Cor 4:7). In Paul's case, the thorn was a big crack in his earthen vessel. Even if Paul didn't need it, the people needed him to have it.

There are two things that especially wow crowds: revelational insight into the truth of God's word, and power in the Spirit to perform signs, wonders, and miracles. Revelation and power. If you have just one of those, people will clamor to get near you. Paul had both. He needed both for his apostolic ministry, but it made for a pretty impressive package. The Lord decided, therefore, to give Paul a counterbalance in his flesh so that people would be gripped with the message rather than the messenger.

Paul was an unusually gifted and capable man. To balance those strengths, God sovereignly and strategically imposed weakness upon his life. Some forms of weakness (such as fasting) are voluntarily embraced, but this affliction in his flesh was involuntarily received. Paul had no choice in the matter. He had to live with the pain and weakness, even though he didn't want to. Chastening is by definition an involuntary imposition of weakness. But God has amazing ways of perfecting His strength through our weakness.

In the Flesh

Paul specified that the thorn was *in the flesh*. While there is much debate about what this *thorn in the flesh* actually was, I am persuaded he meant the words at face value. The issue was in his flesh. Literally. It was some kind of physical infirmity.

Some interpreters have labored strenuously to explain Paul's thorn as being something other than an affliction in his flesh. For example, some teach that the thorn was an individual who resisted him, or that it was persecution he faced everywhere he went. Why don't they want it to be a physical infirmity? I think it's because of their tenacious commitment to the doctrine of divine healing. Since Paul wasn't immediately healed, they don't want his thorn to be a physical infirmity because that would contradict their teaching that God always wants to heal everybody *immediately*. I love their zeal for divine healing, but I think their zeal for that doctrine causes them to improperly exegete this passage. In spite of my zeal for divine healing, I maintain that this thorn was something Paul felt in his flesh. It harassed him in his body. And he wasn't immediately healed of it.

It wasn't just a slight irritation, so he didn't call it a *sliver*. He called it a *thorn*. It was a gnawing, jabbing, curtailing difficulty.

Since the thorn was intended to keep people from exalting him above measure, its effects must have been observable somehow to others. The best conclusion is that Paul's thorn was a physical infirmity that was obvious to others and made him appear somewhat pitiable and unimpressive. Folks were inclined to look at him with reproach and contempt.

When Paul called it a *thorn*, I wonder if he had Isaiah 10:17 in mind, where the Lord described Assyria's aggression against Israel as a *thorn* and *brier*.[1] God used Assyria to chasten Israel, and Isaiah 10 described Assyria as both a *rod* (v. 24) and a *thorn* (v. 17) to Israel. It's chastening lingo. The assurance of Isaiah 10:17 was that the thorn would be devoured by the flame of the Holy One. The thorn was not permanent.

We can't know for certain, but it's possible Paul was referring to his thorn in the flesh in his letter to the Galatians:

> You know that because of physical infirmity I preached the gospel to you at the first. And my trial which was in my flesh you did not despise or reject, but you received me as an angel of God, even as Christ Jesus. What then was the blessing you enjoyed? For I bear you witness that, if possible, you would have plucked out your own eyes and given them to me. (Gal 4:13-15).

Paul's letter to the Galatians was addressed primarily to the churches in Antioch (of Pisidia), Iconium, Lystra, and Derbe—four cities in the Roman province of Galatia where Paul founded churches during his first missionary journey (Acts 13:4-14:23).

For some reason, Paul's infirmity caused him to travel to southern Galatia. Why? Nobody knows for sure. Some have imagined that Paul headed for the higher, cooler elevation of Antioch because of fevers. Others have supposed Paul was planning on traveling *through* southern Galatia to points beyond, but he got slowed down and stopped in Galatia because of the infirmity. Did his thorn possibly restrict his ability to travel as freely as he may have desired?

Paul specifies that the physical infirmity he endured in Galatia was in his flesh. Like the thorn, he said his Galatian infirmity was "in my flesh." Could his physical

1   The NKJV says *thorns* and *briers* but the Hebrew is singular not plural.

infirmity in Galatia have been his thorn in the flesh? It's possible.

Notice in the above Galatians quotation that Paul said, "You would have plucked out your own eyes and given them to me." That statement seems rather random, unless it has some relevance to his physical infirmity. Some interpreters have supposed, therefore, his Galatian infirmity was a problem in his eyes. This theory is not provable but plausible. Was Paul lamed in his eyes?

Paul battled this infirmity while in the Galatian city of Lystra. Interestingly, it's in Lystra that two notable miracles took place. The first was the instantaneous healing of a man who was crippled from birth (Acts 14:8-10). Even though he had a physical infirmity himself at the time, Paul spoke a word of faith, and the cripple took the first leaping steps of his life. Paul could minister divine healing to others while still not experiencing his own healing. Obviously, we don't need to be healed yet ourselves before we can pray boldly for the sick.

The second notable miracle in Lystra regarded the stoning of Paul. Enemies of the gospel stoned him and left him for dead, but after the disciples gathered round him and prayed, he rose up and walked away (Acts 14:19-20). Resurrection life coursed through his entire being in response to the prayers of the saints. It seems he was instantly healed of everything—except that nagging physical infirmity mentioned in Galatians 4:13. That's mysterious. How could he have resurrection life flow through his whole body, but yet not be healed of that debilitating physical infirmity? This is the kind of mystery that surrounds the topic of chastening. God had a purpose for resurrecting Paul, and He also had a purpose for his physical infirmity while in Galatia. If the infirmity of Galatia was the same thing as Paul's thorn in the flesh, then God's purpose for it was that he not be exalted above measure.

The believers in Galatia were well aware of Paul's physical infirmity, and Paul acknowledged that they could have despised him because of it. But he commended them for receiving him and his message, even in spite of his infirmity. It guarded them from exalting Paul above measure, but it didn't keep them from receiving the gospel.

It Was a Demon

Paul said he was buffeted in his flesh by *a messenger of Satan*. That means Satan had sent a messenger on an assignment against Paul. Satan had sent a demon— a spirit of infirmity, if the language of Luke 13:11 is fitting—to harass Paul in his body.

Additionally, Paul notes that this messenger "was *given* to me" (2 Cor 12:7). A demon was given to Paul. But by whom? If the thorn had come directly from Satan, Paul probably would have said something like, "I was attacked," or "I was assaulted," or "There came against me," or as he says elsewhere, "I was hindered." But Paul said the thorn "was given to me." He describes the thorn as a gift. Nothing coming from Satan is ever a gift. Only God gives gifts. The thorn was given to Paul, therefore, by God. *God gave Paul a demon*. How do you find a theological category for that? God gave the permission slip, and Satan sent it. Both God and Satan were involved, which is so typical of chastening.

That God should use evil powers for divine purposes is not a new idea in Scripture. For example, Scripture says that "a distressing spirit from the LORD troubled" Saul (1 Sam 16:14). We don't know whether it was a heavenly or demonic spirit. In another example, Micaiah saw a spirit come before God's throne and say, "I will go out and be a lying spirit in the mouth of all his prophets" (1 Kgs 22:22). So God sent that spirit on that sinister assignment. Again, we don't know whether that was a heavenly or demonic spirit, but I personally suspect it was a demon. If that's true, it came before God's throne similar to the way Satan did in Job 1:6. My point in mentioning these examples is to show that God, in His sovereignty, can use even demons for His purposes.

The demon afflicting Paul didn't enter his soul or spirit or inhabit him. He was not demon-possessed or demonized. Rather, the demon attacked his flesh. It attached to Paul like a leech. And the infirmity jabbed into his flesh like a thorn. A thorn in one's flesh would harass and harangue, but it would not immobilize. That's why Paul called it a thorn, because while it didn't stop him, it certainly did slow and hinder him.

It's possible that Paul had this thorn in view when he spoke three times of being hindered by Satan.

> Now I do not want you to be unaware, brethren, that I often planned to come to you (but was hindered until now), that I might have some fruit among you also, just as among the other Gentiles (Rom 1:13).

> For this reason I also have been much hindered from coming to you (Rom 15:22).

> Therefore we wanted to come to you—even I, Paul, time and again—but Satan hindered us (1 Thess 2:18).

Whether or not he was referring to his thorn, it's clear that Satan was able to hinder his travels to some extent. As an apostle, he was called to travel, and that's precisely the point where Satan hindered him. I can imagine him making repeated attempts to get to Thessalonica or Rome, but just when he was about to buy his ticket, the demon would buffet him in his flesh, the infirmity would flare up, and Paul would have to postpone his plans.

Paul was not alone in this regard. Satan still seeks to hinder believers, especially at the point of their calling.

Paul's Thorn is Relevant to Us

I used to think Paul's thorn was an anomaly, a highly unusual exception that happened to him because of his unique encounters with God. I had heard it said, "Unless you've had abundant revelations like Paul, you don't need to concern yourself with being given a thorn in the flesh." But now I realize Paul's thorn wasn't a rare one-off; it was the sort of thing God has been doing with His servants throughout history. He understands how organically our body is joined to our soul, and He knows how to use physical restrictions to temper the mind, soul, and spirit.

What God did with Paul He's still doing today.

Benjamin Franklin once said, *An ounce of prevention is worth a pound of cure.* That proverb is applicable in the realm of chastening. God's discipline in our lives is sometimes like a preemptive strike. A small chastening today can save us from a large disaster tomorrow.

In the heat of the crucible it may not feel like an *ounce* of prevention but more like a *pound* of prevention. In other words, it can feel too intense to simply be a preventive measure. But when you consider that the fruit from the chastening makes a huge difference in our eternal rewards, the affliction comes into focus for what it truly is—light and momentary in contrast to the exceeding and eternal weight of glory that will come from it (2 Cor 4:17).

Was Paul Ever Healed?

Many people assume Paul was never delivered of his thorn in the flesh. Three times Paul pled with Jesus to take it from him. You'll notice that in His response to Paul, Jesus never said, "No." His response was more like, "Not just now."

When God has you in a season of chastening, you can plead with Him to deliver you, but sometimes His answer is, "Not yet." When God's season of chastening is not yet over in your life, it's not possible to muscle your way out of it by mustering faith. Faith is not a means whereby we strong-arm God. Paul had to wait on God for his healing, not because he didn't have enough faith but because it wasn't yet God's time to remove the chastening. The one who wore the crown of thorns had grace to empower Paul to endure his thorn.

Paul didn't know how to handle the thorn—until Jesus spoke to him. Paul wrote, "And He said to me." When Jesus spoke, the turbulence in Paul's soul was settled and he knew how to walk forward. When you are experiencing a chastening that you don't know how to handle, there's nothing better than a word from the Master's mouth!

Paul was not healed the moment he pled with God for healing. There is reason to believe, however, that Paul was eventually delivered from the thorn. Let me explain.

It was right around AD 55 or 56 that Paul wrote in 2 Corinthians 12 about his thorn. About ten or eleven years later, Paul wrote his second letter to Timothy (which was Paul's final epistle before his death). In that letter, Paul spoke of the physical afflictions he endured while in Galatia. (Timothy was with him on that trip.) Notice what Paul said about those afflictions:

> But you have carefully followed my doctrine, manner of life, purpose, faith, longsuffering, love, perseverance, persecutions, *afflictions*, which happened to me at Antioch, at Iconium, at Lystra—what persecutions

I endured. And out of them all the Lord delivered me (2 Tim 3:10-11).

Paul told Timothy the Lord delivered him out of *all* the afflictions he endured in Galatia. Did Paul already have the thorn in his flesh when he ministered in Galatia? It seems likely (Gal 4:13). If Paul had his thorn at the time he was in Galatia, then clearly he was delivered of that affliction, because he told Timothy he was delivered of *all* the afflictions he endured in Galatia.

Why is this important? Because God's intended way in chastening is that the chastened son eventually be healed (Heb 12:13). Even as it appears from the evidence that Paul was healed of his thorn, God desires to heal you of the chastening affliction that buffets you. Settle for nothing less.

A Strange Old Testament Story

I'm going to add a bizarre Old Testament story here, basically because I don't know where else to fit it in this book. So I'm putting this weird story next to Paul's weird thorn. In the context of the story, King Ahab had just spared from death Ben-hadad, king of Syria, whom God didn't want spared.

> Now a certain man of the sons of the prophets said to his neighbor by the word of the LORD, "Strike me, please." And the man refused to strike him. Then he said to him, "Because you have not obeyed the voice of the LORD, surely, as soon as you depart from me, a lion shall kill you." And as soon as he left him, a lion found him and killed him. And he found another man, and said, "Strike me, please." So the man struck him, inflicting a wound. Then the prophet departed and waited for the king by the road, and disguised himself with a bandage over his eyes. Now as the king passed by, he cried out to the king and said, "Your servant went out into the midst of

the battle; and there, a man came over and brought a man to me, and said, 'Guard this man; if by any means he is missing, your life shall be for his life, or else you shall pay a talent of silver.' While your servant was busy here and there, he was gone." Then the king of Israel said to him, "So shall your judgment be; you yourself have decided it." And he hastened to take the bandage away from his eyes; and the king of Israel recognized him as one of the prophets. Then he said to him, "Thus says the LORD: 'Because you have let slip out of your hand a man whom I appointed to utter destruction, therefore your life shall go for his life, and your people for his people'" (1 Kgs 20:35-42).

This is a terrifying story for everyone involved. It was terrifying to the prophet because, as God's messenger, he had to solicit a wound to his body. It was terrifying to the prophet's neighbor who lost his life for being well-mannered and gracious. It was terrifying to the man who struck the prophet in fearful self-preservation. And it was fearful to King Ahab, who received the prophetic judgment from the wounded prophet.

What kind of implement or weapon was used to wound the prophet? How badly was he maimed? Badly enough to convince Ahab he was injured in battle.

Maybe there is something similar, after all, between Paul's thorn and this prophet's wound. Both of them had to suffer in the flesh in order to carry their message effectively to others.

Sometimes God wounds His prophets. It's a terrifying hour when God's messengers must be struck and wounded in order to be a living parable of their message from God. I believe we live in just such an hour.

Here's my takeaway on this story: Some messages require a wounded prophet.

21

Caricatures of Child Discipline

This book is devoted to the Lord's discipline in our lives. However, before we close, I want to take a couple chapters to deal with the topic of child discipline because the two are inextricably related.

I want to say, from the start, that I vigorously oppose child abuse. The Bible speaks against the mistreatment of our children, and a balanced position on child discipline vehemently resists excessive or abusive punishment. God forbid that anyone should use the Bible's instruction on discipline to abuse their children. Child discipline is the kind and tender shaping and nurturing of a child to become a whole, godly, productive person in society.

But not everyone in the world views it positively.

Child discipline. Correction. Punishment. Spanking. These are controversial, hot-button words today. Since 1979, when Sweden made spanking of children in private homes punishable by law, a host of other nations have enacted similar legislation, sharing in a worldwide trend to disparage and vilify the practice of child discipline through physical, bodily means.

As of January 2016, parents can face criminal charges in forty-nine nations (and counting) for spanking their children[1]: Albania, Andorra, Argentina, Austria, Benin, Bolivia, Brazil, Bulgaria, Cape Verde, Costa Rica, Croatia, Cyprus, Denmark, Estonia, Finland, Germany, Greece, Honduras, Hungary, Iceland, Ireland, Israel, Kenya, Latvia, Liechtenstein, Luxembourg, Macedonia, Malta, Moldova, Netherlands, New Zealand, Nicaragua, Norway, Peru, Poland, Portugal, Republic of Congo, Romania, San Marino, South Korea, South Sudan, Spain, Sweden, Togo, Tunisia, Turkmenistan, Ukraine, Uruguay, and Venezuela.

Additionally, a number of international and national agencies oppose spanking of children. Their desire is to make all forms of bodily discipline punishable by law in every home, school, and nation.[2]

1 https://en.wikipedia.org/wiki/Corporal_punishment_in_the_home
2 Following is a listing of some of those agencies.
   UNESCO recommends that corporal punishment be prohibited in schools, homes and institutions as a form of discipline, and alleges that it is a violation of human rights as well as counterproductive, ineffective, dangerous and harmful to children. www.unesco.org/new/en/unesco
   Save the Children opposes all forms of corporal punishment on children. www.savethechildren.net/alliance/index.html
   The Australian Psychological Society holds that corporal punishment of children is an ineffective method of deterring unwanted behavior promotes undesirable behaviors and fails to demonstrate an alternative desirable behavior. www.psychology.org.au
   The Canadian Pediatrics Society reviewed research on spanking and concluded that it was associated with negative outcomes, and physicians recommended against spanking.
   In the United Kingdom, the Royal College of Paediatrics and Child Health is against spanking and opposes the striking of children in all circumstances. http://en.wikipedia.org/wiki/Corporal_punishment_in_the_home - cite_note-pmid12949335-41#cite_note-pmid12949335-41
   The Royal College of Psychiatrists also takes the position that corporal punishment is unacceptable in all circumstances. www.rcpch.ac.uk/ and www.rcpsych.ac.uk
   The American Academy of Pediatrics believes that corporal punishment possesses some negative side-effects and only limited benefits, and recommends the use of other forms of discipline to manage undesirable behavior. www.aap.org
   International Humanist and Ethical Union: www.iheu.org
   End All Corporal Punishment of Children: www.endcorporalpunishment.org

This worldwide movement to denigrate and criminalize all use of bodily punishment is in response to the abusive practices of some parents, but is in direct opposition to the wisdom of Scripture. God's word specifically enjoins parents to use a rod to correct and chasten their children.

> Chasten your son while there is hope, and do not set your heart on his destruction (Prov 19:18).

> Foolishness is bound up in the heart of a child; the rod of correction will drive it far from him (Prov 22:15).

> Do not withhold correction from a child, for if you beat him with a rod, he will not die. You shall beat him with a rod, and deliver his soul from hell (Prov 23:13-14).

> The rod and rebuke give wisdom, but a child left to himself brings shame to his mother (Prov 29:15).

Many psychologists insist that bodily punishment produces no positive but only negative results in children. That opinion contradicts the Bible's claim that it can deliver children from foolishness, shame, destruction, and hell.

When the Bible talks about using a *rod* on our children, it doesn't mean we should have a club in the house. I explain my understanding of a contemporary rod in the next chapter.

The biblical imagery of a rod is taken from the Israelites' shepherding culture. A shepherd typically carried two wooden objects—a staff, which was a long, thin walking stick with a crook used for providing direction or to lift a lamb, and a rod, which was a shorter, thicker cudgel or club. Its primary purpose was to fend off flock predators and then, secondarily, to discipline wayward sheep.

Center for Effective Discipline: www.stophitting.com
The No Spanking Page: www.neverhitachild.org
Project NoSpank: www.nospank.netUNICEF: www.unicef.org

Some people today oppose the biblical idea of using a rod to correct a child. If we are to oppose it, we must conclude that God's counsel is harsh, that we are kinder and more merciful than He, and we know better than He how to raise our children.

But God's counsel to use the rod is exceedingly merciful. Since disciplining a child will deliver his soul from hell (Prov 23:14), what could possibly be more merciful? Unless you don't believe in the existence of hell, in which case I can understand how physical punishment could seem unreasonable.

Those who advise, "Don't hit your kids," have cynically reduced chastening to *hitting*. They claim it produces aggressive, antisocial behavior, physical injury, inhibits brain development and mental health, threatens the child's sense of security, and is a violation of children's human rights. When they look at spanking, here's what they see: Parents angrily hitting their children in frustration over their mistakes and immaturity.

Now, it's true—some parents *do* lash out at their children in anger and frustration. But that's not an accurate image of what chastening should be, that's the jaded caricature. True chastening is characterized by affection, restraint, wisdom, perceptivity, understanding, and patient resolve.

What is causing the nations of the earth to outlaw the compassionate spanking of children? The answer is in Ephesians 6:12, "For we do not wrestle against flesh and blood, but against principalities, against powers, against the rulers of the darkness of this age, against spiritual hosts of wickedness in the heavenly places." Hell has declared war on chastening. There is a full-on, worldwide, energetic offensive by the powers of darkness to convince the earth that the chastening of children is harsh, repressive, damaging, abusive, cruel, antiquated, and obsolete.

And there's a reason for it. Satan's agenda is to skew and embitter a generation against the goodness and wisdom of God's chastening hand. If a father who chastens his children in kindness can be painted as a tyrant, then the next reasonable conclusion is to view God as oppressive and tyrannical when He chastens.

This is the main reason why the spiritual warfare surrounding the topic of chastening is astonishingly intense. Satan seeks to caricaturize the fatherhood of God so that men will reject, malign, and blaspheme Him.

Satan wants today's generation to have a skewed, distorted view of chastening so they will have no framework for processing the end-time judgments of the Lord. If an entire generation views physical punishment (chastening) as abusive and worthy of legal recrimination, they are positioned to become offended at God for the way He judges the world and chastens His children. The very concept of chastening has come under tremendous fire because Satan wants today's generation to view God as oppressive and tyrannical in His leadership style.

Loving parents don't patrol every action of their children, poised to penalize every infraction with a spanking. But neither are they disengaged, absent, and neglectful, giving little regard to the progress of their children. God is the same way. He is doting, caring, tender, and greatly interested in our welfare. Chastening is a measure used only when needed and is designed for a positive, redemptive outcome.

Today's anti-spanking movement appears, on the surface, to be motivated by compassion for the little ones of the earth. While that's true to a measure, it's actually fueled in a strong measure by a sinister scheme of darkness. The furor isn't simply about the protection of children in abusive families, it's about defaming God's reputation and word.

In response to the caricaturizations of God's goodness, I want to begin by saying what child discipline is *not*. That will help us see what it actually *is*.

Chastening Isn't Abuse

Child discipline, properly executed, is not abusive but remedial and beneficial.

Can discipline be abused? Absolutely. And it often is. That's one reason this topic is so controversial. Some parents get so angry that they lash their children excessively or inappropriately. The number of children who say they were abused by their parents is alarming. But just because some parents sin against their children in their manner of discipline doesn't mean all discipline is wrong or should be banned. If people drive drunk, should we outlaw driving? We don't outlaw driving but drunk driving; similarly, we shouldn't outlaw child discipline but child abuse.

Let me be clear. If a parent abuses a child, it's not chastening. It's abuse. When we validate chastening, we are not giving parents permission to vent their frustrations upon their children. Parents must walk in the fear of the Lord, for we will give account to God for our parenting. In instances where parents have been excessive, harsh, or abusive, we should confess our sin to God, ask forgiveness of our children (when they are old enough to understand), and pray with our children for reconciliation, forgiveness, and healing.

In physical discipline, godly parents seek to guide their children to a soft heart and a submitted will, without crushing their spirit. Proverbs 17:22 says that "a crushed spirit dries up the bones." If we crush the spirit we have become abusive; but if we shape and direct the spirit in wisdom, we are doing our children a great kindness.

True chastening is not abusive but beautiful.

Chastening Isn't a Release for Anger and Frustration

Secondly, chastening isn't a release for a parent's frustration.

Some people view spanking as adults taking advantage of their superior strength to vent their exasperation and frustration on people who are smaller and weaker than they. That is not my view. Chastening is not parents bottling their anger until they burst and explode in an episode of hitting. Rather, chastening is done in a calm and collected resolve, with wisdom and level-headed understanding.

Anger can actually undermine the authority of a parent. As an example, consider the authority of a policeman. If he pulls you over for speeding and then rants at you, it actually diminishes his credibility and reputation. Either way you'll pay the fine; but if he handles you with a cool disposition, you will honor and respect him— even while he's giving you a ticket.

In the same say, the calmer a parent is, the more effective the discipline is likely to be. We want our children to realize we're not striking out in a fit of rage; rather, we're faithful stewards before God, fulfilling our duty conscientiously to raise our children "in the training and admonition of the Lord" (Eph 6:4).

Chastening Isn't Damaging

The opponents of chastening contend that it's damaging to the emotions and soul of a child. They say it can even damage a child's body.

Let me repeat myself. If chastening ever damages a child's body, the parent has been abusive. Spanking may leave some temporary redness on a child's buttocks, but it should never draw blood, break bones, or leave dark bruising. It is legitimate for a society to have laws to protect children from parents who damage their children's bodies.

The point is not to inflict wounds on a child's body. The point is to smack the body with enough force that causes the child to smart. It should produce genuine tears. It should hurt but not damage.

Sincere chastening, carefully administered, doesn't damage the soul, mind, or psyche of a child. In fact, it does the exact opposite. It enables a child to learn a valuable lesson without being damaged. A child learns to forsake behaviors that would have become damaging in their future.

Chastening is the compassionate use of a lesser punishment today to save a child from a greater injury tomorrow. For example, a child is spanked for giving place to rage today, in their youth, so that they are able to control themselves and not destroy, in years to come, other people (such as acquaintances, spouse, children) through uncontrolled rage.

Carefully executed corporal punishment doesn't damage children; what damages them is a parent's undisciplined tongue. If parents don't believe in spanking, then what recourse do they have to corral their children's unacceptable behaviors? The alternative often employed, unfortunately, is the tongue. *The tongue can damage a child much more deeply and permanently than any rod.*

Consider what the Bible has to say about the power of the tongue.

Even so the tongue is a little member and boasts great things. See how great a forest a little fire kindles! And the tongue is a fire, a world of iniquity. The tongue is so set among our members that it defiles the whole body, and sets on fire the course of nature; and it is set on fire by hell. For every kind of beast and bird, of reptile and creature of the sea, is tamed and has been tamed by mankind. But no man can tame the tongue. It is an unruly evil, full of deadly poison (Jas 3:5-8).

There is one who speaks like the piercings of a sword, but the tongue of the wise promotes health (Prov 12:18).

Death and life are in the power of the tongue (Prov 18:21).

Let your speech always be with grace, seasoned with salt, that you may know how you ought to answer each one (Col 4:6).

When parents vent by yelling, raging, cursing, or demeaning their kids, they can do tremendous harm to their impressionable hearts. A rod might leave a temporary red mark on the skin, but words can cut and pierce the soul, producing wounds that can fester and scar for life.

Instead of damaging their kids with their words, loving parents will find a calm and loving way to spank their children, as needed, to help them adopt godly behavior.

Chastening Doesn't Teach Children Violence

We've come to a fourth caricature of child discipline. Some think that, when we spank our children, we are teaching them to hit others who cross them. Actually, the opposite is true. The rod of correction doesn't teach your child to be violent. Rather, it drives the foolishness of violence and wrath from him. One of the things we spank our children for is violence. If our children are aggressive or violent to others by hitting them, they get a spanking to teach them not to hit.

There are two basic categories of things for which we spank our children: behaviors that the Bible proscribes, and attitudes that the Bible proscribes. Whenever we chasten our children, we want to base it upon a biblical passage or principle in order to show our children that what they have done is wrong not just before people, but before God.

For example, it's fitting to spank children for temper tantrums. The Bible clearly speaks against rage, and when our children go into fits of rage, we have a godly duty to discipline them accordingly.

This is all the more reason why chastening must not be done in anger. It's hypocritical to angrily spank a child for getting angry.

Notice how the following passage speaks against outbursts of wrath.

> Now the works of the flesh are evident, which are: adultery, fornication, uncleanness, lewdness, idolatry, sorcery, hatred, contentions, jealousies, outbursts of wrath, selfish ambitions, dissensions, heresies, envy, murders, drunkenness, revelries, and the like; of which I tell you beforehand, just as I also told you in time past, that those who practice such things will not inherit the kingdom of God (Gal 5:19-21).

It's wrong for children to give place to outbursts of wrath, and it's wrong for parents to discipline in outbursts of wrath.

One of the biblical purposes of the rod is to drive foolishness from the heart of a child (Prov 22:15). There is nothing more foolish than giving place to the works of the flesh because, as the above passage states, those who practice such things will not inherit the kingdom of God. We use the rod, therefore, to drive the foolishness of wrath, hatred, and contentions from their lives.

One of the foolish things bound up in the heart of a child is rebellion and disobedience. When a child manifests those foolish behaviors, a godly parent will use proper discipline to drive that foolishness from them. In such instances, we want to explain to our children, "Sweetheart, you're getting this spanking because you disobeyed Mommy. The Bible says, 'Children, obey your parents.' Do you understand what you did wrong?"

It's wonderful when we can quote Scripture in the disciplinary process because it demonstrates our submission to the authority of God's word and helps our children realize that our evaluation of their behavior is supported by an authority higher than just our own opinion. Our submission to God's word teaches them submission to God's word and will.

Chastening Isn't Cruel and Dehumanizing

Finally, opponents of physical correction caricaturize it as mean, barbaric, and dehumanizing. They claim studies and surveys to substantiate their conclusions.

Rather than dehumanizing, however, chastening actually infuses dignity into the soul. It demonstrates to children that we love them enough to endure a temporary unpleasantry in order to achieve a positive and enduring benefit.

> Train up a child in the way he should go, and when he is old he will not depart from it (Prov 22:6).

The Hebrew word for *train up* comes from the root word meaning *to develop a thirst, create a desire*. Training and discipline are designed to instill in a child an appetite for righteousness. Far from being cruel, the act of chastening can direct a child toward godly character and self-control.

Chastening produces a marvelous opportunity to infuse a child with confidence and identity. In the process of the punishment, the heart of a child is made soft and open to instruction and affection. What sin tried to harden in the heart of the child, correction and repentance will now soften. With the spanking comes a marvelous window for character formation. It's a moment when both parent and child are profoundly soft and close. In that moment, words can be expressed to a child that form strong foundations of confidence, character, and identity. "I love you so much. I totally forgive you. You are now clean before God. You have such a good heart. You want to do good, and I love that about you. You are growing up to be such a godly person. I'm so proud of your willingness to change. Thank you for receiving me. You have an amazing destiny in God."

Chastening is not cruel; the absence of chastening is cruel. When a child sins but then is not coached on how to unload their guilt, they carry it into their future. *That's* cruel. A parent holds the key to a child's exoneration, and the cruel thing would be to provide no relief for a child's guilt. Chastening provides a child an opportunity for penance and penitence. Sins are confessed, the burden is removed, the forgiveness and light of Christ shines, affection is exchanged between parent and child, and the child leaves the exchange with a heart that is free, clean, unencumbered, and happy.

This is not cruel and dehumanizing, but gracious and dignifying.

Chastening Is Caring Correction

Having said what chastening is not, let me now say the same thing in positive terms. *Chastening is the tender and affectionate shaping of a child's soul so they might grow into complete, healthy, productive adults.* Sometimes it's the kindest, most loving thing a parent can do.

Spanking is the calm, intentional, strategic chastening of our children, in the proper time and way, in order to raise them up into their fullest potential. It represents the willingness of a loving parent to do whatever is necessary to raise a child properly, even at the risk of that child misunderstanding. In the moment, a child might feel wronged or unjustly punished. But the intention of love is to help the child eventually understand the parent's noble purpose.

According to Proverbs, the abusive parent is the one who withholds the rod: "He who spares the rod hates his son, but he who loves him is careful to discipline him" (Prov 13:24). Children are arrows (Ps 127:4), and it is a parent's responsibility to make them straight. Straight arrows, when deployed, hit the mark of their calling and purpose.

Our heavenly Father handles His children in the same way. He will confront negative behaviors in our lives to save us from destruction. If God handles us that carefully, shouldn't we do the same for our kids?

22

Practical Suggestions for Child Discipline

Having defended the biblical practice of child discipline, now I want to get practical and offer suggestions on how to chasten our children in their youth. Why is this necessary? Because some of us grew up in a home where there was no spanking, and others in a home where discipline was violent or excessive. I hope to be helpful, therefore, by giving some practical guidelines on how to discipline our children in a biblical way.

Be Willing to Spank

Some believers were indoctrinated against spanking before they came to Christ by people who did not acknowledge the wisdom and authority of God's word. Now that they are disciples of Christ, they can find themselves torn between the humanistic advice of their past and the truth of Scripture.

Choose truth. Allow God's word to form your values and shape your convictions. As Paul wrote, "And do not be conformed to this world, but be transformed by the renewing of your mind, that you may prove what is that good and acceptable and perfect will of God (Rom 12:2).

If you vowed in your soul to never spank your children, simply repent. Determine to raise your children according to the wisdom of God's word.

Chasten Sparingly

Spanking is not the only tool a parent has for correcting and shaping children. Nor is it always to be the first response. Discerning parents will know when it's time to spank.

There are two primary means for correcting children: physical punishment (chastening), and verbal instruction (rebukes). Jesus uses both with us: "As many as I love, I rebuke and chasten" (Rev 3:19). Paul acknowledged both means when he wrote, "And you, fathers, do not provoke your children to wrath, but bring them up in the training and admonition of the Lord" (Eph 6:4).

I spoke of this earlier, but let me repeat that the words *training* and *admonition* are meaningful. *Training* is the Greek word *paideia*, which points to the education and training of a child in order to inculcate discipline. Figuratively, it carries the idea of chastening or chastisement. The Greek word for *admonition* is *nouthesia*, to call attention to, which by implication means rebuke, warning, or admonition. In broad strokes, *paideia* emphasizes non-verbal chastening, and *nouthesia* emphasizes verbal correction.

Over the course of a child's upbringing, parents use *nouthesia* (admonition) a whole lot more than *paideia* (training) to coach a child toward maturity. So let me be clear. Not only is chastening *not* the only way we discipline our children, it's the *lesser* means used. Verbal instruction plays a much more dominant role in the development of our children.

Training and admonition are inversely proportional, based upon the maturity level of our children. Let me explain. In their early childhood, training is used rather heavily and verbal admonition is not used extensively—particularly in those early seasons of life when children understand a physical swat much more than a verbal rebuke. Then, as children grow and mature, the proportions of these two ingredients change. Training (nonverbal correction) begins to fall off, and it is replaced with large amounts of verbal admonition. Why? Because as our children mature, they grow in their ability to absorb and respond to verbal correction.

The same general trend is also true in our walk with Christ. Generally, the Lord uses progressively less chastening and more instruction as we mature and demonstrate the ability to respond to His voice.

Use the Least Means Possible

Chastening always seeks to achieve a noble, upright goal in the life of a child. *Always employ the least severe means possible to achieve the desired end*. We shouldn't fall short of the desired end by being too lenient, but neither should we continue to chasten when we have reached the desired end in the child's heart. Do only what's necessary, and then it's enough.

Be Sensitive to a Child's Maturity Level

Each child matures differently. Therefore, there is no set age when a parent should begin or cease to spank. The age differs with each child, according to their maturity and temperament. Proverbs 13:24 says, "He who spares his rod hates his son, but he who loves him disciplines him promptly." The meaning of the Hebrew word for *promptly* is *early*. Early in life. This goes along with how The Living Bible renders Proverbs 19:18, "Discipline your son in his early years while there is hope. If you don't you will ruin his life."

Don't spank children when they are still too young to absorb the significance of a swat. As they grow, children come to a place where they begin to comprehend the significance of a little swat. Loving parents will discern how much their children are able to comprehend as they grow and will adjust their chastening practices accordingly.

We are always compassionate toward our precious children. Many times we opt in favor of being lenient and gracious because we are tender toward their weaknesses. Thank God that He is also gracious with us!

Correct Sinful Actions

Children should be corrected when they do something that is contrary to the Lord's guidance in Scripture. If they violate a biblical precept without knowing it was wrong, we instruct them in that precept. If they already knew that action was wrong, but did it anyways, then the correction needs to be stronger.

One of the fundamental principles we teach our children early in life is that of Ephesians 6:1, which is based on one of the Ten Commandments (Exod 20:12).

> Children, obey your parents in the Lord, for this is right (Eph 6:1).

Every child needs to know this Scripture, and that disobedience incurs negative consequences. When enforcing biblical expectations, parental follow-through is essential. For example, suppose a parent says, "If you do this, you will get a spanking," and then suppose the child does it anyways. That parent needs to be careful to follow through on their word. Don't get frustrated and repeat the same warning but only louder. Follow James 5:12, which says, "But let your 'Yes' be 'Yes,' and your 'No,' 'No.'" Simply deliver on your word.

Explain to your children that when they disobey they are sinning not only against you, but also against God. Be sure they understand they are being disciplined for *sin*.

Always keep this in mind: Delayed obedience is disobedience. If a child responds only after you have reiterated your call several times, that is not obedience. Obedience is responding to your call the first time (Matt 4:20). Children that don't obey immediately should be rebuked or chastened.

Some examples of sinful behaviors we discipline are disobedience or breaking known rules (Eph 6:1), lying (Col 3:9), stealing (Exod 20:15), violent behavior toward another (Gen 6:11-13), causing strife between kids (Rom 13:13), swearing (Col 3:8), name-calling (2 Kgs 2:23), complaining (Phil 2:14), sexually inappropriate conduct (Col 3:5), etc. In each instance, always have a Scripture to support your disciplinary action. You'll notice violent behavior is in the list. The Bible speaks clearly against violence, so when a child hits another person in an intentionally aggressive way, that kind of violent behavior must be corrected. Notice that causing strife is also in the list. If a child is doing something intentional that is producing strife in a relationship with another child or within a group, then the producing of strife must be disciplined. Don't wink at sibling tension. Never allow a child's sinful behavior to compromise the spirit of peace that rests upon your home.

We don't spank kids for making innocent mistakes. We don't chasten, for example, if a child loses control of a household object, drops it, and it breaks accidentally. On the other hand, if the child knew he was not allowed to touch that object, but picked it up anyways, then he may get a spanking—not for breaking it, but for the disobedience of picking it up.

The first step in the disciplinary process is to help the child identify and understand how he sinned. If the child is old enough to understand, then point to the biblical passage or principle which is the basis for your discipline.

Correct Sinful Attitudes

We chasten our children, therefore, for sinful actions. But that's not all. We also discipline them for sinful attitudes. It's not enough to correct only wrong behavior; we must also correct wrong emotional responses.

For example, a mother once told her son who was misbehaving to sit down. After finally sitting down, the boy answered, "I may be sitting down on the outside, but on the inside I'm still standing up!" That story illustrates that children can behave in a way that is technically correct, but do it with a wrong attitude. Even if their behavior is correct, sinful attitudes must be addressed.

We explain to our children why certain attitudes are sinful. We never exasperate them by disciplining them for something they didn't know was wrong. We explain the wrong, and then if they continue to sin, we bring correction.

Let me mention a few sinful attitudes which parents should correct. This is not a complete listing, but just a few examples to show how to identify sinful attitudes according to God's word.

Chasten children for losing their temper (Jas 1:20; Col 3:8). Galatians 5:20 identifies "outbursts of wrath" as sinful. Children must learn to control emotions of anger and not give place to them. If they lose their temper, deal decisively with the situation until the anger has dissipated and there is authentic contrition.

Correct children for arguing. Philippians 2:14 says, "Do all things without...disputing," Arguing is not a benign activity to be tolerated; it's giving place to sinful attitudes and must be addressed.

Confront rebellion (1 Sam 15:23). We want to cultivate a submissive, obedient spirit in our children (1 Pet 5:5).

Don't allow your children to pout. Pouting is just an internalized form of anger (Col 3:8). We are told to, "Rejoice in the Lord always" (Phil 4:4), so sometimes it's appropriate to tell your children to snap out of it—fast.

Correct disrespect toward adults. Leviticus 19:32 says, "You shall rise before the gray headed and honor the presence of an old man, and fear your God." Coach your children to honor adults. If they refuse to greet adults with honor, then rebuke them.

Use a Rod

When the Bible speaks of using a rod, the implication seems to be that we should use a neutral object to spank our children. It's tempting for parents, in the haste and convenience of the moment, to use their hand in disciplining their children. For example, it can be easy to slap a mouthy child, but it's better to slow our reflexes and use an implement other than our hand. Occasionally it's understandable if we need to give a kid a quick swat on the rump with our hand because of the moment, but make that the exception. Our hand is for tenderness, reassurance, and blessing—not for slapping. Let your children always associate your hand with tenderness.

What kind of "rod" might we use? Perhaps a wide leather belt or a smooth wooden spoon.

The purpose of the rod is to hurt. Scripture teaches that pain is a deterrent to wrong behavior. Solomon said it clearly, "Blows that hurt cleanse away evil, as do stripes the inner depths of the heart" (Prov 20:30). Spanking that is painful produces good behavior and helps cleanse the heart. If it's not painful we miss the point.

Stay Calm

If your emotions are heated in the immediacy of an infraction, remember what God said to Israel in Exodus 33:5, "I could come up into your midst in one moment and consume you. Now therefore, take off your ornaments, that I may know what to do to you." In the spirit of that incident, sit down with your child, be silent, cool down, and take some time to ponder what the next step should be.

Someone might say, "But that's why I don't spank. I don't want to vent my anger on my children." Refraining from chastening is not the right response. Rather, deal with your anger issues, and then chasten your children in wisdom and tenderness.

Don't yell at your children. If you do, you yourself are introducing strife into your home. Repent, and stop yelling. Repent for allowing their sin to control your emotions. Don't raise your voice—you hold the rod. Every time you lose your temper with your children, apologize to them and ask them to pray for you in accordance with James 5:16.

Elements of the Disciplinary Process

When spanking your children, consider using some of these measures.

▸ Provide the dignity of privacy. Try to discipline a child away from the eyes and ears of others.

▸ Some circumstances require delayed discipline, but in the spirit of Ecclesiastes 8:11, attend to it as soon as reasonably possible.

▸ Explain the reason for the chastening. Be sure they understand their sin. Make it a teaching moment.

▸ Afterwards, hold the child. Express profuse affection. Show that your relationship is fully restored.

▸ Pray together. Let the child repent. Bestow a blessing.

▸ Change the mood immediately. The sin is forgiven and forgotten. It's time to laugh and play.

When we go through this process with our children, we feel many of the emotions that God feels when He chastens us. Like Him, we feel incredible love for our child. We feel the tension of wishing we didn't have to chasten while knowing that, if we really love our child, we'll do it. We feel the reach of a longing heart toward our child. And then we realize: This is how God feels toward us! He is such a good and kind Father.

The Master Key to Raising Godly Children

No parent is equal to the task of bringing up their children in the training and admonition of the Lord. The challenge is bigger than any of us. We call upon God, therefore, for help with every step in the journey. Only with His help can we properly raise our children.

Someone reading this book might think, "I've blown it. I didn't chasten my children when I should have." There is no condemnation for past failures. Just confess it, receive forgiveness, and increase your prayers for your children. God can redeem what is lacking when we confess and surrender our past wrongs to Him. In Joel 2:25, the Lord said, "I will restore to you the years that the swarming locust has eaten," meaning that He is capable of restoring things from our past that never came into fruitfulness because of our negligence. God can redeem years of neglect. So just pick up where you are and move forward with God.

Even if we parent our children perfectly, our perfection is still not good enough. Why? Because we live in a war zone where the enemy is always on the prowl to devour our children. Our best is never enough. We desperately need God's help.

Therefore, I want to share what I consider to be the *master key* to raising godly children. It's simply this: As you pray with your children, lay hands upon them and place the Holy Spirit upon them. Bestow a blessing upon them. The priestly blessing of Numbers 6:24-26 might be a helpful guide.

The abiding presence of the Holy Spirit resting upon our children is *the difference*. Place His name and Spirit upon them.

John the Baptist grew up to be a great, godly man. But I suggest it wasn't because of his parents. His parents were elderly when John was born, and generally speaking elderly people don't make ideal parents. They tend to be inflexible, not very playful, not always real engaging, and not exceedingly tolerant of noise and activity.

I am suggesting that John grew into such outstanding godliness not because of his parents but in spite of his parents. The key was with the Holy Spirit. Gabriel foretold of John, "He will also be filled with the Holy Spirit, even from his mother's womb" (Luke 1:15). That's what made the difference in John's life—he was filled with the Holy Spirit. Pray, therefore, for the Holy Spirit to fill your children. Bless them with His presence. He makes all the difference.

Here's a sample prayer, as you lay hands upon your child: *Heavenly Father, I ask You to place Your name and Your Holy Spirit upon my daughter now. Fill her with the Holy Spirit. Holy Spirit, I am asking You to come upon her, live in her, and never leave her. Always help her to live in obedience to Your word. Make her into a godly woman who loves Jesus with all her heart. I ask this in Jesus' name. Amen*

23

Answering Questions and Objections

In this chapter, I answer some of the thorniest questions and strongest objections believers often have on the topic of the Lord's chastening. I am not claiming to have the perfect or most complete answers to these questions, but I will give it my best. Even if you don't agree with my answers, I hope this chapter will help to get everything "out on the table" so we can look at these things carefully and rightly divide the word of truth (2 Tim 2:15).

Please be patient when some of the answers are repetitive of content earlier in this book. The repetition is intentional because I realize not everyone reading this chapter will have read the entire book.

Also, I realize this chapter is long. Rather than split it into two parts for readability, I just put all the objections into one chapter. Hunker down, let's do this.

Does God ever chasten His children with sickness?

In identifying the nature of chastening, Scripture uses words like *wound*, *lame*, *scourge*, and *afflict*. The idea of "being sick" is present but not primary in the texts. More commonly the imagery is that of being lamed or wounded.

In chapter 11, I explained how *lame* in Hebrews 12:13 seems to describe a condition in which believers are pained, restricted, constrained, inconvenienced, and distressed, but not so distressed they're unable to pursue God. God doesn't chasten to render us incapable of functioning spiritually, but to render us desperate for an authentic relationship with Him.

Many forms of sickness render the sufferer incapable of pursuing God with a clear heart and mind. For example, conditions such as migraines, nausea, chronic fatigue, and severe pain can render the sufferer incapacitated, which is not God's way. Furthermore, life-threatening diseases such as cancer and congestive heart failure don't enable a pursuit of God—how can you pursue Christlikeness if you're dead? Therefore, I am persuaded that God rarely uses severe sickness to chasten His children. Most of that comes from the thief, who steals, kills, and destroys.

Having said that, I know God is sovereign, and He will not be limited in the means He uses to further His purposes in our lives. If He wants to use sickness, He can. He allowed Satan to use his disease of choice—boils—to afflict Job. Somewhat similarly, Hezekiah was afflicted with a boil that made him so sick he nearly died (Isa 38). The sickness was most certainly intended by God to deepen his heart for his posterity.[1] Sadly, Hezekiah didn't seem to be changed by the affliction, even though he was healed. God showed with both Job and Hezekiah that He can chasten with disease (in this case, boils) if He wants to.

In another instance, God wanted to use a disease in Asa's feet to redirect his heart. Instead of seeking God for healing, however, Asa consulted physicians and died in his affliction (2 Chron 16:12).

1   I expound on Hezekiah's story in my book, *The Fire of Delayed Answers*.

In Psalm 118:17-18, the writer spoke of being chastened with a sickness that almost took his life, but then he rejoiced in the Lord's salvation. So that was a rare instance of God chastening with sickness.

God struck Miriam with the dreaded disease of leprosy, and then healed her (Num 12:1-15), obviously to make a point. Paul "was given" a demonic affliction that beat on him, paining his flesh like a thorn (2 Cor 12:7-10). However, the Bible uses *affliction* not *sickness* to describe Paul's thorn. (I deal with Paul's thorn in chapter 20.)

The biblical instances of God using sickness to chasten are very few. Therefore, I believe we can conclude that sickness is rarely used by God as a means of chastening. Usually God uses other means, such as affliction, infirmity (lameness), other people, financial pressures, or circumstances.

Does sickness draw people closer to God?

In most cases, no. It usually drives people toward despair, languishing, grief, and death. It's the devil who oppresses people with sickness and disease (Acts 10:38). Jesus came to heal and deliver people from Satan's works.

Sickness can motivate us, however, to cry out to God. Sometimes backsliders are motivated by sickness to return to the Lord. Sometimes, believers are motivated by sickness to press into the Lord for healing. That response pleases the Lord. Sometimes, God will allow the devil to hit a believer with a trial because God sees a redemptive end for it. A saint can come through a trial closer to God than ever. What Satan intended for evil God can redeem for good.

During His earthly ministry, Jesus never made anyone sick but only healed the sick. If Jesus chastens by

wounding us, why didn't He wound anyone during His earthly ministry?

Jesus the King came to demonstrate what the kingdom looks like when the King is with us. When the King is present, everyone who comes to Him is healed instantly in His presence. Every time. It was essential that Jesus demonstrate and establish that truth. This is why our hearts yearn so intensely for the kingdom of God to come. When He is with us, everything that is broken and wounded is healed. Jesus healed everybody *who came to Him* to demonstrate unequivocally that it's His will to heal *everyone* who seeks His healing in sincerity. It was essential that His earthly ministry establish this truth without question.

Jesus did, however, lame people in times past. For example, virtually all scholars agree that when Genesis 32:24 says, "Then Jacob was left alone; and a Man wrestled with him until the breaking of day," that the Man was Christ Himself in a pre-incarnate form. It was Jesus who reached out His hand in the wrestling match and lamed Jacob in his hip.

Every time God chastened in the Bible, it was done with the Father and Son working implicitly together. There never was a chastening in which Jesus was non-participatory.

It was in the New Testament, after His ascension and glorification, that Jesus said to John, "As many as I love, I rebuke and chasten" (Rev 3:19). It is impossible to deny—Jesus chastens His beloved ones.

During His earthly ministry, Jesus never made anyone sick in order to teach them something, but healed everyone. Are you saying He now makes people sick in order to accomplish a deeper work in their lives?

The church of Jesus Christ has always responded well to persecution, often finding its strongest spiritual vitality in times of its greatest opposition. Persecution has an inherent pruning power. It culls away lukewarmness and promotes spiritual fervency.

Chastening has that same inherent pruning power. Even in contexts where the church is suffering no persecution, God is not without His means to ignite His people. He can chasten in our lives to produce deep spiritual change. Affliction itself doesn't change us, but if it drives us into the face of Christ, the pursuit of Jesus in the word and prayer is life-transforming.

Are there times when it's God's will for us to be sick?

It seems to be rare, but yes, there are rare instances.

But I also think the answer is no. Let me use an illustration to explain my meaning. Suppose I have a son who is being antagonistic toward his siblings and, after repeated infractions, I consign him to his room for a couple hours. My intention is to use the confines of his room to chasten him so that he will mature in the way he relates to his siblings. Is it my will that he be limited only to his room? Actually, no. My will is that he relate to his siblings in kindness, and be free to roam and play. But because of his immature behavior, I am using his "room arrest" to try to attain my actual will for his life, which is mature behavior. Until he grasps that, my temporary will is his room arrest.

So while sickness or infirmity might be God's temporary will for a season of learning and maturing in faith, His ultimate will for our lives is that we grow up into the Head, become complete in Christ, and be whole and free to serve. Therefore, it's God's will to heal.

If sickness or infirmity makes us a better believer, wouldn't that mean we should ask for even more of it?

This question might suppose that if a little is good, a lot is better. That's not true when it comes to medicine, vitamins, vaccines, or food, and it's not true when it comes to chastening.

The scriptural evidence is that, when being chastened, we should ask for healing and deliverance, not a more grievous trial.

If God is partly responsible for someone's infirmity, would it be wrong to ask for healing? Would that be asking God to do something contrary to His will?

No, it wouldn't be wrong to ask for healing or deliverance. As stated in chapter 12, there is no contradiction in asking God to deliver from a calamity He orchestrated. When He sends a calamity, He wants us to turn to Him with all our hearts and call on His name for deliverance.

If someone who is sick, infirm, or afflicted asks me to pray for their healing, how can I know whether they are being chastened by God or attacked by the devil?

Sometimes, God will give you discernment to know the spirits that are operational in a given affliction (1 Cor 12:10). If God gives you that discernment, you can pray with greater authority and understanding.

If God doesn't give you discernment, then here's my advice: Pray for healing. Pray for healing *every time* that a sick or lame person comes to you—unless God specifically gives you a different way to pray. Go after divine healing aggressively. Don't let the possibility of chastening make you tentative. Be bold and offer the prayer of faith!

Let your first impulse be to assume that the affliction is demonic. If God wants you to view the situation differently, He can reveal that to you. In general, my orientation is to pray against the works of the devil, believe for healing, and not concern myself with any chastening aspects. I don't think we need to be burdened or distracted with any way in which God might be chastening in someone's life, unless the Lord chooses to grant us discernment into the trial.

Apart from divine information or Holy Spirit impressions, it's impossible for us to know whether an affliction is partially a chastening of the Lord. In every prayer situation, lean on Jesus for direction and pray according to what you see the Father doing (John 5:19). The Holy Spirit has been given to help us pray according to God's will (Rom 8:26-27). Follow the lead of the Holy Spirit as you pray for the sick person (Rom 8:14).

If an afflicted person asks me to pray for their healing, and I sense they are under the Lord's chastening, how should I pray?

Unless specifically constrained and redirected by the Holy Spirit, pray for their healing—because God wants to heal and deliver. Ask for God's will to be done in their lives, even as His perfect will is done in heaven.

Jesus never said to anyone, "You need to have this affliction for more time still, because God hasn't finished using this crucible redemptively in your life." Therefore, I don't think we should say things like that, either. Rather, pray for healing.

Even when God has designed a chastening prison for someone for a season, the process of contending for deliverance is an important element in the journey. Contend earnestly with the prisoner for deliverance to come and for all of God's purposes to be realized. Pray for God to receive maximum glory from their story.

Are there times when it's not God's will to heal some-one right now?

Yes. For example, when Lazarus became sick, it was not Jesus' will to heal Him at that time because He wanted to perform an even greater miracle—resurrection.

But in the vast majority of cases, God wants to heal. If someone is not healed, it's probably not that God wills them to be sick; there's probably something else hindering the healing, and we should seek the Lord for the way to overcome that hindrance.

Unless the Holy Spirit clearly directs you otherwise, pray every time for healing and deliverance. The kingdom norm that Jesus modeled is for healing—every time, and right now.

If there are occasional times when it's not God's will to heal a certain person right now, why did Jesus heal everyone immediately?

Excellent question!

Jesus healed everyone who sought His healing touch to demonstrate the heart of the Father. He showed that it's the Father's heart and desire to heal everyone who comes to Him with a sincere heart, every time. If Jesus had left even one seeker unhealed, we would always question God's will every time we're asked to pray for a sick person. But now we have no question—now we know it's God's will to heal everyone, in every situation (except for those who don't want His touch). Jesus' example strengthens our faith.

Get in the presence of Jesus and you will be healed. Every time. Why? Because He is the Healer, and healing is just what He does. Let me illustrate this truth with a story in John's gospel that I love. Lazarus was a friend of Jesus who had gotten deathly sick. His sisters sent a messenger to Jesus, summoning Him to come and heal him. When Jesus got the message, He remained where He was. Jesus actually waited where He was until Lazarus had died. Once Lazarus was dead, Jesus launched on the trip for Bethany, heading for Lazarus's tomb. And here's what Jesus said to His disciples about this: "And I am glad for your sakes that I was not there, that you may believe. Nevertheless let us go to him" (John 11:15).

Why was Jesus glad He was not in Bethany when Lazarus became sick? Because if He had been there, they would have asked Him to heal Lazarus, and He most certainly would have. Because Jesus always heals everyone who comes to Him and gets in His presence. Everyone. Every time.

Jesus was glad He was not there to heal Lazarus because the Father wanted Him to do something even more spectacular—raise Lazarus from the dead. That spectacular resurrection would strengthen the faith of His disciples—"that you may believe."

Jesus' point is clear: If He is present, and someone takes sick in His presence, He will heal every time if called upon.

Get in Jesus' immediate presence and I assure you, you will be healed! Because He always heals everyone. Immediately.

Getting in the immediate presence of Jesus becomes the quest of the chastened believer who makes that goal his pilgrimage.

The Lord said, "My people are destroyed for lack of knowledge" (Hos 4:6). Does that verse mean, at least in part, that some believers die in their infirmities because they lack knowledge about God's will to heal?

Yes, that is one meaning of that verse. Some believers

take the truths about God's sovereignty to an extreme and suppose that in His sovereignty He has chosen not to heal them. However, God in His sovereignty has revealed that it's His desire to heal—always! It's possible for believers who lack knowledge to passively accept an infirmity that God intended for them to resist and overcome.

We must hold passionately to the sovereignty of God without passively falling into a form of godliness that denies the power of our glorious gospel (2 Tim 3:5).

Okay, so some believers are afflicted because they are in a chastening process with God. If they ask me to pray for their healing, and I don't know God's timing for their release, how can I pray in faith? Isn't faith based on knowing God's will regarding healing?

With this question, we are at the heart of the issue. This is the central issue for those who have little room in their theology for the chastening of the Lord. Their objection is that teaching the chastening of the Lord, at least as it's taught in this book, undermines faith for healing. Their zeal is to champion and preserve the glory of divine healing.

First, I want to say that I applaud their zeal for divine healing. I share it fully! I love that they resist anything that would undermine authentic kingdom faith. I feel the same way. I am contending with them for an explosion of the glory of God in the earth, where no disease known to man will be able to stand in the presence of His glory. Amen, come to us in Your power, Lord Jesus!

To pray effectively for people, we must pray in faith. Anything that weakens or undermines the prayer of faith is no friend to the kingdom of God. If we teach the chastening of the Lord in a way that guts believers of their faith for divine deliverance, then we have taught the doctrine improperly. Hebrews 12 ends its teaching on chastening with the words, "rather be healed." Healing is always the last word in chastening.

One of the mysterious questions that is often asked, even by those who see more miracles in their healing ministries than most, is *why are some people not healed*? The answer is mostly veiled from our understanding. I think the answer, in part, lies in a biblical understanding of chastening. When we understand what Hebrews 12 teaches about this topic, we realize that some saints are in a specific pilgrimage with God and their healing will unfold as they continue to walk forward in God.

So if you're praying for someone you think might be in a chastening of the Lord, pray according to what you *do* know: God wants to heal them! Don't concern yourself with what you *don't* know (such as, is this God's time?). Pray boldly for an immediate miracle, in accordance with 2 Corinthians 6:2, "Behold, now is the accepted time; behold, now is the day of salvation."

When those being chastened by the Lord are not healed in the moment, the doctrine of chastening informs us that healing is *definitely* God's will for their lives. So instead of giving up and concluding, "I don't know if you'll ever be healed," we're able to say, "God is going to heal you. Keep asking, keep seeking, keep knocking. Never relent, never give up. You are headed for an encounter with the glory of God. Press in more than ever! Go after the prize."

Rather than undermining faith, therefore, the doctrine of chastening actually *increases* faith for healing. It strengthens our confidence to keep contending for breakthrough, knowing that healing is inevitable. And if God chooses to heal tomorrow instead of today, it's only because He knows the story will be even more powerful because of the wait.

Therefore, when the sick come to you, pray the prayer of faith!

"And the prayer of faith will save the sick, and the Lord will raise him up" (Jas 5:15).

If God wants me lame right now because He's chastening me, how can I have faith for healing?

God wants to heal you. But here's one reason why it's His will that you be lame right now: He wants you to be motivated by the lameness to pursue faith, healing, and oneness with Christ. Without the lameness, you would relax your pursuit. The lameness will cause your spirit to search diligently (Ps 77:6), driving you into a passionate pursuit of the word of faith in Scripture. It's not the trial that changes you; it's the desperate pursuit of God in the trial that changes you. God knows how to lame you in a way that will set your spirit searching with utmost diligence.

You can't devote yourself to unceasing prayer without being changed. Unrelenting prayer is life-transforming. It's the context in which faith grows.

God never intended for His chastening to cause you to resign yourself to coping with pain for the rest of your days. He meant for it to motivate you to press violently into His heart for the healing that's yours.

Live in His word, night and day. Let the word of Christ dwell in you richly. You will grow in faith as you immerse yourself in God's word (Rom 10:17). Jesus has assured us, "If you abide in Me, and My words abide in you, you will ask what you desire, and it shall be done for you" (John 15:7). Pursue that promise of Christ with all your heart, soul, mind, and strength. His promise cannot fail.

What you ask shall be done for you! Never relent until you attain it.

As you devour the Scriptures and pray without ceasing, you will grow in faith. Like a mustard seed, faith will grow in your heart until it becomes mountain-moving faith (Matt 17:20). This is what God wanted for you all along, but He knew chastening was necessary to help you get there.

How can God be good at all times while also orchestrating evil calamity in our lives?

Please return to chapter 1 for my comments there. But let me say here that God is so good, He will do whatever it takes to secure our affections and cause the garden of our hearts to become as fruitful as possible. For example, the Shulamite in Song of Solomon 4:16 recognized that if the garden of her heart was to bring forth maximum fruit, she would need not only the warm summer breezes of the south wind to refresh her garden, but also the cold winter blasts of the north wind. Winter can feel evil at the time, but it's vital in the cycles of growth and fruitfulness. Later, when the harvest is reaped, we will be grateful for the way God's goodness took us through all the seasons.

If God chastens using affliction, disease, infirmity, or lameness, how does that reconcile that with James 1:17, which says, "Every good gift and every perfect gift is from above, and comes down from the Father of lights, with whom there is no variation or shadow of turning"? How can we say that disease and infirmity is a "good gift and perfect gift"?

Affliction, disease, infirmity, or lameness are not "good" or "perfect," to whatever degree Satan is involved.

We said in chapter 18 that sometimes God uses Satan as a rod in His hand to chasten His children, as He did with Job and Paul. Anytime Satan gets involved, the waters are muddied. He always tries to cause more distress than God intended. Satan always overplays his hand, as discussed in chapter 19.

In most cases of chastening, both God and Satan are involved. However, there are rare occasions in which God alone is the laming agent. I have two Bible stories in mind here. The first is the laming of Jacob's hip. Jesus Himself wrestled with Jacob at Peniel (Gen 32:24), and Jesus was the only causative element in giving Jacob his limp. Jacob's limp came to him exclusively from above, from whence we receive "every good gift and every perfect gift" (Jas 1:17). I conclude, therefore, that Jacob's limp was a good and perfect gift for him.

The other story I have in mind is when the Lord lamed Zacharias by striking him mute for ten months. That happened during an encounter with Gabriel, a mighty angel from above (Luke 1:20). Satan was not involved in any way. The muteness came from above. I conclude, therefore, that Zacharias's muteness was a good and perfect gift for him.

Even when God chastens, His dealings in our lives are good and perfect.

Is God glorified by making me sick, infirm, or afflicted?

Not necessarily. Some believers become casualties in the midst of chastening, and instead of God's redemptive purposes being realized, Satan's agenda sidelines them. Paul spoke of "the falling away" (2 Thess 2:3) that will happen at the end of the age. One reason some believers will fall away is because they won't understand

God's good purposes in chastening. They will agree with the adversary's accusations, become bitter against God, and fall away. In such cases, God's desire to be glorified through the chastening will not be realized.

God wants you to endure in faith to the end, that He might be glorified through your trial. He'll be glorified when you are healed! It's possible, however, for God to be glorified in your life even during your chastening— if you will engage by faith with His purposes. You don't have to wait for the chastening to be finished before God is glorified in your life. Romans 4:20 says Abraham gave glory to God during the twenty-five years he waited for God to give him his promised miracle baby. In other words, Abraham kept telling people, "God is going to fulfill His promise." Even in the journey, therefore, while you feel the reproach of your "unfinished-ness," God will gain glory through your obedience and witness. Just staying in faith in your infirmity, by itself, glorifies God.

How do I reconcile God's will to prosper me with God's design to discipline me?

There is no contradiction between the two. Let me explain.

In his third epistle, John offered this prayer, "Beloved, I pray that you may prosper in all things and be in health, just as your soul prospers" (3 John 2). Clearly, God wants to prosper us. However, we know from the biblical record (the book of Judges is especially clear on this point) that we don't do so well with prosperity. Prosperity often makes us soft, comfortable, passive, lazy, and lukewarm—sometimes becoming the very reason that God must chasten in our lives.

God disciplines so that He might prosper us. One purpose of His chastening is to make us so disciplined

THE CHASTENING OF THE LORD

in our souls that the prosperity will not ruin us. If spiritual disciplines become a part of our DNA, then we will maintain spiritual discipline in the midst of prosperity and health. This is what John meant with his qualifier, "as your soul prospers." The soul prospers only to the extent to which we maintain the spiritual disciplines of fasting, prayer, and word immersion. John was saying, "I want you to prosper, but only to the degree that your soul is prospering through spiritual disciplines." John knew that if our material prosperity outstrips our prosperity of soul, we're likely to fall back into lazy lukewarmness.

Rather than being contradictory, the relationship between God's discipline and prosperity are actually symbiotic.

If I'm facing a trial, how can I know whether to submit to it because it's from God, or resist it because it's from the devil?

I deal with this question in chapter 19, but let me add a couple comments here. When our trial is entirely from God, it's a rather straightforward thing to submit to Him. We rest in His goodness and wisdom. And when our trial is from the devil, we're usually not confused about what to do—we know to fight him with every reserve in our being.

Our confusion and struggle usually surround those calamities in which both God and Satan are active instruments. Let's return to the example of Job. God was involved in Job's calamity because He started the fight with Satan and oversaw the entire proceedings. Satan was also involved, however, viciously assaulting Job with bereavement, plundering invaders, loss, and disease. Job was torn between both God and Satan. When both are involved, you don't want to submit to it—because the last thing you want to do is submit to something the devil is putting on you. But you don't want to resist it, either, because you don't want to resist God's formative dealings in your life. In cases like this, when you feel like you can't submit or resist, you find yourself completely perplexed about what to do next.

It's the perplexity of being torn between the two that accelerates the Lord's purposes in the chastening. All you can do is tremble in His presence and throw yourself upon His mercy. When you don't know how to hold on any longer, He will hold you. His mercy is enough.

In chastening a son, a caring earthly father wouldn't go so far as to wound or lame his son. Why would God lame His sons? Is He a sadistic Father?

No, He is not sadistic. He is the most doting, caring, involved, engaged Father you will ever know. He loves His sons enough to do what is necessary to help them enter their fullest destiny.

There are many reasons why God's chastening is so intense, but for now consider these four factors: God's intensity, our brokenness, our great inheritance, and the wartime context. Let's do one at a time.

God's intensity: Our heavenly Father is extremely intense. So much so that He is literally a living flame of consuming fire. He is Jealous, righteous, holy, and eternal. In other words, He's a whole lot more intense than your earthly father. He's not a mortal in his thirties, He's the everlasting Creator of the universe. His rod is a whole lot bigger than your earthly father's! The fact that we even *survive* His chastening is a miracle in itself.

Our brokenness: We have been broken so deeply by sin, at so many levels in our souls, that sometimes strong measures are required by the Father to change us all the way through.

Our great inheritance: When you consider how weak we are, and how great the heights to which God is lifting us, you realize how strongly God must work in our lives. The intensity of the chastening is reflective, therefore, of the glory of the inheritance for those who respond well. The highest things come with a price tag.

The wartime context: God is doing this glorious work in our lives in the context of a war. There are rules of engagement to which the Lord adheres in His war with Satan. Satan is always crying, "Foul! Not fair! You're using Your advantage unfairly by using this person in such a powerful manner!" (In Zechariah 3:1, this is how Satan opposed the way God was using Joshua.) God answers by pointing to the intensity of the chastening: "It's not unfair. Look at the price he paid to get where he is! He more than paid the price for this entrustment." The chastening is intense, therefore, so we can qualify for a promotion in the army of God.

There are other reasons why God's chastening is sometimes so intense—see chapter 14 on the three purposes of chastening. My point here is simply this: When we gain understanding into how and why God is chastening, we will worship Him for His compassionate mercy in our lives. We should have been consumed (Lam 3:22), but instead, here we are with broad influence (Ps 18:19), standing on high places (Ps 18:33), with arms that have been trained to bend a bow of bronze (Ps 18:34). His grace is stunning!

We should not suppose we human fathers are more merciful than our heavenly Father. We are believing a lie if we think God would be a better Father if He took His chastening cues from us. If He were to discipline the way we do, we would still be groveling in the miry clay of this earthly plane.

Is it okay to accept my infirmity as my lot in life, realizing that God is using it to make me a better person?

In chapter 12, I show a graph to illustrate the paradox between faith-oriented believers and sovereignty-oriented believers. Most of us tend to favor one side. The person asking the above question would probably favor the sovereignty side of the spectrum.

For those who are inclined to favor God's sovereignty, they are more likely to accept an infirmity as their lot in life. Rather than feeling a need to contend for healing, they are more likely to rest in God's sovereignty and surrender their lives to God's goodness and providential care.

For those who favor the faith side of the spectrum, they are more likely to clutch the promise of Hebrews 12:13, "but rather be healed," and contend for the Lord's promised healing.

God enjoys each of His children for their uniqueness. So be yourself, whether trusting or contending, and know that the Lord delights in you in the journey. The main thing is to be led of the Holy Spirit in how you respond to your trial.

But I also want to say that I haven't written this book to make anyone okay with no healing. I'm not seeking to decrease but to increase your expectation for divine healing.

When Jesus said, "Take up your cross daily," did He mean, "Embrace disease daily"?

I don't believe that's what Jesus meant. To take up your cross, in my understanding, is to die daily to the desires of the flesh, the desire to preserve our own lives, and the carnal tendency to control and direct our own course in life. There are things we don't enjoy or want to do, but we embrace them willingly in obedience because of our love debt to our Redeemer.

If God is disciplining me with infirmity, and the process in me is still incomplete, is it possible that no amount of praying will get me healed right now?

I suppose that's a possibility. Faith for healing is a gift from God. If God is not yet releasing faith for a certain healing, we can't manufacture that faith in our own zeal. We must continue to wait upon Him expectantly, pressing violently into faith, knowing the day is coming when He will enable us to offer the prayer of faith.

However, I don't see Jesus saying, "I'm not ready to heal you yet, so it really doesn't matter how passionately you pray. No matter how you pray, I'm not going to heal you right now." Rather, I see Jesus saying, "I really want to heal you. Even now! But there are things in you that are preventing you from touching Me in faith. I want My chastening to help you see those things. Rise up and come after Me!"

Whenever the prayer of faith is offered, through the enabling of the Holy Spirit, healing will most certainly happen—whether the faith is exercised by the person being prayed for, or the person praying for them. In our prayers, we are in pursuit of this kind of mountain-moving faith. Never relax your pursuit until you touch it!

How do we see the chastening of the Father modeled and taught in the earthly ministry of Jesus?

I see the Father's chastening modeled in Jesus' life in His scourging, crucifixion, death, and descent to hell. Then I see the Father's healing in the glorious resurrection of Christ.

During Jesus' earthly ministry, He rebuked His

disciples often, but we see Him doing no chastening at that time. Perhaps His chastening was not necessary at that time because of His physical presence with them. It seems that His chastening was to come later. It wasn't until after His resurrection that He said to John, "As many as I love, I rebuke and chasten. Therefore be zealous and repent" (Rev 3:19).

In the letters to the seven churches, Jesus warned of actions toward His churches that we never saw during His three-year ministry on earth. For example, in Revelation 2:16, Jesus spoke of fighting against the believers in Pergamos with the sword of His mouth—something He never did when on earth. Furthermore, in Revelation 2:23, Jesus said He would kill the children of Jezebel with death—something He never did when on earth. I submit that it isn't inconsistent, therefore, to see Jesus doing something in Revelation 3:19 (chastening His loved ones) that He didn't do during His earthly ministry.

When you illustrate your understanding of chastening, Bob, you often cite the example of Job. Is it possible to establish a solid theology on this topic based on the life of someone who lived in the Old Testament era?

I am persuaded that an accurate theology of chastening must be consistent with the witness of *all* Scripture on this topic, from Genesis to Revelation. I have sought to use the entire Bible in this treatise on this subject.

And I will defend the example of Job. The fact is, God set the book of Job as the cornerstone of Scripture (it was the first Bible book written). He did that intentionally because the cornerstone of truth and revelation is precedent-setting, to which all truth must align. Since God placed that book first in Scripture, I am bold to align my understandings with that book—even if some builders reject that cornerstone and say you can't build truth on it.

Jesus was never sick, nor did He ever make anyone sick or lame while on earth. How, then, do you see Job's experience consistent with the life and ministry of Jesus?

If we think there's a contradiction between Job's life and Jesus' life, then we're missing something, because Scripture is a complete unity. To see Job in the life of Christ, I go to the crucifixion. When you see the cross in the book of Job, you realize God put the cross into the very foundations of Scripture. In the case of both Job and Jesus, the most righteous man on earth suffered the most of anyone on earth. Job said, "Naked I came from my mother's womb, and naked shall I return there"— which describes the cross. Just as Job came through to a place of honor and vindication, Jesus was resurrected from the dead. There is no contradiction for me to see Abba Father chastening both sons. To summarize, I see Job in the life of Christ in this manner:

▶ Christ's earthly ministry corresponds to Job's early prosperity and success.

▶ Christ's crucifixion and death corresponds to Job's trial.

▶ Christ's resurrection corresponds to Job's restoration and exaltation.

Also, please look again at chapter 15, where I show that even as Job's cross qualified him for greater spiritual authority, Jesus' cross qualified Him to be given all authority in heaven and on earth. In both cases, their chastening was *qualifying*.

If we say that infirmity is sometimes God's will for our lives, aren't we rendering void the work of the cross and, specifically, the healing that His stripes purchased for us (1 Pet 2:24)?

No. We were healed by His stripes on the cross, and that healing is available to us—now. When we are chastened by the Lord and then healed by Him (Heb 12:13), the basis of that healing is the stripes Jesus bore. The power of the cross is eternally effectual!

I have an infirmity. The possibility that it has been given to me by God is really killing my faith. How can I even believe for healing now?

If a truth from God's word is killing your faith, perhaps your faith was not as solid as you might have thought. Sometimes God removes false props from our theology—what feels to us like the gutting of our faith—in order to rebuild our faith on immovable foundations that will withstand the greatest storms of life.

God has healing for you—even if your trial is a chastening (Heb 12:13). Pursue faith, and go after your healing until it is realized in your life. Healing is yours!

Again, if your infirmity is a chastening, one of the Lord's primary purposes in your trial is that you attain mountain-moving faith. Let the pain of your infirmity motivate you to pursue the faith of Jesus more fervently than ever.

Let me point to an interesting Scripture that might help. Paul wrote, "And since we have the same spirit of faith, according to what is written, 'I believed and therefore I spoke,' we also believe and therefore speak" (2 Cor 4:13). Paul was quoting from Psalm 116, saying he had the same spirit of faith as the writer of Psalm 116. Here's the verse Paul quoted: "I believed, therefore I spoke, 'I am greatly afflicted.' I said in my haste, 'All men are liars'"

(Ps 116:10-11). The psalmist was a man of faith, and his faith caused him to speak. Because faith speaks. What did he speak? "I am greatly afflicted." Now, to some that would not qualify as a statement of faith, but of unbelief. But Scripture says it was a confession of faith. He was saying, "I am afflicted of God, and I believe God has a purpose for this affliction. This is going somewhere. It's not over." Then he went on to say, "All men are liars," because others were looking at his affliction and misdiagnosing it. They saw him as unbelieving, or under divine judgment. But he was claiming to be favored of God—in a trial that God had designed for holy purpose. So in the haste of his soul he categorically called all men liars. He was a man of faith living under an affliction.

The point is, when you're afflicted with an infirmity, God wants you to stay in faith. Believe that God has holy purpose for your journey. Go after all that God has for you—including healing.

If you are not healed today, don't be discouraged. Be assured that healing is your portion. Be encouraged, stay in the race, grow in faith, and pursue Jesus until you touch the hem of His garment. Just one touch is all you need.

If Jesus always wants to heal those He lames, why was Jacob not healed of his limp?

I don't know. But I will make a couple observations. Jacob's limp didn't hinder his spiritual destiny. Even with it, he entered into the fullness of the Lord's redemption for his life. He got all his sons back, he was established in prosperity in Egypt, he blessed Pharaoh, and received the funeral of the millennium. Jacob's limp was a mark, given to him by Christ, that in turn left a profound mark upon his sons. The limp didn't immobilize him, but it marked him as the father of the nation of Israel. It was a trophy of his encounter with God that his posterity never forgot. Whenever they saw their father walking, they were likely to remember, "He never walked like that until the day he saw God." Furthermore, it became the trademark of the nation of Israel. Jacob's limp has always spoken to Israel's identity and legacy.

I will also point out that Jesus alone gave Jacob his limp. The devil was not involved at all. So the limp was given to him in perfection. It was a perfect memorial of God's hand on his life.

Even though Jacob wasn't healed, I believe chastened children should claim the assurance of Hebrews 12:13, that God wants the lame part to be healed.

The fact that Jacob remained unhealed underscores that, when it comes to the Lord's chastening, we are peering into an area that is somewhat shrouded by paradox, mystery, and sovereignty. *Nobody* has perfect understanding into all the depths of God's heart—especially me. That means that we must remain humble, pliable, leaning on our Beloved, and confident in His goodness and lovingkindness.

> Oh, the depth of the riches both of the wisdom and knowledge of God! How unsearchable are His judgments and His ways past finding out! "For who has known the mind of the LORD? Or who has become His counselor? Or who has first given to Him and it shall be repaid to him?" For of Him and through Him and to Him are all things, to whom be glory forever. Amen. (Rom 11:33-36).

Let me add one more thing, based upon Micah 4:6. "In that day," says the LORD, "I will assemble the lame, I will gather the outcast and those whom I have afflicted." This verse speaks of those whom God has afflicted. It seems to me, therefore, that the verse is speaking of chastened believers—made lame because God has afflicted them.

Here's the promise in the verse: "In that day...I will assemble the lame." The lame, by virtue of their handicap, are naturally isolated, dispersed, and hidden throughout society. There is only one thing that would cause the lame to assemble: A release of divine healing. When God visits His people with His promised healing, and people are coming out of their wheelchairs, leaving their prosthetics behind, and the blind are casting away their walking sticks, the lame will assemble from all over to be healed. I assure you, Jesus is going to visit His church with divine healing. And when He does, the lame will assemble to His great name and be healed of every infirmity and affliction.

Praise His holy name! That Micah 4:6 day is coming!

If we fail to heed the Lord's chastening, will He continue to chasten in our lives until we finally get it?

God's Spirit will strive with us for a long time because He is so long-suffering, but there can come a time when He stops speaking. We should keep in mind the warning of Proverbs 29:1, "He who is often rebuked, and hardens his neck, will suddenly be destroyed, and that without remedy."

Does God hit?

The answer, remarkably enough, is *yes*. When Isaiah spoke of how God chastened Israel to get their attention, he wrote, "For the people do not turn to Him who strikes them, nor do they seek the LORD of hosts" (Isa 9:13). When Ezekiel prophesied God's judgment upon Jerusalem because the people refused to obey the Lord, he wrote, "Then you shall know that I am the LORD who strikes" (Ezek 7:9).

God wanted the people of Israel to know in no un-
certain terms that He is the Lord who strikes His people
to correct them. "The Lord who strikes"—what a name!
God spanks!

What was Paul talking about in 1 Corinthians 5:5 when he said to deliver a man over to Satan for the destruction of the flesh so that his spirit may be saved?

Paul was addressing an instance where a believer
was living in open, unrepentant sin. If that believer were
to remain in that lifestyle of unrepentant sin, he would
lose his life in the judgment to come. Therefore, Paul
urged the church to deliver that believer over to Satan
while there was still hope. Satan would afflict the man in
his flesh (Satan is always glad to afflict when he is given
permission), and the hope is that the man would come
to his senses, repent, and be saved from eternal judgment. In this instance of chastening, we see both God
and Satan at work together—God, by removing His pro-
tective shield, and Satan, by afflicting this disobedient
believer in his flesh.

Someone once asked, "Are the consequences of an addiction a result of God's chastisement?"

No. Sin produces death (Rom 6:23), and is often ac-
companied by the negative consequences of our harmful choices. In such cases, we should diligently seek the
Lord's healing because I believe Calvary's provision includes redemption from the damaging effects of our
former sins.

Here, then, is the conclusion of the matter:

▶ Chastening is God's compassionate use of non-verbal means to correct and discipline us for our progress and maturity.

▶ We shouldn't blow off His corrections, nor should we be disheartened by them. Rather, we should repent and change because we realize how much He loves us.

▶ We're comforted when He doesn't leave us to ourselves because that means we really are His children and not bastards (sons of the devil).

▶ It's helpful to understand that a mix of five causative agents can be behind our trial: God, Satan, people, ourselves, and living in a broken world.

▶ His chastening trains us and produces in us a rich spiritual harvest: eternal life, righteousness, holiness, fervency, clear vision, Christlikeness, wisdom, intimacy, and spiritual authority.

▶ Those who are lame will be healed as they stay in the race.

▶ The doctrine of chastening, properly taught, increases our faith for divine healing.

▶ Although God uses chastening to punish and purify, His greatest purpose is to qualify us for a higher entrustment in the kingdom.

▶ In light of the glorious benefits of chastening, we're filled with gratitude when He does whatever it takes to possess the entirety of our hearts.

▶ Understanding how God fathers us will help us parent our children in compassion and wisdom.

▶ Thanks be to God, who is helping us *remember* this marvelous truth about His glorious purposes for our lives. *He is so good!*

24
Joel's Letter

In closing, I want to share a letter my oldest son, Joel, wrote me in 2014. This was his greeting to me on my birthday that year. This letter is a look at chastening through the eyes of my son. He was thirty years old when he wrote this, and I was fifty-seven. We didn't edit his letter in any way. I hope it's a blessing.

I am beyond grateful for you. To be quite to-the-point, I can't thank God enough for letting you suffer for the last 20-something years. Without that, I would have never known how to weather the storms of life. We've endured some difficult trials over the last handful of years, and while I feel I've come through some of these with a leaning heart, I know that it is not because of my own understanding, perspective and faith. When the storm of your life hit the shores of your heart, you didn't just panic and strive to survive. You built a shelter for me (and our family) in the midst of the storm. I did not connect with it until I became ill years ago, but you built a house on a solid rock and brought us all into it. Once there, you displayed radical commitment to enduring through trials. You showed us how to pray. You taught us that there was no plan B, there was only God, His loving chastening, and His ultimate goal to conform us into the likeness of Christ. Because of you, I have been able to see the hand of God in my own trials, and I have not lost heart, even when I was at my flesh's end. You taught me how to forgive and turn the other cheek. You taught me how to love my neighbor, even when they are unlovable. You taught me how to care for the poor and weep with those that weep. You even taught me how to rejoice with those that rejoice; even when the rejoicing causes us pain. And even then, you showed me the envy in my heart towards others, and again, in that, showed me how to love. You showed me how to zealously pursue the call of God on my life, yet cautioned me of the dangers of thriving on the praise of man. You showed me how to care about what God cares about, and forsake the self-seeking I am prone to. You showed me how to hunger and thirst for righteousness, and you showed me how to repent.

You are a good father, and I can't express the gratitude in my heart that God did not let us get off the hook with a boring, predictable story. I hope I speak for everyone here when I say that we are grateful to have been grafted into your story. Thank you for leading us, loving us, and watching us grow with the delight that only a true father can have for his children.

I love you dad. Happy birthday. Joel

All of Bob Sorge's Titles

To order Bob's materials:
- Go to www.oasishouse.com
- Call 816-767-8880 (ask about quantity discounts)
- Write Oasis House, PO Box 522, Grandview, MO 64030-0522

Go to www.oasishouse.com for special package discounts, book descriptions, ebooks, and free teachings.